An Optimistic
Look at the Global
Financial Crash

JUBILEE
on Wall Street

David Knox Barker

Foreword by **Billy Graham**

LWD

Published by Long Wave Dynamics, LLC, 3rd Edition (2009)

This publication is designed to provide accurate and authoritative information
in regard to the subject matter covered. It is sold with the understanding that the
author and the publisher are not engaged in rendering legal, accounting, financial,
investment or other professional advice.

ISBN: 0-9825283-1-0
ISBN-13: 9780982528310

FROM THE DUST JACKET

Jubilee on Wall Street: An Optimistic Look at the Global Financial Crash reviews our global economic and financial crises, and presents in clear terms a picture of what the future may hold. Contrary to proponents of gloom and doom, financial market analyst and world-systems analyst David Knox Barker shows that there are positive forces at work that can create The Great Republic–a new golden age that embraces not global socialism and wealth redistribution but true international free-market capitalism.

In *Jubilee on Wall Street*, Barker explains how the long wave theory, introduced and developed by Russian economist Nikolai Kondratieff, and validated by System Dynamics at MIT, has proven to be a precise forecaster of economic and financial events. The long wave shows how cycles of boom and bust have occurred throughout history–as far back as Leviticus and the insightful laws regarding debt cancellation in the Year of Jubilee.

Barker takes us through a brief historical overview of financial crises, bringing into focus the last two hundred years. He delves into the "seasons" that mark the wave's contraction and expansion. He examines the impact of wars, the role that banks have played, and the influence on stock markets worldwide. He shows the sure disaster if we engage in trade wars. He debunks the myth about the long-term safety of fixed-income securities, and takes a look at the commodity markets and the creation of a new system of international digital gold currency.

In prior editions, Barker accurately predicted the deflationary debt collapse, crashing stock markets, the international banking disaster, and the crisis of capitalism with remarkable accuracy. His latest book offers an optimistic view of the future founded on the theory that the economy thrives on "new beginnings born of adversity caused by prior mistakes and the crises they create." From these crises, he points to the advent of new ideas and technologies, creating a better world economically, politically, and spiritually.

ABOUT THE AUTHOR

David Knox Barker is the founder of Long Wave Dynamics, LLC and publisher of *The Long Wave Dynamics Letter.* He is a writer, inventor, entrepreneur, financial market analyst and world-systems analyst. Barker has written on the impact of the long wave on financial markets and the international political economy for twenty-five years, and has applied long wave analytics to entrepreneurial business development decisions throughout his career. He also serves as the founder and CEO of ALP Life Sciences, LLC, a life sciences research and development company currently working on a revolutionary application of nanobiotechnology known as the Nanoveson™ project. Barker was founder and CEO for ten years of a successful life sciences research and marketing services company. He received his bachelor's degree in finance and a master's degree in political science. Barker is happily married to a remarkable wife, and they are the parents of three great kids.

DEDICATION

This book is dedicated to the memory of the legendary and magnanimous market analyst and philosopher PQ Wall (1931–2009). PQ's life demonstrated that destiny is real. Just one of PQ's many contributions to cycle research is the Wall cycle, a remarkable cycle that is $1/144^{th}$ of a long wave "Jubilee" in length. The true nature of the Wall cycle is one of the most important discoveries in the history of cycle research and financial market analysis; the Wall cycle is a miniature long wave. And this book is dedicated to you, the reader. You and your life's purpose are essential to the powerful force of human action. Your destiny is real.

ACKNOWLEDGEMENTS

This book represents the impact of many teachers, friends, colleagues, family members, writers and others that have made a difference and spoken into my life over the years. They have all played a role in my ongoing education and, therefore, in the writing of this book, and are hereby granted full immunity. My teachers and professors were many, but a few who went the extra mile to put up with my wide-ranging pursuit of answers were Al Lucksavage, Ray Jones, Edward Allen, Jawad Bargothi, Mark Stern, and Waltraud Q. Morales. Where would we be without our teachers? Object-oriented paradigm discussions with John Bremser improved the long wave analysis found in this new edition. Steve Aceto's wisdom and counsel over the years has made this a better book, and the author a better person. The writings of market timing legend PQ Wall and my discussion with him over the years have had a major impact on my approach to financial market analysis and cycle research. Immanuel Wallerstein must be recognized for the beautiful irony of his wisdom and his World-Systems Analysis, in which he so starkly demonstrates the consequences of capitalism's now culminating compromises and from which I have borrowed, in an attempt to show the captains of capitalism the way home, from so far out at sea. Jay Forrester is acknowledged for creating and giving us System Dynamics, which will surely yield many of the answers required in the years to come, and he is also thanked for the use of his charts. Thanks to Ron Griess at TheChartStore.com, for the charts that help tell the long wave "Jubilee" story. Thanks to Nick Laird at ShareLynx.com for the Dow/Gold ratio chart, it is a great chart. Thanks to the Friday morning coffee cabal, who motivated me for this new edition more than they know. Stephan and Gigi, thank you for all the encouragement over the years, and for your daughter. Thank you Berdjette and kids for your patience. You are my heroes. Nikolai Kondratieff, you did not die in vain, the world is now beginning to see and understand the ebb and flow of the long wave.

"There is a tide in the affairs of men.
Which, taken at the flood, leads on to fortune;
Omitted, all the voyage of their life
Is bound in shallows and in miseries.
On such a full sea are we now afloat,
And we must take the current when it serves,
Or lose our ventures."

William Shakespeare

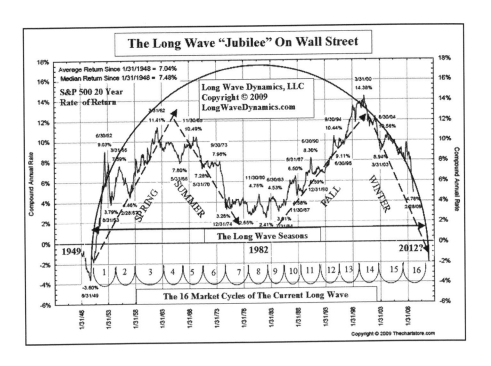

CONTENTS

Part IV   The Future

FOREWORD

by Billy Graham

During the past decade, I have been in many of the countries of the world and talked to businessmen, heads of labor unions, political leaders, religious leaders, etc. I am finding that there is a great uncertainty, and even fear, on the part of almost everybody when we think of the global economy, especially as it affects us personally.

The Bible could almost be a textbook on economy. Its teachings on this subject have been greatly overlooked by economists and religious theologians.

David Knox Barker's book, *Jubilee on Wall Street: An Optimistic Look at the Global Financial Crash,* is not a religious book, but it brings out the teachings of the Bible on economic practices of biblical times and the prophecies concerning the economy of the future. The Bible is relevant to our global situation today and its teachings need to be taken seriously.

Mr. Barker has written a book that is so fascinating that it's difficult to put down. I would recommend people of all walks of life who are concerned about their finances and the finances of their country to not only read, but study this book.

AUTHOR'S NOTE

This book has been a work in progress for the better part of half of a long wave "Jubilee" cycle. My introduction to the long wave in the global economy came over 25 years ago as an undergraduate finance student upon reading a speech delivered by Julian Snyder. Snyder was founder and editor of the Switzerland based *International Moneyline.* Snyder's speech was delivered to the Wharton Business School Club of New York on June 14, 1983 and published in the August 1983 issue of *Vital Speeches of the Day.* Snyder's reference to the economic long wave was brief, but the idea that international free market capitalism ebbs and flows in economic long waves resonated with me as a young student in a profound way.

Further research into the long wave revealed the evidence for the long wave in prices, debt, production, interest rates, and stock markets in the global economy. The idea that each global long wave advance is powered by a new wave of advances in technology and invention, primarily focused on advances in communications and transportation, is supported by history and the data. The evidence indicates that the long wave phenomenon is a critical force at work in the ebbing and flowing tides of the global economy.

The current global crisis cannot be understood without the long wave perspective. An understanding of the long wave view brings order to what appears to be chaos. It explains the patterns that we all recognize. This new edition of *Jubilee on Wall Street* is, therefore, updated and offered to readers for its relevant insight into the current global crisis.

My first effort at writing on and explaining the subject of the long wave was an undergraduate finance paper for Dr. Ray Jones, who also had an interest in the long wave debate. As an aspiring freelance finance writer–with enthusiasm for the subject of the long wave, but little practical, real-world experience– I researched and hammered out the first edition of this book in short order after graduation. It was with great expectations that

I wrote to Julian Snyder in Switzerland and requested he write an introduction for the book.

My expectations required adjustment. Mr. Snyder graciously wrote back and suggested the book needed more work and was a bit premature. He was generous. Of course, he was clearly right on both points, as evidenced by this new edition over two decades later. However, despite Snyder's misgivings and advice, the first edition of this book was published and released in August of 1987, just a few months before the stock market crash of October 1987 as *Jubilee on Wall Street; An Optimistic Look at the Coming Financial Crash.*

Clearly the stock market crash of 1987 was not the anticipated financial crash of this global long wave, but merely the stock market adjustment of a regular business and market cycle in the long wave fall season. Over the years I have observed the long wave force of a global debt collapse building in a crescendo with every regular business cycle. The global long wave financial crisis has now arrived in full regalia. We are clearly now deep into a global deflationary long wave winter season and a global debt bust deflation.

A number of years after the first edition of this book, my thesis for a master's degree in political science took on the subject of disequilibrium in international political economy from a long wave perspective. Research on the thesis was used to update this book for a second edition, which was published in hardback by Irwin Professional Publishing in 1995, now a division of Times Mirror, under the title *The K Wave: Profiting from the Cyclical Booms and Busts in the Global Economy.* The print run of the hard back edition was limited and was soon out of print. It should be noted that the 1995 edition projected the end of the current long wave to come in 2009, the year of the release of this new edition. Used copies of this 1995 edition are rarely available. The price for a used copy has been steadily rising in recent years. Seeing a used copy with an asking price of over $1,000 in early 2009 inspired me to accelerate work on this new edition. This new edition is intended to clarify my current analysis of exactly where we now find ourselves in this global long wave. Actually, if you must know, my wife threatened to sell my last copy of the 1995 edition if I didn't complete this new edition.

For the new edition, the decision was made to return to the original title of *Jubilee on Wall Street*. The role of Wall Street and the global focus on Wall Street as culprit during the current global deflationary debt collapse and the clear Jubilee debt principles at work make the original title more fitting at this time.

Like a calendar year, the long wave is characterized by four seasons. Over the years I have never changed my view that the recession of the early 1980s marked the halfway point in this current long wave (i.e., the turn of the overheated economic long wave summer season into the economic long wave fall season of corporate efficiency and financial speculation). This key turning point is remarkably obvious in many of the charts you will find in this book.

Evidence presented in this book suggests the present economic long wave began in 1949. This long wave start date was first identified by Robert Prechter of Elliott Wave International (elliottwave.com). Getting the start date of the long wave correct is essential to relevant long wave analysis. We are now clearly in the final global winter season of the long wave.

My target end date for the current long wave winter and the beginning of a new long wave and spring season is now 2012. However, the forecast in the 1995 edition for the end of the global long wave in 2009 has to be respected; there remains one cycle count that suggests 2009 as the end of the long wave. Although such an accurate projection from 15 years out would have been a feather in my forecasting cap, strong evidence suggests the current long wave winter season has a few years remaining.

The powerful long wave forces of excessive debt and overproduction, which drive crisis and price adjustments in global markets, have not sufficiently corrected for the beginning of a new global long wave. Based on the long wave analysis presented in this book, the most likely outcome is that this long wave winter season unfolds in the form of a "W", or double-dip global crisis, with a weak global recovery from the 2009 global market and economic lows, that gives way to the final global economic and financial market declines of this long wave in 2012. However, some national markets and economies will likely begin their next long wave advance prior to that date. To follow my ongoing analysis of the long wave ending and new long wave beginning scenarios, please visit LongWaveDynamics.com for the latest thinking and analysis on this crucial topic.

You can receive a current update on my analysis of the long wave dynamics now driving markets and where we are in the long wave family of cycles from my long wave research and market analytics firm, Long Wave Dynamics, LLC. Additional information can be found at LongWaveDynamics.com.

Every monthly issue of *The Long Wave Dynamics Letter* keeps readers current and updated on the long wave family of cycles and the additional information presented in this book. The plan to update my thinking on the long wave for a 50th Jubilee anniversary edition of *Jubilee on Wall Street* is on my calendar.

David Knox Barker
Summer 2009

PROLOGUE

Earlier editions of this book predicted many aspects of the current global crisis years ahead of their development and in detail. Many of the projections have proven to be precise. However, some of the forecasts were wide of the mark, excluding this author from the status of a prophet, thankfully. Nevertheless, the salient, accurate insights of prior editions make the new edition of this book uniquely eligible to review the current state of the global crisis and its implications, and to consider what the future may hold.

Most will appreciate the fact that this book proposes that a truly new global economy, with remarkable potential and opportunity, is already in the works and will emerge with explosive force from this global crisis. Since earlier editions predicted this global crisis in detail, this edition turns to the expectation of the rise of a new economy.

In the planning for this new edition counsel was sought from a wise, lifelong friend about including a foreword by Billy Graham in a book such as this on a global financial and debt crisis and economic long wave. This advice was sought before the current global financial crisis was in full tilt and the wheels were coming off global financial markets.

My friend's counsel was that if this crisis was going to be limited in its sphere of impact then, no, but if the global crisis is expected to rise to the level of the defining archetype event for our generation, an event that transcends mere financial and economic concerns to contain defining moments in all our lives, then a foreword by Mr. Graham would be appropriate. Events since this advice have clearly accelerated this global crisis to a level of being the "archetype" event of this generation (i.e., universally present in the psyche of all).

In the interest of full disclosure, it is only proper to share with you that Mr. Graham's eldest granddaughter is my beautiful, charming wife, Berdjette. Since my grandfathers both passed away when I was young, he has, over the years, filled the role of the perfect grandfather to me as well, for which I am eternally grateful. He is the most gracious and genuinely humble human being I have ever encountered and his sincere concern and life's purpose to help others to experience peace in their lives and fulfill their unique purposes in life is an inspiration to us all.

Shortly after the 1987 stock market crash Mr. Graham invited me to lunch to discuss the first edition of *Jubilee on Wall Street*. It was a great time of conversation and discussion with Mr. and Mrs. Graham at their mountain home. Mr. Graham has always been interested in global economic and financial news and current events. Over the years there has typically been a copy of the *Wall Street Journal* and *Financial Times,* in addition to the *New York Times* and other daily papers, on the kitchen table. In recent years, as his eyesight has faded, these papers are no longer a part of his daily routine, although he still enjoys discussing the economy and financial markets.

Mr. Graham was genuinely interested in the connection between the Year of Jubilee and long wave theory and the clear relevance of scriptures, written thousands of years ago, to modern economic life. Later in the afternoon, following that lunch, Mr. Graham's office called and informed me that he had just spoken with former president Richard Nixon. Evidently, President Nixon was also very interested in the content of this book regarding the economic long wave, in light of the crisis hitting international financial markets at the time. Nixon requested a copy of *Jubilee on Wall Street* be sent to him by overnight courier.

This request from President Nixon for the first edition of this book was particularly appreciated, since my earliest memory of financial crisis and financial market events was the news broadcast I watched with my father in 1971 that reported Nixon's closing of the gold window. No longer could foreigners trade dollars for gold at $35 per ounce. U.S. citizens did not have the privilege of trading their dollars for gold at the time, only non U.S. entities and individuals could trade dollars for gold. It is my view that dollar backing for gold was not Nixon's primary interest and concern; it was the outflow of U.S. gold reserves from the U.S. vault at Fort Knox.

This little piece of Nixon history is the perfect prologue to the subject matter of this book because of the importance of Nixon's closing the gold window to the outcome of the current international crisis and the clear emergence of digital gold currency (DGC). This action by Nixon set global forces in motion that continue to build to this day and are now more relevant than ever. For the first time in world history DGC provides a powerful potential check to unsound fiscal and monetary policy around the globe. This will be discussed in more detail in this book in chapters on gold and the banking system regarding the rise of a new international currency option in the form of digital gold currency. DGC is an option that is growing rapidly as this global long wave crisis accelerates and investors and sovereign governments seek safety and protection from the raging global financial storm.

Most view Nixon's closing the gold window negatively, but they do not appreciate the whole picture that only comes with time. Thousands of tons of gold in Fort Knox would not be there today if Nixon had not acted. I believe that Nixon stopped what could be viewed as the greatest gold heist in history. This gold is a national treasure and resource that may well play an important role in our national security and prosperity, as well as in the realization of what I term The Great Republic–the rising system of international political economy that will provide the greatest economic opportunity and advances in history.

More distant history may view President Nixon very differently in light of the new global economy that lies ahead. The digital gold currency that is now emerging will likely play an important role in the next global long wave advance. There are powerful forces at work that will lead governments to create their own DGC systems to compliment their fiat currency systems. There are reasons to believe that the U.S. Congress and Treasury will also realize gold's critical role and offer DGC in parallel to the Federal Reserve's fiat dollar system. Such a dual gold/fiat currency system actually makes a great deal of sense and would accelerate global economic growth. It will also make the Federal Reserve's job of managing a stable monetary policy far more manageable, thus allowing the Federal Reserve to maintain its essential independence from the political process.

Fort Knox represents potentially the largest and safest digital gold currency bank vault in the world. A change of this scale will take some clarification of the U.S. Constitution in the form of a constitutional amendment. A move to turn Fort Knox into the world's largest digital gold bank vault could be a boon to the U.S. and global economy. Although DGC represents a completely separate currency from the dollar it could secure the role of the U.S. fiat dollar as the world's reserve fiat currency for years to come, which will continue to play a vital and lead role in the global economy.

For the second edition of this book, published in 1995, eight years after the release of the first edition, I asked Mr. Graham if he would write a few lines for the dust jacket. He graciously wrote a number of paragraphs, however, only two lines were used by the publisher from what he had written on the dust jacket of the second edition. When I began to consider updating this book for another edition, in light of the economic long wave crisis entering its critical years, I came across the unpublished material he had written for the second edition. It struck me that his words are far more relevant now than when he wrote them. His reference to fear on the part of almost everybody regarding the global economy seems more poignant, even prophetic. Fear is now a pervasive and dominant theme concerning the global economy and financial markets.

Like so many of his generation, the Great Depression on the farm left indelible memories that impacted Mr. Graham's entire life. When he was recently asked about his most vivid memories of the Great Depression, he told of seeing the effects of the Great Depression in his father's eyes. This memory moved me to the core, as it is occurring once again in homes around the world as we all struggle to deal with this global crisis. Children are seeing the effects of this crisis in their parent's eyes and, no doubt, parents are also seeing it in the eyes of their children.

Over dinner on the mountain in 2008, the emerging debt crisis assailing Wall Street and the world was discussed with

Mr. Graham. We also discussed the idea that a new updated edition of this book may be appropriate and help people of all walks of life understand the causes of this global crisis and give them a clear hope for the future. I asked him if the material he had written for the 2nd edition could be used as a foreword for a new updated edition, and that I saw no need for him to add to what he had already written due to its prescience. He graciously agreed and encouraged me to pursue a new edition, and he was keen on a return to the original title of *Jubilee on Wall Street*. The material he had written for the second edition is now the previously unpublished and unedited foreword in this new edition, with the only change being the title's return to *Jubilee on Wall Street*.

After encouraging me to pursue this edition, with his renowned quick wit and great sense of humor, Mr. Graham shared one of his characteristic anecdotal stories. He told of a man that took a flight from Los Angeles to New York in response to an advertisement for a job position that required specialized education, expertise and experience. The man in the story traveled to New York specifically to tell the potential employer that he was not the man for the job. Mr. Graham was clearly suggesting that he is not an expert on the subject matter of the economic long wave or the current global financial crisis. Nevertheless, most of us will agree that Mr. Graham is something of an expert on the waywardness of the human heart, and has a talent for redirecting us toward what really matters in times of personal and national crisis. We discussed that the magnitude of the global crisis and the misguided human action that caused it may in fact indicate that the long wave is ultimately driven by forces that transcend financial, business, monetary and political decision making. The long wave may ultimately be driven by the unfulfilled needs and, therefore, the unchecked ambitions of the human heart.

No matter how you slice it, we are experiencing a global debt driven deflationary recession, or depression, depending on which country you call home. However, this book suggests there are, in fact, solid reasons and clear evidence for great optimism that a remarkable and prosperous future lies directly ahead.

The forecast for the rise of a new global economy with phenomenal potential for growth and prosperity is not merely based on the fact that recessions and depressions run their course in due season. This prediction is founded on a theory that demonstrates that the global economy thrives on new beginnings–especially those born of adversity and caused by prior mistakes–and on the crises they create. The forces of the long wave are coupled with the sweeping raw power and potential of great new ideas and with the clarity of thought that comes from a clean slate on which to work. We are now experiencing the economy's version of not just Jubilee on Wall Street, but a truly global Jubilee.

PREFACE

"In the end, the only way out of all this global debt may prove to be a Biblical debt Jubilee."

Ambrose Evans-Pritchard,
The Daily Telegraph, January 2009

Every fiftieth year, on the Day of Atonement, let the trumpets blow loud and long throughout the land. For the fiftieth year shall be holy, a time to proclaim liberty throughout the land to all enslaved debtors, and a time for the canceling of all public and private debts. It shall be a year when all the family estates sold to others shall be returned to the original owners or their heirs.

What a happy year it will be! In it you shall not sow, nor gather crops nor grapes; for it is a holy Year of Jubilee for you. That year your food shall be the volunteer crops that grow wild in the fields. Yes, during the Year of Jubilee everyone shall return home to his original family possession; if he has sold it, it shall be his again!

Because of this, if the land is sold or bought during the preceding forty-nine years, a fair price shall be arrived at by counting the number of years until the Jubilee. If the Jubilee is many years away, the price will be high; if few years, the price will be low; for what you are really doing is selling the number of crops the new owner will get from the land before it is returned to you.

You must fear your God and not overcharge! For I am Jehovah. Obey my laws if you want to live safely in the land. When you obey, the land will yield bumper crops and you can eat your fill in safety.

Leviticus 25: 8-19

INTRODUCTION

This book presents the evidence that there is actually an enlightening comprehensive theory of global economic, financial and political development that clearly explains why we now find ourselves in the greatest global debt bust in human history. The theory is known as the economic long wave. In this book you will learn that the current global financial and economic crisis is clearly the manifestation of the winter season of the global long wave.

Renowned Harvard economist, Joseph Schumpeter, the author of the two-volume set, Business *Cycles*, observed that the long wave is the single most important tool in economic prognostication. If he is right (and this author wholeheartedly agrees with him), then the most important topic of financial and economic study and discussion that will help us come to terms with and understand the cause and way out of the current global financial and economic crisis is a thorough review of the economic long wave. The most important questions that can be asked at present are regarding what the long wave is telling us about the current global crisis.

The long wave has a multifaceted basis in the writings of the Russian economist, Nikolai Kondratieff, in the 1920s, the more recent research at the System Dynamics Group and MIT, the ancient and remarkably insightful Levitical laws regarding the Year of Jubilee, the overwhelming evidence of history, and the current global crisis itself. The current global situation was, in fact, predicted by many who follow and understand the long wave.

The central tenets of the long wave are more applicable today than at any time since proposed and introduced to the world by Kondratieff in 1926, on the eve of the Great Depression. Over the years a significant number of prominent national and international financial and business publications have printed articles discussing the potential existence of a long wave of prosperity and depression. Among the publications carrying such articles have been *The Wall Street Journal, Barron's,*

The Economist, BusinessWeek, National Affairs, Forbes, and *The London Financial Times,* to name a few. To the surprise of many readers, these articles always mention a number of prominent economists, financial analysts, and academic institutions that take very seriously the evidence of a long wave, a cycle that passes through the global economy at regular intervals. However, in the end, most of the articles typically conclude that, although compelling, the theory is outdated for our modern high-tech economy with built-in government safety nets. Such conclusions require reconsideration in light of recent global developments.

The theory of the economic long wave explains in detail how a new vibrant global economy will emerge beyond this crisis and the clear implications for various investment instruments. Only the theory of the dynamic long wave, which has been recurring in global market economies for hundreds of years, provides the much needed insight into the greatest global economic and financial collapse since the Great Depression.

Economic and financial crises have devastated the global economy and financial markets along with unsuspecting investors on a recurring basis throughout history. This fact is undisputable. The real question is whether there is evidence of a long wave in such unfortunate events. A closer look at the evidence reveals that those who take the long wave lightly are making a mistake, with potentially severe financial and economic consequences. The accounts and portfolios of most savers and investors are reduced to mere fractions of their previous values, often to nothing, when the periods of depression inevitably come knocking at the door of global prosperity during the decline of the long wave.

The study of economic long wave presented in this book is driven by four key areas of interests for any student of the long wave: Part I, the overwhelming evidence of the long wave's existence; Part II, the profound influence of the long wave on all aspects of the global economy and society; Part III, the long wave effect on various investment instruments; and Part IV, the impact of the current long wave crisis on the future and the struggle between competing world systems, one of which will secure its dominance as we emerge from the current global crisis. These four key areas of long wave inquiry are reflected in the four sections of this book.

The ability of aggressive fiscal and monetary policy to lengthen, but not eliminate, business cycles has been confirmed by System Dynamics research at MIT. The good news regarding these fiscal and monetary policy propagated bubbles that extended the boom years is that the global financial crisis will likely be compressed as compared to the Great Depression. The implications for the global economy and individual participants are profound. In short, we are far closer to the end of this long wave winter than during its parallel long wave global financial panic of the early 1930s, and, therefore, we are far closer to catching the rising tide of the next global long wave advance. The beginning of a new long wave will be a very positive and transformational force that proves to be a powerful new beginning for the global economy.

The global debt crisis and degree of global debt deleveraging taking place is unprecedented. Every nation and almost every individual on the planet will be affected in some way by this crisis. Global debt in all forms is astronomically high and is weighing down consumers, businesses, governments and taxpayers. Debt must be reduced. The crisis is truly a modern day Jubilee–a period of global debt reckoning and financial collapse–that is driven by debt deleveraging and is bringing the global economy and financial markets to their knees. This modern day Jubilee has come to Wall Street and all financial centers around the globe. Only the theory known as the economic long wave provides the evidence and framework to explain the unfolding debt crisis.

Professor Nouriel Roubini, one of the few who clearly and articulately anticipated this global debt crisis, is the widely followed, Harvard-educated Ph.D. economist, Chairman of RGE Monitor, and economics professor at the Stern School of Business at New York University. One seldom-discussed aspect of Roubini's analysis is that he is one of the lone voices that recognizes and cuts to the core the greatest issue of this global debt crisis and its only option for resolution. His clear insight is summarized when he stated, "The only real solution to the problem of over indebtedness is to reduce the value of the outstanding debt."

This statement effectively highlights the fundamental principles at work in the Jubilee debt forgiveness and the booms and busts of the economic long wave. Dr. Roubini has also been one of the few to point out the intrinsic contradictions of socializing risk and privatizing profits in a capitalist system, which will surely lead to great long term structural problems for capitalism. Too much debt weighing down households, businesses and governments is not only the heart of the problem; it is what drives the long wave. The amount of debt in the system exceeds the ability for household, business and government incomes to repay it and, therefore, for the economy to expand.

It should be remembered that taxpayers are also the ones ultimately responsible for all public debt, and not just their mortgage, home equity line, credit card, auto and college loan debt. The Jubilee principle of a year of debt cancellation to keep debt from reaching excessive levels takes on a new perspective in light of the debt levels we have reached and the debt collapse now sweeping the globe. Private debt, including household and business debt exceeds $25 trillion. It is estimated that including existing government debt, plus future government obligations and entitlements, the amount of debt in the U.S. exceeds $50 trillion. Government has no money of its own. All debts will ultimately be repaid by individuals. Even corporate taxes that go to pay off government debts are all ultimately paid by individuals who buy a company's products, a very simple concept that many do not grasp. That puts each American's total private and government debt obligations at over $150,000. Welcome to modern day debt slavery. However, we are now experiencing a modern day Year of Jubilee. But if debt is not allowed to default and be wrung from the system through bankruptcy and reorganization, the pain will be long and drawn out further than it has to be and the next advance will not be as powerful as it otherwise would be.

The debt problem is global. Most developed and periphery countries are suffering from the same debt contagion and collapse in real estate values as the United States. The global financial problems produced by the amounts of debt going bad represent the crux of the most severe international systemic crisis since the Great Depression.

Once you understand the basic concepts of the long wave that invariably reduces debt through bankruptcy, failure and deleveraging every 50-to-70 years, you will have a better understanding of the global predicament. The insightful parallels with the principles of the Jubilee calling for debt forgiveness will become clear. However, the international debt crisis that continues to spread will only be minimally impacted by the relatively small amount of officially sponsored debt forgiveness compared to the total debt that threatens the U.S. and global economy. The greatest amount of debt forgiveness in this long wave is expected to ultimately come through failure, bankruptcy and foreclosure, on the part of individuals, companies and governments around the globe.

Some have suggested that this book and the Jubilee principal advocate the redistribution of wealth. This feedback comes from those who fail to understand the principles and implications of the Jubilee–the basic theme of this book. The long wave is international free market capitalism's naturally occurring Jubilee mechanism. Capitalism is the greatest system ever devised in this history of humanity to drive human growth and development. The Jubilee as outlined in the book of Leviticus reveals what could be viewed as a natural law of excess debt, production and prices due to human action in a capitalist market based economic system that corrects naturally with the long wave. The Jubilee is also a call to better stewardship of our resources and individual accountability.

During the Great Depression, one of the new deal entities was the Home Owners Loan Corporation (HOLC) which purchased mortgages and reduced the debts of households. The key here is that debt levels were reduced, a government sponsored partial Jubilee was provided to households and administered by the government. The Obama administration announced a Homeowner Stability Initiative (HSI), but its implementation has been slow. It is not clear if the amount of debt will actually be reduced for home owners. This or a similar plan will likely be implemented and greatly expanded in some form before this long wave crisis has run its course, potentially on a scale far larger than HOLC in the Great Depression. However, it will likely only be able to help a small portion of indebted households that are facing foreclosure, but is certainly in the spirit of the Jubilee, unless it is only used to transfer the debt to taxpayers.

Government stepping in with various bailouts is troubling for anyone who believes in the basic tenets of free markets and capitalism. The depth of this long wave crisis is created by a combination of human greed and government intervention in mortgage markets without requisite regulation in the late stages of a global long wave, but there is far more than greed at work. Various other levels of creeping state capitalism and interventionism run amuck exacerbated the heights of incredulity seen in this cycle. A global crisis multiplied many times over by state capitalism and intervention requires a role be played by the state to unwind the leverage and disaster.

The fact that many pundits have been blaming the free market, *laissez-faire* capitalism for the global financial and economic crisis needs to be addressed. It's true that the long wave and its market forces are essential, but government intervention and state capitalism's sponsorship of trillions of dollars in the speculative debt bubbles that have burst during this long wave winter season have made conditions far worse than they would otherwise have been.

We haven't had a true free market system for a long time, so allowing a true free market solution to this crisis was not an option. A true free market based solution to what is a crisis of "state" capitalism would have been widespread bankruptcy, merciless and swift retribution and punishment for bad business decisions, in short, immediate and total global systemic financial meltdown. The government had no choice but to step in with various bailouts or there would have been an uncontrolled unwinding of global debt with spreading global financial contagion. Those who smugly called to let the free market sort it out did not understand the implications of such a cavalier position.

However, the necessary bailouts should have been managed with far more prudence and common sense. Most accept that some bailouts were required, but there is outrage at bailouts that had no provisions to prevent paying out billions in bonuses to the managers that helped create the disaster. It is unconscionable that working grandmothers and their grandchildren are going to pay for million-dollar bonuses to financial managers who are responsible for the greatest financial blunders in history. Entities that were effectively gambling with uncovered puts should have never have had their gambling winnings covered by taxpayers when the house failed.

It appears as if politicians do not realize that these political failures are producing far reaching tsunamis of populist outrage that will sweep the country in future elections. The politicians believe voters will forget. Those who dismiss populist outrage and the consequences do not have long enough memories themselves, or a sufficient grasp of history. Their review of relevant history should perhaps go back a bit further than a few decades. I would suggest a bit of French history, starting with Bastille Day.

Let me be clear, this author is an advocate of free markets, pure undefiled free markets; however, what is not really appreciated by most free market proponents is that the real market takes no prisoners. It shows no mercy. You cannot throw a pen-raised, corn-fed, fatted calf into a fight with a hungry grizzly bear. That would simply not be sporting. Those who suggest letting the free market have its way in this crisis, likely do not fully appreciate the implications of the argument they are making in this long wave crisis. If we allow the market to swing the pendulum that far that fast, socialism or even neo-Marxism will look like an attractive alternative for many struggling people—real people with real pain and frustration. We are already witnessing a rush to embrace aspects of socialism by redistributing wealth to try and create demand.

The fact of the matter is that advocates of free markets are now in a most precarious position in the greatest global chess match of ideas in all of human history. Proponents of free markets must now be willing to sacrifice a few game pieces for past mistakes, or risk losing their Queen.

In short, this crisis is a time for a bit of pragmatism on the part of proponents of free markets, if there ever was one. Government intervention and stabilization of the debt crisis is required in various forms. The plan should be to get the global economy out of the ICU and allow international capitalism to survive until the next long wave advance kicks in. We must fight for a return to true free markets as soon as possible. Creeping state capitalism and interventionism that creates future moral hazard, malinvestment and economic dislocation must be fought at every level. Only true free markets will realize the full potential of the global economy. Government must be made more efficient and radically reduced on all fronts and we must fight to establish a genuine global system of free market international capitalism. Socialization of risk and privatization of profits in the form of state capitalism and interventionism that got us into this mess must be fought across the board.

I realize it is not the popular position at present, but the depth of this crisis was not caused by free markets, but by creeping "state" capitalism in the U.S. and intervention in combination with the decline of a long wave winter season. Free markets cannot be allowed to take the blame in the long run. However, pragmatists must be fully aware of the risks now faced by the economy and even the stability of governments, due to decades of compromise. By compromising in the past, there is a risk that this crisis pushes not just the U.S., but the entire developed world into the arms of a renewed form of global socialism, which is beyond the point of no return to true free market international capitalism for our civilization. We will address this clear and present danger in this book.

The U.S. government, which played a major role in creating the excessive global debt boom, was right to step in and attempt an orderly unwinding of the greatest debt bubble ever accumulated in human history. Most of the politicians calling for a total free market solution have themselves been enjoying the spoils of creeping state capitalism collecting in their reelection coffers for decades. After decades on the dole, advocating and accepting creeping state capitalism and intervention, the politicians who only pay lip service to free markets have forfeited their right to stand up for limited government at this critical time. They do not appreciate how violently and swiftly the vigilante traders and true free market international capitalism will handle this long wave global debt crisis.

The key in the years ahead for proponents of international free market capitalism is that we rapidly make the change from pragmatism to realism. The U.S. and other developed country governments must be forced to back off the socialist limb required to address this crisis as quickly as possible. However, the advocates of socialism are already rising up globally to seize the opportunity of this crisis and seize power wherever possible. We simply cannot allow a move to even greater state control beyond this global debt crisis. If history is any indication, it is going to be a tough fight.

Creeping state capitalism and our mixed system of state intervention and free market economy produced malinvestment, overexpansion and overproduction of everything from houses to cars to toasters. Market participants hooked their corporate and banking wagons to the state sponsored gravy train of insured mortgages that should have never been lent and various other government intervention based enterprises of state capitalism. A lack of regulation and greed also clearly played a major role and created a multiplier to the moral hazard produced by state capitalism and intervention at every level.

The statement has been repeated often in recent days that credit is the life blood of capitalism. This is simply not true. The life blood of free market capitalism is the ingenuity and talent of people; it is the equity capital and cash flow their hard work produces. The importance of credit is overemphasized these days.

What is most disturbing about recent events is the lack of a coherent explanation of how we managed to get ourselves into this mess. The list of the usual suspects–and some not so usual–is long: unmanaged risk, liar loans, inadequate regulation, collateralized debt swaps, no-money-down schemes, loose monetary policy, uncontrolled fiscal policy, too much debt, trade imbalances, hedge fund leverage, short sellers, debt/equity ratios, and the list could go on. If you step back, you realize these are all actors in this great debt crisis and played their roles.

Fortunately, the long wave makes sense of the global crisis being played out before us. The long wave is the single economic theory that takes a broad enough view, has a long enough history of evidence, and is thereby able to unravel this global crisis and make sense of it.

Kondratieff was studying Western grain production and prices when he stumbled onto some disturbing evidence. His findings ultimately led to what has come to be known as the long wave theory, popularly also referred to as the Kondratieff Wave or long wave. After taking a close look at the agricultural data he had collected, Kondratieff began to see the emergence of a long wave in the rise and fall of agricultural prices and production in the market economies of the West. Fascinated with this phenomenon, he began to study other segments of the economy and markets, such as interest rates, land prices, debt, industrial production, and labor prices. He saw that they too followed a distinct long wave of boom and bust.

Kondratieff did extensive research on what he found in the data and published his findings in a paper in 1926, which he delivered in a speech at the Moscow Institute of Economics. Kondratieff's research showed distinct long waves rising and falling in the global market economy from 1789 until his research ended in the mid-1920s. He became convinced of a long wave of prosperity and depression in the international capitalist system. He postulated that if his theory was correct, the free market system was headed for a decline in the 1930s. But he also concluded that the bust and the changes it spawned would, in time, give birth to a new advance of ideas, inventions, growth, and prosperity for market economies that would far surpass the previous advance.

Stalin was pleased with the notion of the impending collapse of the Western world's economic system as projected by Kondratieff for the 1930s. However, he was not happy with Kondratieff's predictions that the system would rebound stronger than ever. Something else troubled the Stalin regime even more than Kondratieff's prediction of the West rising to new heights after its next purifying fall. Kondratieff also concluded that lacking a free market for finding appropriate price and production levels, the planned communist/socialist system would naturally and of necessity become inefficient and stagnant, a permanent winter season. Kondratieff argued for more freedom for prices and production in the economy. In time, logic dictated that a planned communist economic system would fail because of the fundamental contradictions, basic economic relationships, and lack of market forces. The history of Soviet demise tells us Kondratieff was correct.

Kondratieff's struggle for more economic freedom in Russia (he opposed Stalin's agricultural collectivization programs) coupled with the idea that the free market system in the West would come back even stronger than ever during its next long wave advance was intolerable for the authorities. Kondratieff's research was, in effect, praising the inherent self-rejuvenating, long wave of the free market system, while predicting trouble, and in time failure, of a rigid, planned economy.

Kondratieff was rewarded for his research with imprisonment in a slave-labor camp, where he died in 1938. Alexander Solzhenitsyn recorded the death of Kondratieff in his book, *The Gulag Archipelago.* Kondratieff's death came only after his predicted economic and financial collapse in the West had occurred in the form of the Great Depression. The foundations for the new economic and financial beginning in the West, which Kondratieff predicted would come after a depression, were already being established when he died. The ultimate victory in the struggle of global economic and political ideas was already being won in the free market for ideas and capital in the West.

In light of the collapse of the Soviet Union and the recognized superiority of the market system over the planned communist system, Kondratieff's work takes on prophetic dimensions. His research is now finding new respect within Russia and in other countries around the globe. However, if the past gives any clues to potential financial crises and economic trouble in the future, the validity of the free market international capitalism will be brought into question and challenged again-just as it was by communism and socialism during the Great Depression.

A dangerous new world of international bureaucratic interventionism–or, what some would consider the threat of a Global New Deal–may well be the challenge to potentially stifle international capitalism. It will be argued during a crisis that there wasn't enough intervention and government control. It will be argued that the pain created by the market demands even more government involvement, but on a global level.

Among the respected institutions that are interested in the long wave is the prominent Massachusetts Institute of Technology (MIT). The System Dynamics Group in the Sloan School of Management at MIT is dedicated to studying the dynamics of economic, political and business relationships and was created by Jay Forrester, the renowned MIT researcher who also holds a patent to random access memory. The program's computer-generated models provide powerful evidence of a long wave lasting 50-to-70 years. Recent experiments with the model by Forrester have demonstrated that accommodative monetary policy toward the end of the long wave will extend it by an additional decade or more, but the end of the long wave and the inevitable debt reckoning still come. It cannot be avoided.

The System Dynamics Group at MIT is sponsored by dozens of major corporations, who are interested in the application of system dynamics to real world problems. They are also interested in the evidence, pro and con, of a long wave of boom and bust. Businesses are keenly interested in any solid research on a possible economic long wave, its origins and effects, especially in relation to their particular business operations and profitability. This book will take a brief look at the research at MIT.

An interesting thing about the long wave is that, during every new wave, a new core nation leads the next advance and, therefore, experiences the greatest speculative bubbles in stocks, real estate, and industrial expansion. Evidence would indicate that France was the leader of the long wave peak in the 1810s; England was the leader of the peak in the 1870s (although England wasn't as speculative as previous leaders, its empire was lost during the decline); and the United States was the leader in the 1920s. It is clear that Japan was on the front edge of the most recent long wave economic advance and financial speculation as evidenced by their economic contagion for almost two decades now. China will invariably lead the next advance and is, in many respects, already out of the blocks; but it will also suffer great economic pain during the current decline.

Joseph Schumpeter believed there were 18 business cycles in each long wave. More recent data, charting technology and evidence suggests there are only 16 business cycles in every economic long wave, which was first recognized by PQ Wall (www.PQWall.com). The stock market crash of 1987 was obviously not the major long wave financial crash anticipated in this long wave, but only the decline of one of the 16 smaller business cycles now expected to make up a complete long wave. The 16 business cycles discussed here are not necessarily identified by the official government recession statistics, but are evident in major stock market indexes.

During the last long wave the U.S. stock market appears to have peaked during 1929, in the 11th business cycle of the total 16 business cycles that make up every long wave. It is interesting to note that during this long wave, Japan, the leader of stock market speculation this time around, appears to have peaked in 1989, which was also the 11th business cycle of the 16 business cycles expected in the current long wave.

Since the early 1980s, I have been counting off the cycles. The global economy is now projected to be in the final cycle number 16 before we get the next long wave under way. This final cycle promises to be full of major financial and economic developments before this long wave ends and a new one begins.

In this long wave, the U.S. and other global markets have peaked in much later business cycles than typically expected in a long wave, due to excessive and aggressive fiscal and monetary policy that pumped liquidity into the system at the first hint of financial and economic trouble on the downward slope of the long wave. These injections of liquidity sought to avoid the smaller business cycle downturns. Fiscal and monetary stimulation have become more aggressive as the economic and market risks of the inevitable adjustment continued to grow. It is now clear that these smaller cycles were all building greater forces of systemic debt risk into the larger global long wave. It is now clear that the current long wave has crested and is now plunging into the unknown of a global systemic debt crisis.

The good news is that this long wave winter season may be far shorter than most, but the debt bust will be severe. The government stimulated the economy deep into this winter season. The flip-side of a global long wave winter is that, following these tough years of debt liquidation, we will enjoy the beginning of a powerful new global long wave expansion. Unlike the last long wave, when communism was threatening the borders of international capitalism, and global markets were actually shrinking, we now have capitalism spreading to huge new markets around the world.

The BRIC countries of Brazil, Russia, India and China, and dozens of smaller countries, are relatively new markets for the expansion and spread of international capitalism (i.e., they provide better returns on capital for older industries). These markets will likely suffer during this long wave winter, but as the next long wave gets underway, these markets are expected to recover quickly with growing internal demand, and pull the U.S. economy into a major recovery and global boom. The powerful economic growth that will explode as these economies enter the next long wave advance should not be underestimated. The new long wave expansion will bring the implementation of breakthroughs and advances in all areas of science and technology that will be deployed globally. The next long wave advance, led by these relatively new entrants into the global economy, could produced a global boom that will shock and astound.

This book proposes that there are three primary options available for the global economy to emerge from this global crisis (though only one of these options will prevail in the years ahead): The first option, which I believe has a very small probability of occurring, deserves vetting and review due to recent events that demonstrate the potential for the rise of global socialism, and government ownership of production. There are those who advocate a new world order of global socialism and believe this global long wave crisis will provide the opportunity to shift national and international political institutions as well as national and international law in this direction. In light of the recent lurch toward socialist solutions to this crisis by governments all over the world, including the U.S., this option deserves review, but is not expected by this author to get real traction, and it is doomed to failure if it does. The second option is a redistributive world empire, where the middle class bears the tax burden of wealth redistribution for the social safety net, but also bears the costs of the socialization of risks and the privatization of profits for an elite class of managers and politicians. Production is primarily privately owned. Unfortunately, this appears to be the direction world leaders are currently taking us and is the most likely outcome. Fortunately, there is a third option–what I term The Great Republic. The Great Republic is the ascendence from this global systemic crisis of a new form of genuine free market international capitalism. The idea behind The Great Republic was first presented by Adam Smith in the *Wealth of Nations* with the concept he coined as, "The Great Mercantile Republic." There are a number of reasons why a new global economy in the form The Great Republic with free access to information, financial capital and human capital will emerge more free and stronger than ever from this global systemic crisis.

Hope springs eternal. My hope for a better economic future for all lies in the rise of The Great Republic. There is reason to believe The Great Republic has real potential to rise out of wreckage of this global crisis. Ironically, such a system also has the potential to enhance the sovereignty and economic power of any nation state that embraces it and allows it to flourish, although The Great Republic will exist beyond the reach of manipulation and coercion of national governments. The Great Republic would be driven by the free flow of information and unfettered global access to products, services, capital and human talent.

Although fiat currencies will still be prevalent and may dominate trade activity, the digital gold currency (DGC) of The Great Republic will provide an independent check on the risks of government fiscal policy run amuck. Central bank response to fiscal policy makes effectively managing fiat money a very difficult if not impossible task. The digital gold currency of The Great Republic will force smaller and more efficient national governments. It will mercilessly and transparently punish bad fiscal and fiat monetary policy by crushing national and regional fiat currencies that are mismanaged in their gold price, which it will otherwise not oppose. Digital gold currency that is secure and can be used in national and international transactions is now possible due to the Internet. Such a currency closely resembles the U.S. Constitution's requirements for currency, but prevents such a currency's manipulation and inevitable mismanagement and destruction by Congress.

The early trends in this global crisis are toward a redistributive world empire. One of the great problems with a redistributive world empire is the disturbing trend toward the privatization of profits and the socialization of risks. This trend must be reversed. Fortunately, a redistributive world empire, even with all its faults, is a better alternative than world socialism. On the bright side, Rome, the last redistributive world empire, did last in a fairly stable form for hundreds of years, before it collapsed into the dark ages of human ruin and misery. We must now back away from our lurch toward a redistributive world empire as quickly as possible, but it will be difficult.

Upon review of the evidence presented in this book, you may come to agree that the long wave provides highly relevant and timely insight into the global crisis now unfolding. The intent is to provide relevant information pertaining to your investments and a review of World-Systems Analysis for the future political, economic and financial system options that will lead us out of this crisis.

Long wave analysis suggests that we have now sailed into the tough final years of a long wave winter season. A required period of debt deleveraging and liquidation is in full force. However, as surely as winter follows fall, bringing death and decay, so the winter, of necessity, gives birth to spring and new life. A new long wave advance promises to get underway shortly that promises to take international free market capitalism and all participants to new levels of accomplishments and success.

PART I
THE FOUNDATION

Chapter 1:

A BRIEF HISTORY OF FINANCIAL CRISIS

"Every generation, no matter how paltry its character, thinks itself much wiser than the one immediately preceding it, let alone those that are more remote."

Arthur Schopenhauer

"Study the past if you would divine the future."

Confucius

Financial crises have no doubt been occurring ever since the human race decided that a better life was possible by participating in the trade of goods and services with fellow human beings. Markets were created to facilitate trade and disequilibrium was invented. The primary approach of this book is to provide the evidence for the long wave that lies in the past 200 years of history. However, to limit our observations to that era alone would be shortsighted. A review of the more distant history of financial crisis will actually help put the current global crisis in perspective.

This chapter is to be a brief and hopefully enjoyable overview of the Ancient, Roman, Medieval, and Renaissance history of human conflict with the economy and the inevitable recurrence of systemic financial shock to economic systems. We will look at a number of fascinating facts and stories. This chapter is meant to help build a framework for our study by presenting anecdotal evidence that as humans we have regularly engaged in systemic financial crisis throughout history. Historical crises provide great insight into our current global crisis. If such a look back at financial history holds no interest for you, then by all means, proceed to the next chapter.

There is clear evidence that the rise and fall of the economic forces wrought by human interaction have been with us since the history books have been kept. The rise and fall of economies within societies and civilizations in many ways appear to be subplots in the entire story of human development. To assume humanity has become immune from such historic tendencies may be the height of human arrogance. All you need to do is pick up a paper or turn on the news to realize we are in the soup once again.

Recorded economic declines of ancient history have haunting similarities with modern declines and depressions. This chapter takes a look back into history so that we may gain a broad-based perspective on the issues of prosperity and depression, boom and bust. The economic advances and declines we will review in this chapter played an important role in the emergence of the economic world we live in today.

Many have a hard time imagining the Pharaoh of Egypt in the year 2500 B.C. pacing his gold-laden throne room, worried over the current trade imbalance or the dwindling of the treasury, due to extravagant public works projects. Whether due to our preoccupation with the present or simply a lack of broad enough liberal education, it would seem there is a prevailing view that ups and downs in the economy are a fairly modern problem. The fact of the matter is, for thousands of years, humanity has been plagued with the seemingly uncontrollable economic downturn–just when life was beginning to seem comfortable.

What are the forces that cause kings to fall from their thrones, banks to shut their doors, and previously sane men to leap from tall buildings? Are there natural laws that govern the rise and fall of economies and financial markets, or does humanity hold the key that controls the forces that can and will bring whole nations and civilizations to their knees?

The noted historian Otto C. Lightner (1922) wrote a major work titled, *The History of Economic Depressions*. This chapter summarizes Lightner's insightful work. Lightner owned and managed a number of successful newspaper and publishing companies. During the Great Depression, he was the publisher of *Hobbies* magazine, based in Chicago. He said that since very few people had money during the Great Depression, they should have a hobby. The public agreed. His magazine did very well and Lightner prospered during the period. We have seen this again in the current global crisis, when gardening is enjoying a major resurgence.

The Lightner museum is located in what was the Alcazar Hotel in St. Augustine, Florida. The Alcazar sits across the street from what was the famous Ponce de Leon Hotel. St. Augustine was considered the American Riviera in the late 1800s. The Alcazar Hotel was one of the most lavish and opulent in the country in its day. The Great Depression proved to be more than the hotel could endure. It closed its doors after the winter season of 1931.

During the Great Depression, Lightner became a collector of everything from rare art work to musical instruments. He bought fascinating items at greatly reduced prices from the estates of former millionaires. Many of the items were relics of the roaring 1920s. His collection became so large that, in 1946, he bought the vacant Alcazar Hotel for $150,000 and turned it into a museum to store his collection. Lightner's book (1922) gives an insightful perspective into the problem of changing economic forces and the havoc they played on humanity's plans over the centuries.

We will begin our quest for answers on the ancient shores of the Mediterranean Sea. Going as far back as 6000 B.C., the Mesopotamians made incredible economic advances. They appear to have experienced the peak of a great civilization around 4000 B.C. They engaged in substantial trade and commerce. Some historians say they had banks similar to those of the present day before vanishing as a culture. Around the year 2000 B.C., the Egyptian civilization dominated as a commercial empire on the scale of one of the few major empires.

Egypt is the first clear example in recorded history when the economy of a civilization repeatedly rose and fell in cyclical fashion, yet maintained its identity. It is recorded that ancient Egypt reached incredible levels of economic development, which then declined. During periods of depression, the rulers put armies of hundreds of thousands of unemployed to work building pyramids. Egyptian history was scarred by four severe economic declines and subsequent revivals. During these ups and downs, the empire was never conquered by its enemies. Other civilizations probably experienced such swings from prosperity to depression, but the historic evidence of such economic shifts is missing.

Babylon emerged as the commercial leader in the region of the lower valley of the Tigris and Euphrates Rivers. But in time even the Great Babylon succumbed to the forces of economic decline, and the empire crumbled. In considering the decline of Babylon in the first half of the final millennium B.C., we see this clearly. According to Lightner (1922):

> It was only when the Europeans found a new path to India across the ocean and converted the great commerce of the world from a land to a sea trade that the royal city on the banks of the Tigris and Euphrates began to decline. Then, deprived of its commerce it fell a victim to the two-fold oppression of anarchy and violence and sunk to its original state-a stinking marsh and barren land.

The Assyrians emerged from the carnage left by the Babylonian demise and built an empire that also stretched into Egypt and Asia Minor. In time, disorganization and then anarchy brought down the Assyrians as well. After the Assyrians, the Persians, led by Cyrus the Great, became the dominant and ruling people in the region.

During the Heroic Age of Greece, the city states rose to commercial and artistic supremacy. The Greeks are known for their innovation in politics and philosophy, as well as their openness and creative spirit in dealing with the issues and obstacles of life. For thousands of years, leaders attempted to avert the erosion of faith in their commercial systems unsuccessfully; but in the year 594 B.C., Solon, the Athenian statesman and law giver, took radical measures that had never before been attempted. The plan Solon used to bring order to Greece's economy is very much like the plan laid out for the Year of Jubilee. Whether Solon borrowed the plan or came upon it spontaneously, its application as a cure for a worsening situation was unique. While the Year of Jubilee was to be applied as preventive medicine, Solon was applying his plan as Athens lay on its financial and economic deathbed.

Lightner (1922) wrote that when a great depression struck Athens in 594 B.C., creating public panic, Solon produced a bold plan that rescued Athens from its dire predicament. Debt and poverty oppressed the poor of Athens. Selfishness and greed were considered normal, expected behavior on the part of the higher classes. Extracting the last dime in interest from the poor for their debts seemed the highest aim of the wealthy. This should ring a bell with recent news on banks and their credit card policies and accusations of usury. By birth, Solon was a member of the aristocracy. However, during the course of his life, he had learned the ways of exploitation by merchants through interest on debt. He understood the plight of the common people and he knew the cure. The situation had grown so bad that neighboring city states were planning to attack Athens in its weakened state of economic depression.

Solon took action. Every citizen who had been sold into slavery was restored. All debts secured by individuals and property were canceled. All debts on land were canceled.

Looking forward in history from the time of Solon, we find that the laws enacted by him have been reenacted by many nations and leaders during times of economic depression right up to the present day. No doubt we will see similar actions in the future as well. In 2009, what could have been considered as a Jubilee law was proposed in the U.S. that would have allowed bankruptcy judges to reduce the mortgage debt of homeowners, but it stalled.

It was many years after Solon had saved Athens from distress with his radical changes, debt cancellation, and innovations that Greek civilization finally fell from dominance in the ancient world. Alexander the Great ruled the remnants of Greek civilization through the Macedonian Empire in the fourth century B.C. He led the overthrow of the then-declining Persian Empire in 328 B.C.

It would be fascinating to have a detailed historical account of the demise and destruction of these ancient empires. Perhaps it was a few dry years and the devastation of the wheat harvest that brought the Assyrians to ruin; possibly the Persian leaders had an extravagance for villas on the Mediterranean and a weakness for wine and women. Even without perfect records, we know that there were major shifts taking place in the commerce of the world and market forces that led to the fall and decline of these empires.

It would be easy to drift into the dangerous game of finding one villain for all the problems and afflictions that bring about the rise and fall of civilizations. But every factor plays its role and is only enhanced and strengthened by other factors as they slowly weave their way together and around the very life of the civilization they are seeking to destroy.

The rise and fall of empires and civilizations beyond the control of the men at the helm, and occasionally women, was not confined to the Mediterranean region and Southwest Asia. Counterparts of the Far East were not immune from the disease of decline that in time infects all cultures who have come together to form both political and economic ties in their quest to build a stable society.

Evidence indicates that from the first Chinese dynasty around 2200 B.C., its people experienced periods of great prosperity and, in turn, trade decline and depression. The cause of these declines is not completely known. We do know, however, that the printing press and mariner's compass were discovered and used by the Chinese and were then lost and forgotten during periods of economic crisis and chaos. The Chinese will likely experience their largest financial crisis in a few thousand years during this long wave winter.

The Roman Empire began to emerge as the dominant political and economic force in the world in the first century B.C. Eventually Rome expanded its borders to engulf most of the civilized world. In its prime, Rome reigned supreme as the seat of world government. The Via Sacra was the Wall Street of the world.

We can gain a number of insights into today's problems from an account of a Roman crisis in the year A.D. 33, as told by Lightner (1922, p. 20-22). If detailed records were available, maybe the long wave would be evident. Just trade a few of the banking names for Bear Stearns and Lehman Brothers.

When we make a hasty survey of the Roman Empire to find the symptoms of decay there is brought to light as the outstanding feature industrial stagnation and commercial ruin. The year 33 A.D. was full of events in the ancient world. It marked two disturbances as the outgrowth of the mob spirit. The first was in the remote province of Judea where one Christus was tried before Pontius Pilate, was crucified, dead and buried. The other event was the great Roman panic which shook the empire from end to end. The consternation accompanying the latter died down and it was soon forgotten, but the murmurings of the former swept down the centuries until, bursting into flames, it enveloped the world.

A description of the panic reads like one of our own times: The important firm of Seuthes and Son, of Alexandria, was facing difficulties because of the loss of three richly laden ships in a Red Sea storm, followed by a fall in the value of ostrich feather and ivory. About the same time the great house of Malchus and Co. of Tyre with branches at Antioch and Ephesus, suddenly became bankrupt as a result of a strike among their Phoenician workmen and the embezzlements of a freedman manager. These failures affected the Roman banking house, Quintus Maximus and Lucius Vibo. A run commenced on their bank and spread to other banking houses that were said to be involved, particularly the Brothers Pittius. The Via Sacra was the Wall Street of Rome and this thoroughfare was teeming with excited merchants. These two firms looked to other bankers for aid, as is done today. Unfortunately, rebellion had occurred among the semi civilized people of North Gaul, where a great deal of Roman capital had been invested, and a moratorium had been declared by the government on account of the disturbed conditions. Other bankers, fearing the suspended conditions, refused to aid the first two houses and this augmented the crises.

Money was tight for another reason: agriculture had been on a decline for some years and Tiberius had proclaimed that one-third of every senator's fortune must be invested in lands within the province of Italy in order to recoup their agricultural production.

Publius Spintler, a wealthy nobleman, was at that time obliged to raise money to comply with the order and had called upon his bank, Balbus Ollius, for 30 million sesterces, which he had deposited with them. This firm immediately closed their doors and entered bankruptcy before the praetor. The panic was fast spreading throughout all the province of Rome and the civilized world. News came of the failure of the great Corinthian bank, Leucippus Sons, followed within a few days by a strong banking house in Carthage. By this time all the surviving banks on the Via Sacra had suspended payment to the depositors. Two banks in Lyons next were obliged to suspend; likewise, another in Byzantium. From all provincial towns creditors ran to bankers and debtors with cries of keen distress only to meet with an answer of failure or bankruptcy.

The legal rate of interest in Rome was then 12 percent and this rose beyond bounds. The praetor's court was filled with creditors demanding the auctioning of the debtor's property and slaves; valuable villas were sold for trifles and many men who were reputed to be rich and of large fortune were reduced to pauperism. This condition existed not only in Rome, but throughout the empire.

Gracchus, the praetor, who saw the calamity threatening the very foundation of all the commerce and industry of the empire, dispatched a message to the emperor, Tiberius, in his villa at Capri. The merchants waited breathlessly for four days until the courier returned. The Senate assembled quickly while a vast throng, slaves and millionaires, elbow to elbow, waited in the forum outside for tidings of the emperor's action. The letter was read to the Senate then to the forum as a breath of relief swept over the waiting multitude.

Tiberius was a wise ruler and solved the problem with his usual good sense. He suspended temporarily the processes of debt and distributed 100 million sesterces from the imperial treasury to the solvent bankers to be loaned to needy debtors without interest for three years. Following this action, the panic in Alexandria, Carthage and Corinth quieted.

And so, under conditions very similar to those existing in the Twentieth Century, business of the Roman Empire resumed its normal aspect and the Via Sacra went its normal way, the same as Wall Street has done on many an occasion after the storm has passed. How similar was the business of the world in that year of the crucifixion of Christ to that of present time!

The Roman Empire dominated the world with the longest period of peace and prosperity ever recorded. But eventually, under the Caesars, corruption and decline set in. Rome's decline as a world empire was scarcely noticeable for the first few hundred years. But in the year A.D. 476, Rome was finally sacked by the Barbarians and the Empire came to an end.

Many attribute the fall of Rome to over taxation, which disgruntled the people and caused unrest, allowing the Barbarians easy victories as they moved toward Rome. The over-taxation and growing inefficiencies of the great bureaucracy had dramatic effects on trade as the volume of the Empire's trade began to slow.

There is a popular belief that moral decadence and the erosion of a nation's value system are the causes of political and economic decline. The decline of Rome is often attributed to this erosion. There is definitely evidence that supports this hypothesis. Too much success can remove the competitive edge from a society and lead to a lazy, pleasure seeking mentality. There is no doubt that an erosion of values destroys the internal structure of an economic system, which will eventually lead to the fall of the civilization. But we must be cautious as we look for the cause of decline and not narrow our vision to any one element. All factors must be taken into consideration as we study the forces that move the global economy and turn even the greatest civilizations into forgotten heaps of rubble.

As the world moved from the glory days of the Roman Empire into the period known as the Middle, or Dark, Ages, it is hard to track the rise and the fall of commerce. The years of Greek and then Roman dominance of the world were marked by great advances in art, science, literature, and commerce. Around the year A.D. 500, the world economy and culture took a radical turn for the worse, a turn that lasted a thousand years.

The ruthless reign and rampaging of the Barbarians stifled any hint of a resurrection in business or the advance of past civilizations. While areas of the Arab world flourished during this period, in Europe there were virtually no books written, and the scant trading that existed between tribes of Western Europe was more often than not interrupted by wars and infighting among the various peoples. The study of this period goes far to show the depth to which humanity can sink. Lightner (1922) noted that simply not being killed and having a sheepskin coat in winter was the height of luxury for most people during the tenth century. Let's hope this is not a repeat for the height of luxury in this long wave winter season.

During the stagnant years of the Middle Ages, a new component to the economic equation was introduced. Religion, taking control of the politics of the day, soon began to have an enormous impact on commerce. The Catholic Church was becoming more and more powerful during this time; it was, and is still, often blamed for holding the world in economic bondage during this period. Wealth that was generated during this time seemed to find its way into the treasury of the Catholic Church and was spent on the extravagances of the Pope.

However, late in the Middle Ages the tables began to turn, and an extraordinary era in the economic progress of the world was ushered in. The Crusades were military campaigns from 1096 to 1291 that were financed by the Catholic Church and government to free the Holy Land from Islam for the Christian cause. The Crusaders did more to stimulate world trade than has any event in history before or since.

Many of the crusaders were motivated by a desire to wrest the Holy Land from the infidels. However, most of the crusaders were homeless men who had nothing to lose and everything to gain. The economic distress was such at the time that most of the warriors were willing to fight for bread and future reward if they were victorious.

Troops traveling from west to east and back ignited the economies of the regions they passed through. New ideas on world affairs were spread. Money was put into circulation. A new system of trade and commerce emerged. There are those who claim the long wave can be tracked back to this period, but the data is not sufficient.

Civilization was slowly working its way out of its darkness, stagnation, and decline and slowly but surely a new day was dawning. The many regions and countries of the world were once again beginning to associate and trade with one another, while at the same time, domestic business activity was on the rise. Art and literature were beginning to emerge again and there was a growing support for education.

Late in the Middle Ages, Holland and Spain emerged as the leading commercial countries of the Western world. Something unique was beginning to happen in these countries. The guild, the predecessor of today's union, was coming into being. As early as the 15th century, depression was attributed by historians to the monopolistic, price-fixing, and protectionist policy of these guilds. The association of commercial interest as a unified front that had its beginning at this time is one of the many elements that play a role in today's rise and fall of the economic cycle.

Modern debit and credit banking can be traced to the last few centuries of the Middle Ages.

During this time, the doctrine stating that it was sinful to take interest lost its force. Economic leaders convinced the clergy that money secured through loans could be put to good use. The financiers convinced the Catholic Church that borrowed funds through debit and credit banking would lead to legitimate development.

During this period, Antwerp was recognized as the financial center of the world. However, lending money to royal debtors, who then proceeded to lose their wars and were thus incapable of repaying their loans, was a grave mistake. These bad loans led to a panic and depression, during which the center of the financial world moved to London, where it remained for five centuries, until the First World War, when it moved to New York. Tokyo was passed the torch of financial leader and speculator of the world in the 1980s, but the torch was quickly passed back to New York for the grand finale of this long wave in the late 1990s.

As the Middle Ages gave birth to the Renaissance, enormous changes were taking place in every area of life. Renaissance means "rebirth" and, indeed, this period was just that, as sweeping changes came to politics, religion, and commerce. Humankind was beginning to explore the ideas of individualism and human freedom and financial control, as the idea of self-rule and self-control surfaced for the first time since the Greeks.

During this time, the industrial and commercial classes began to emerge. Before this period, laborers had been slaves. The quality of their breeding or intelligence didn't matter. Sometimes it was the fortunes of war and sometimes the changes in trade that made them join the ranks of laborer.

Things were changing at the end of the medieval period. Humanity was struggling upward to a state of freedom; whereas trade and commerce had once been considered degrading for the ruling classes, now it was becoming dignified and of growing importance. Lightner (1922) postulated that the world emerged from feudalism due to the demands of commerce. He believed that a need for stronger central government emerged in an attempt to ward off the evil effects of trade declines and local depressions.

Early in the 16th century, with the rise of the Renaissance and mercantile era, economic declines and depressions began to take on new characteristics. Previously, depressions were on the order of trade declines, which moved slowly and gradually into a state of economic despair and confusion. Political folly was often the cause of these declines, as is still true today, but not to the same degree as in previous centuries.

When the personal gains of individualism and freedom began to emerge with the Renaissance, there also emerged a willingness to take a chance and speculate. The art of speculation that arose during this time has stayed with us to the present. The propensity to speculate is another one of the strands that weaves its way into the rope that time has shown will eventually choke the life out of an economic system. One of the first and certainly one of the most fascinating escapades in speculation history occurred around 1630-1635 in Holland.

Lightner (1922, 37-39), quoting Selfridge, relates the story of the tulip mania. Replace the word "tulip" in the quote below for the word "house," and you will have a great description of the collapse of the contemporary housing bubble that has brought Wall Street and the global economy to its knees. However, as we are discovering, when houses are traded like tulip bulbs, the consequences can even be more far reaching.

> The tulip was a rare flower which had been introduced into Western Europe from Turkey and grown in the horticultural collection of Counselor Herwart of Augsburg. The plants were seen by the collectors' neighbors who desired some of their own. The blooms became their pride and others were infected with the desire to possess them. Before long the single little flower had turned everything topsy-turvy; the public had caught the fever and started speculating in tulips. All Europe became involved and the flower gradually

found its way at first into the gardens of wealthy people and later to all classes. Holland was the center of the tulip trade and in that country, as well as most others, it became the requisite of society to possess a collection of tulips.

But the speculative side was probably the most romantic.

The state of the people's mind was such that they wanted excitement and speculation. We read of a trader of Harlem who gave half his fortune for a single bulb ... Stock jobbers made the most of the mania. Few kept their heads and fewer kept aloof from the mania. At first-and it was at this immediate period that the disease reached its virulent form–everyone had infinite confidence in the values and the speculators gained. The market broadened and, as is so often prayed for nowadays by Capel Court and Wall Street, the public came in. Everyone seemed to be making profits from tulips and no one dreamed that prices could fall. People of all grades converted their property into cash and invested in the flowers. House and lands were offered for sale at ruinous rates or assigned in payment of purchases made at the tulip market. Foreigners became smitten with the frenzy and money from abroad poured into Holland. The fever of speculation was superseded by an equally intense fever of pessimism. The whole country was involved and it became imperative that something be done to prevent general bankruptcy. The Government was appealed to. The Government did the usual thing. They discussed the matter for three months and concluded they could not solve the problems. Those who had tulips must lose and lose they did. This applied to nearly everyone. Holland suffered fearfully. Her people, many of them at least, had to begin the accumulation of savings or of fortunes all over again and for years the commerce of the nation languished.

There were numerous economic upheavals throughout Europe during the remainder of the 17th century. In 1640, Charles I sent British commerce into a tailspin by seizing the bullion deposited in the Tower of London. France in 1661 was in great distress due to an enormous trade imbalance with England, Holland, and Spain. In 1672, Charles II sent shock waves through the business community by refusing payment out of the exchequer. The first modern-day run on banks occurred when the Dutch fleet sailed into the Thames. Consternation reigned in London at the sound of their guns. Anyone who had any money at the time had it deposited with the goldsmiths-the bankers of their day. Unfortunately, the government had borrowed the money. The government didn't seem to offer a great deal of security at the time.

In the 18th century, the crisis of 1720 was the first general crisis throughout all of Europe. This crisis was precipitated by the collapse of speculative companies, the South Seas Company in England being one of them, supposedly organized for development in the New World among other ventures. This is known as the South Seas bubble era of speculation. Fortunes from all over Europe were lost. Economic activity and speculation were muted for decades.

In England, December 6, 1745 is known as "Black Friday." A rumor of French invasion touched off a panic. Citizens rushed to withdraw their money from the Bank of England. Virtually all businesses were forced to close down due to the crisis. Merchants hurriedly met and agreed to accept bank notes. A resolution was passed urging the citizens and all merchants to do the same. The resolution was signed by 1,140 businesses and depositors.

England was the victim of another crisis in 1772, which brought with it 525 corporate failures. After the signing of the treaty with America, England found itself again in crisis in 1783. Cornwallis had surrendered to Washington, and the British fleet had been conquered by the admiral of France. Peace brought new markets and a strain on British gold reserves and finances. The year 1789 brought with it the French Revolution and the commercial demise that was inevitable for that nation before its next great advance of Napoleonic conquest.

There were certainly also economic expansions and collapses in the Orient, Africa, the Middle East, and South America, about which we know little or nothing. Coming to the close of the 18th century of global economic history and looking back since the demise of Rome, we see that crises and depressions tended to be local or national in their scope of influence. Occasionally these downturns crossed national borders, but this was the exception, not the rule.

Most argue that there was not sufficient data available to show distinct economic and financial cycles until the end of the 18th century, although booms and busts have long been a reality of commerce. Some argue that there was sufficient data to demonstrate regular cycles in earlier periods.

Evidence indicates that there has always been a rise and fall in the world's economies. However, since late in the 18th century, when better records have been kept, the evidence is even more compelling. A disturbing and fascinating long wave of expansion and contraction has become increasingly obvious for those willing to take the time to examine the evidence.

Nikolai D. Kondratieff 1892–1938

Chapter 2:

KONDRATIEFF'S LONG WAVE DISCOVERY

"Cycles are meaningful, and all science that has been developed in the absence of cycle knowledge is inadequate and partial. ...any theory of economics, sociology, history, medicine, or climatology that ignores non-chance rhythms is as manifestly incomplete as medicine was before the discovery of germs."

Edward R. Dewey

"He who floats with the current, who does not guide himself according to higher principles, who has no ideal, no convictions– such a man is a mere article of the world's furniture–a thing moved, instead of a living and moving being–an echo, not a voice."

Amiel

"The long waves, if existent at all, are a very important and essential factor in economic development, a factor the effects of which can be found in all the principal fields of social and economic life."

Nikolai D. Kondratieff

Nikolai D. Kondratieff was born in 1892 in Russia, where he grew up and was educated during the turmoil of the fall of the Russian monarchy and the emergence of a communist totalitarian dictatorship. Kondratieff graduated from Petersburg University School of Law in 1915. Before radically changing his views, Kondratieff was a member of the left-wing Socialist Revolutionary Party in 1917.

Early on, Kondratieff's interests were turned toward the study of economics and markets, which proved to be his livelihood as well as contributing to his premature death. It was reported in an article on Kondratieff in *National Affairs* (1988, 56), that soon after the revolution, "Kondratieff was no longer a student with socialist-revolutionary leanings, but an eminent scientist, a shrewd and accurate analyst."

At some point, Kondratieff's interest turned from Soviet economic planning–he had worked to develop the first five-year agricultural plan–to the more fascinating analysis of the regular rise and fall of the international capitalist system. Kondratieff became the director of the Institute for Market Studies under the People's Commissariat for Finance.

Early on in his career, as Kondratieff looked over the history of the capitalist system and the data on developments in the global economy since the late 1700s, he saw something quite different from what his peers and predecessors had seen. Kondratieff saw emerging from prices, interest rates, production, and human nature the rise and fall of what has come to be known as the Kondratieff wave. Just as most economists of his day—and, indeed, today–Kondratieff had limited his vision and study to short-term analysis and had never stepped back and taken in a sweeping, all-encompassing view of global economic history. His discovery surprised him.

Kondratieff formulated his views over a number of years. In a footnote at the end of his famous paper, "The Long Wave in Economic Life," which first introduced the notion of long waves to the world, Kondratieff (1951, 42) wrote, "I arrived at the hypothesis concerning the existence of long waves in the years 1919-1921." He noted that he had written the article during the winter and spring of 1925. In February 1926, Kondratieff read a paper on his findings at the Moscow Institute of Economics.

Kondratieff wrote of what he observed to be long wave economic cycles (see Table 2.1). He observed two and one-half cycles. The first cycle began in a trough (economic low point) in 1789 and ended with a trough in the 1840s. He wrote of a plateau period, the long wave fall season, which followed the advance or peak of the cycle. History indicates that the plateauing fall season always gives way to a long wave winter season. Kondratieff himself never appears to have used the seasonal analogy in long waves,

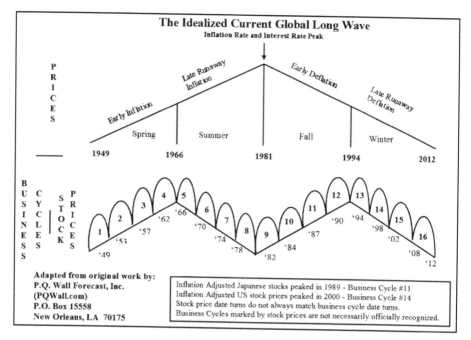

Chart 2.1 The Idealized Current Global Long Wave

which likely originated with PQ Wall and his study of Oswald Spengler's seasonal approach to cultural epochs.

To gain a clear understanding of the long wave plateau, it might help to conceptualize a geographical plateau. You have a steep and lengthy climb to the top of a plateau, an area that brings apparent stability for a time. After crossing the plateau, you come to the edge where you face a steep drop and decline. In like fashion, the economy builds up and expands through the years with rising prices and increasing debt levels, climbing to great heights of output, production, and efficiency. After moving through great advances and expansion, the economy has outdone itself, quite literally. The economy then makes a gallant effort at trying to adjust through capital restructuring. This is the disinflationary fall plateau season of the long wave.

It would be nice if we could stay at these lofty heights forever. The problem is that the economy has been pushed too far and is producing too many goods in every area. With too many companies producing too much, you begin to see falling prices in raw material sectors of the economy. The shift from an inflationary advance to a disinflationary plateau marks the changing of the long wave season from summer into fall.

Falling raw material and commodity prices are first welcomed after coming through a period of inflation. During the fall there is the illusion that the economy is improving and becoming very stable since inflation is under control. The fall offers really only an Indian summer boom before the bust. The financial markets are flooded with cash during the fall because economic growth slows and expansion is no longer demanding as high a level of capital commitment. Almost every area of the economy has been stimulated beyond the world's true needs and demands.

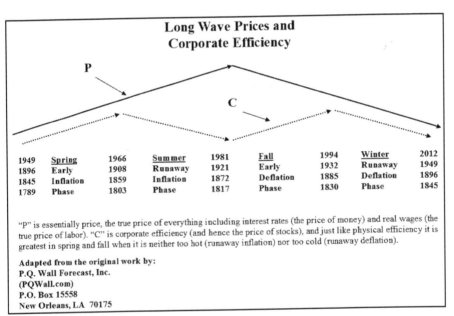

Chart 2.2 The Long Wave Seasons in Prices
and Corporate Efficiency

There is still some substantial development and real expansion going on in the fall, but overall the free market system has taken the advance too far. Because of the great amount of cash in the economy with no place to go, and due to increased corporate efficiency due to falling prices of raw materials, the fall season always sees booming stock markets throughout international capital markets. Lower interest rates, disinflationary pressures, and slowed outlays all have the effect of freeing cash for global stock markets.

The second cycle observed by Kondratieff began its upswing in the 1840s and hit the fall season in the early 1870s. After the fall, it began its decline to the bottom of the long wave winter trough in 1896. The 1880s and early 1890s experienced a global deflationary depression.

The third cycle began its spring season in 1896 and reached the peak of its summer season in 1920. Kondratieff's research covered this period. The cycle appears to have experienced its fall season through the 1920s and shifted from fall to winter in the early 1930s as international capital markets crashed, right on schedule. Kondratieff (1951) acknowledged that the dates of turning and peaks are flexible, give or take a few years, and are not intended to be dogmatically and rigidly interpreted.

After reviewing all the data and information he had collected, Kondratieff (1951, 30-33) made the following observations:

(1) The movements of the series which we have examined running from the end of the 18th century to the present time show long cycles. Although the statistical-mathematical treatment of the series selected is rather complicated, the cycles discovered cannot be regarded as the accidental result of the methods employed. Against such an interpretation is to be set the fact that these waves have been shown with about the same timing in all the more important of the series examined.

(2) The cycles accelerate or retard the rate of growth in series that don't show a trend.

(3) There is a very close correspondence in the timing of the wave movements of the series in the individual countries, in spite of the difficulties present in the treatment of these data. Deviations from the general

rule that prevail in the sequence of the cycles are very rare.

(4) Although for the time being we consider it to be impossible to fix exactly upon the years that marked the turning points of the long cycles, and although the method according to which the statistical data have been analyzed permits an error of five to seven years in the determination of the years of such turnings, the following limits of these cycles can nevertheless be presented as being those most probable:

First long wave	1. The rise lasted from the end of the 1780's or beginning of the 1790's until 1810-1817.
	2. The decline lasted from 1810-1817 until 1844-1851.
Second long wave	1. The rise lasted from 1844-1851 until 1870-1875.
	2. The decline lasted from 1870-1875 until 1890-1896.
Third long wave	1. The rise lasted from 1890-1896 until 1914-1920.
	2. The decline begins around 1920 [and ends in 1949 after Kondratieff's analysis was published and his death].

(5) Naturally, the fact that the movement of the series examined runs in long cycles does not yet prove that such cycles also dominate the movement of all other series. Our investigation has also extended to series in which no waves were evident. On the other hand, it is by no means essential that the long waves embrace all series.

(6) The long waves we have established relative to the series most important in economic life are international; and the timing of these cycles corresponds fairly well for European capitalistic countries. On the basis of

the data that we have adduced, we can venture the statement that the same timing holds also for the United States.

Based on the series Kondratieff used, such as interest rates, government bond prices, and commodity prices, and his own conclusions, the evidence clearly suggests that the end of the third long wave advance came around 1920. The fall season of the decline phase lasted from 1921 until 1930. The winter season lasted into the late-1940s.

World War II came within the long wave winter season and helped to alleviate the economic stress of the downturn by cranking up the military industrial complex. The force and effect of war on the global economy must be recognized as an all-important element in the cycle.

The end of the third long wave decline, based on interest rates and prices adjusted for inflation appears to have come in 1949. The fourth long wave cycle advance, based on the evidence emphasized by Kondratieff's earlier work, began by 1949. Spring ended and the summer season began in the mid-1960s, and then heated up with inflation in the 1970s. The global economy peaked in terms of its greatest years of long wave expansion growth in the 1980-1981 recession, with a blow off in prices and interest rates.

Evidence indicates we entered the long wave fall season in the early 1980s. The 1980s and the 1990s were once again the disinflationary plateau which is best understood as the fall season of the long wave. Japan began the shift from the fall to the winter season when the Tokyo stock market cracked and began to tumble in December of 1989. Sometimes, it can get exceptionally cold in late fall.

The plateau fall season appears to have lasted from 1981 to 2000 in the U.S., although Japan appeared to have already left the fall season and entered the winter season of the decline much earlier. In the U.S. it appears as if aggressive government spending and aggressive monetary policy, in addition to the Internet bubble, allowed stock markets to advance into the first two business cycles of winter. These are business or market cycles

No. 13 and No. 14 out of an expected 16 cycles in a long wave. In the included idealized charts of the long wave the fall season is marked by the shift from business cycle No. 12 to business cycle No. 13. In actuality in Japan the shift came earlier, in the U.S. it came later.

Table 2.1

The Long Wave and Its Four Seasons of Development

- Important phases, dates and general trends
- All dates are approximations, give or take two to three years
- Each long wave season averages 12 to 16 years (ideally 14 years)
- Each long wave season tends to have four regular Kitchin cycles
- Kitchin cycles fluctuate from three to four years each in length

The Long Wave Spring Seasons

1789-1802
1845-1858
1896-1907
1949-1966
2012-2026?

Trends During Spring:

- Stocks Up, Bonds Down, Commodities Up
- New Optimism Arises in General Population
- Economy Grows Solidly
- Stock Prices Rising Consistently
- Very Low Inflation but Steady Advance
- Raw Material and Commodity Prices Rise Slowly
- Real Estate Prices Rise Slowly
- Interest Rates Begin to Rise

- New Technologies and Inventions Create New Industries
- Banking System Healthy with No Failures
- Recessions Shallow and Brief and Recoveries Strong & Long

The Long Wave Summer Seasons

1803-1816
1859-1871
1908-1920
1966-1981
2026-2040?

Trends During Summer:

- Stocks Down, Bonds Down, Commodities Up
- Inflation Heats Up
- Military Conflicts Arise
- Debt Levels Increasing
- Stocks Stagnate Nominally and Crash in Real Terms
- Rising Expectations
- Rising Prices Coax Industry into Overshooting World Demand
- Runaway Inflation In Late Summer
- Raw Materials and Commodity Prices Spike Up at End of Summer
- Farm Land Prices Peak
- Interest Rates Peak
- Rate of Long Wave Economic Growth and Expansion Peaks
- Primary Recession at End of the Long Wave Summer

The Long Wave Fall Seasons

1816-1829
1872-1884
1921-1929

1981-1994
2040-2054?

Trends During Fall:

- Stocks Up, Bonds Up, Commodities Down
- Fall Comes After Primary Long wave Recession
- Worldwide overcapacity
- High Debt Levels Continue to Grow
- Global System Awash in Cash
- Financial Speculation
- Real Economic Growth Pace Slows Significantly from Long Wave Advance
- Interest Rates Decline
- Global Stock Markets Boom
- *Laissez-faire* Political Posture and Deregulation
- Early Deflation and Disinflation
- Falling Raw Material, Commodity and Farm Land Prices
- Commercial and Residential Real Estate Prices Peak in Late Fall
- Slower Capital Investment Pace
- Banking System Weakens and Failures Begin
- Trade Protection Pressures Build
- Psychological Optimism for Society (Roaring '20s and '90s)
- Economic Growth Slower than Spring and Summer
- Greed Runs Wild
- Individual Investors Follow the Herd into Stocks
- Final Speculative Stock Blow off at End of Fall
- Record New Stock Offerings

The Long Wave Winter Seasons

1830-1844
1885-1896
1932-1948
1994-2012?
2054-2068?

Trends During Winter:

- Stocks Down, Bonds Up, Commodities Down
- Global Stock Markets Enter Extended Bear Markets
- Interest Rates Spike In Early Winter, then Decline Throughout
- New Stock Offerings End
- Economic Growth Slow or Negative During Much of Winter
- Some Runaway Deflation and Falling Prices
- Commercial and Residential Real Estate Prices Fall
- Trade Conflicts Worsen
- Social Upheaval and Society Becomes Negative
- Bankruptcies Accelerate and High Debt Eliminated by Bankruptcy
- Stock Markets Reach Bottom and Begin New Bulls in Winter
- Overcapacity/Overproduction Purged by Obsolescence and Failure
- Greed is Purged from System
- Recessions Long and Recoveries Brief
- Free Market System Blamed and Socialist Solutions Offered
- Banking System Shaky and Fails
- A New or Restructured Banking System Introduced
- New Technology and Inventions Developed and Implemented
- Real Estate Prices Find Bottom
- New Work Ethics Develop Since Jobs are Scarce
- Interest Rates and Prices Bottom
- Debt Levels Very Low after Defaults, Bankruptcy and Forgiveness
- View of Future at Low Ebb
- Bright Spots Appear and Social Mood Improves
- There is a Clean Economic Slate to Build On
- Investors are Very Conservative and Risk Averse
- A New Economy Begins to Emerge

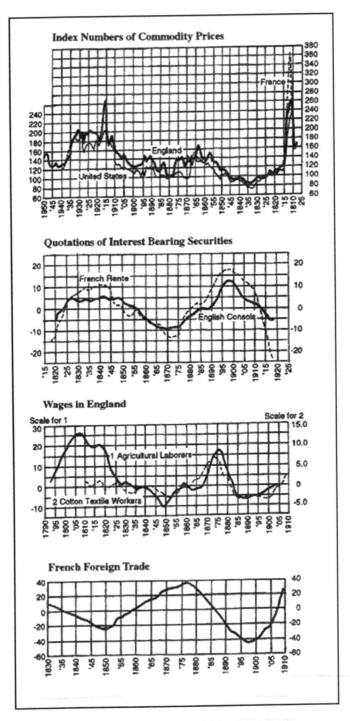

Chart 2.3 Kondratieff's Original Charts

Remember that all nations do not move in perfect unison within the long wave, although we are currently witnessing a synchronized global decline. International free market capitalism is increasingly tightly bound together by the ever-growing interdependence of the global economy. Global financial markets and the debt-ridden economy are, therefore, able to reach higher levels of excess than in the past before their collapse. The emerging global marketplace allows the global economy to expand further and reach far greater heights than nations reached independently during past cycles, however, the global economy and close association of nations cannot stop the inevitable.

Many countries and markets will bottom and be pulling into the next advance before the end of the winter season. Kondratieff expressed the belief that the dynamics of free market economics are not linear (moving in a straight line), continually progressing upward. Kondratieff clearly saw the world economy as cyclical (advancing in cycles). Kondratieff acknowledged that each cycle advanced and developed the economy further and brought it to new heights, but clearly taught that this advance was a cyclical advance and not a linear advance,

Kondratieff believed in the existence of the intermediate 7-11-year cycle that many economists still recognize today; however, Kondratieff taught that reducing the system to this cycle only was simplistic and a broader long wave scope should be superimposed onto the development of the system. Kondratieff recognized and was open to the necessity of flexibility in the system and said, "the long cycle fluctuates between 45 and 60 years."

Here he also pointed out the flexibility of the intermediate 7-11-year cycle, relative to its length, is far greater than the long wave. Another cycle accepted today and recognized by Kondratieff is based on the work of Joseph Kitchin who showed a cycle that fluctuates between three years and four and one-half years. Relative to its length, the long wave is more precise than smaller cycles. The Kitchin cycle is the regular business cycle that our research suggests is ideally 42-months, but fluctuates long and short by Fibonacci ratios in time. Fibonacci ratios are also evident in price.

The Fibonacci sequence is 1, 2, 3, 5, 8, 13, 21, 34, 89, 144, etc. Leonardo Fibonacci was the 12th century mathematician who converted the Arabic numeral system for use in Europe and who discovered the remarkable power of the sequence. Fibonacci ratios are derived by dividing numbers in the Fibonacci sequence with each other. The most important ratio is 1:1.618 or 61.8%, the golden ratio, and 38.2%, the inverse golden ratio. These ratios show up in many natural phenomena, especially stock price activity in cycles, which we will discover are merely fields of human action reflected in prices.

There is increasing evidence that there are four Kitchin cycles or regular business cycles in each of the four seasons of the long wave cycle. This means there are 16 business cycles in each Kondratieff cycle.

The foundation to Kondratieff's theory, and the element considered to be one of the most important aspects of his research, is the cycle's impact on the rise and fall of prices. The movement of prices is key to understanding the long wave and the effect the long wave has on investments. Raw material and commodity prices in recent decades have closely followed the outline Kondratieff laid out for the rise and fall of the cycle. However, in the early 2000s we saw a commodity spike, which now appears to be retracing rapidly in the face of the risk of global deflation. Raw material and commodities include wheat, oil, iron, coal, beef, cotton, soybeans, lumber, pork bellies, etc.

National Affairs (1988, 58), a formerly prominent Soviet publication, reported that Kondratieff

like few economists of the time, perceived that the market was irreplaceable as a meeting place for demand and supply, as a procedure for comparing consumers' desires with production's potential. Kondratieff–again like few people in both our country and the West–realized the importance of prices as a most reliable and irreplaceable information system telling producers what consumers want from them.

Prices reflect the nature of the cycle. Raw materials and commodities, especially agricultural commodities, constantly rise during the long wave advance and peak in price during the primary recession and the shift from the summer to the fall season. Clearly, this was evidenced in the 1920 recession and the 1980-1981 recession. The collapse of raw material and commodity prices usher in the fall period of early deflation and disinflation in the economy. When this occurs, the agricultural and raw materials industries are thrown into deep recession and depression. Remember what happened in the oil and agricultural industries globally in the 1980s. They were also in a depression in the 1920s, long before the rest of the economy took the plunge into depression in the 1930s.

The deflation doesn't hit retail prices and wholesale prices until the end of the fall plateau and the beginning of winter when the secondary recession pushes the economy over the edge and into the long wave decline. Then prices decline until the long wave winter reaches bottom. It is also important to note that deflation or falling prices hit agricultural land during the primary recession and the beginning of the fall season. Deflation and falling prices in commercial and residential real estate prices come at the end of the fall season and accelerate as the long wave winter sets in and as the speculative bubbles around the globe begin to burst. When the long wave debt crisis hits is when real estate declines the most in price.

Falling prices of raw materials and commodities are an important point because they lend energy to the financial speculation and booming stock markets that take place during the fall season. The wholesalers who sell to the retailers and the retailers who sell to the final consumer experience increased corporate efficiency during the fall season. This is because the costs to produce the goods they sell are going down. Remember raw materials prices are falling, therefore, the costs of production for everything from a loaf of bread to a car is going down. Did gas prices at the pump ever fall as fast as the price of oil? The middlemen and retailers were making a killing while the companies that pulled the raw material out of the ground were in deep trouble.

Due to aggressive fiscal and monetary policies in recent years, retail prices rose later into this long wave fall and winter season than long waves of the past. During the fall season, long wave consumer spending and demand has yet to peak and keeps wholesale and retail prices rising. The raw materials industry is hurt during the fall season while the wholesalers and retailers are watching their profit margins explode as consumer optimism surges with the debt binge. Improving margins for most companies along with a global economic system awash in cash creates the financial boom of the long wave fall season. Society is coaxed into a natural speculative frenzy that ends in a bust. Eventually, the collapse of prices hits the wholesale and retail level. All the debt that must be paid off with high retail revenues begins to unravel and default in the long wave winter, just as it happened to the raw-material producers when the prices they received fell during the fall season.

The price of oil affects the price of almost everything else. The price of oil should be watched closely during this long wave winter. Lower prices sound good for consumers, but eventually lower oil prices will help bring a leveraged global economy to its knees. Global assets are financed based on inflated values and anticipated future rising prices during the good times of the long wave advance. Real estate is proving to be the most important asset ushering in the deflation of this long wave winter season. When the long wave decline sets in and asset values fall, the international banking system that financed these assets faces potential collapse. Real estate and energy prices will play a major role in the unfolding deflation.

We are all aware that a price collapse in every sector of the world economy will bring the stock markets crashing and almost all global economic growth to a halt. The incredible amount of debt, throughout every area of the economy, only magnifies the collapse.

Kondratieff (1951) was quick to bring wages and the amount of global trade into the long wave. Kondratieff analyzed the weekly levels of wages in the English cotton and textile industry as well as the number of agricultural workers. To observe the relationship of trade to the long wave, Kondratieff looked at the sum of French exports and imports. True to form, the levels of wages and trade rose as the cycle rose and declined as the cycle declined.

Kondratieff (1951) got very brave in his analysis of the capitalist system and took a look into production. His analysis of prices, interest rates, and wages he considered to be value-based characteristics and felt the true test would come in a purely physical (production) series (year-to-year studies of the same group).

For his analysis, Kondratieff (1951) picked coal production and consumption, along with the production of pig iron and lead in England. The physical series held true. Although sections of the data were missing, there appeared to be an obvious long wave trend.

Kondratieff (1951) mentioned other series in which the long wave appeared evident. A number of such series were as follows: the deposits and the portfolio of the bank of France; deposits at the French banks, English imports, and total English foreign trade; coal production in the United States and Germany, as well as the whole world; lead production in the United States; the number of spindles in the cotton industry in the United States; cotton acreage in the United States; and oat acreage in France.

A major reason for Kondratieff's (1951) conclusions on the long wave comes from the historical rise and fall of interest rates. He believed analysis of interest rates should be based on yields from government bonds because of their stability relative to other instruments, so he looked at yields and prices from the French *rente* and the English *consol* (both are government bonds). True to form, the prices of bonds follow the long wave.

Although Kondratieff did not use the United State's yields and prices, they closely follow the French and English model. Interest rates reach their peak as the long wave summer season peaks before the primary recession and beginning of the fall season. Bond prices reach their lows as rates reach their peak with the beginning of fall and bond prices reach highs close to the end of the winter season of the long wave.

Of course, interest rates have a direct impact on economic activity and the expansion of all sectors of the economy. The

highest interest rates in the cycle indicate the end of the long
wave advance. Summer has ended, and the fall has begun;
interest rates collapse. Remember the high interest rates in the
early 1980s before the collapse? The same thing occurred in the
early 1920s. This was a sure sign we had entered the fall season
of the cycle and were headed for global corporate efficiency and
financial speculation. Fall is the only season when stocks and
bonds boom together.

In observing the fluctuation of interest rates, Kondratieff
(1951, 26) remarked, "The periods of these cycles agree rather
closely with the corresponding periods in the movements of
wholesale commodity prices."

After Kondratieff had exhausted his statistical studies of the
long wave cycle, he began to look at the empirical (practical,
nonscientific) characteristics of the rise and fall in free market
capitalist countries.

Kondratieff (1951, 33-34) introduced this area of his study
with the following statement:

> From another point of view, the historical material
> relating to the development of economic and social
> life as a whole confirms the hypothesis of long waves.
> Several general propositions which we have arrived at
> concerning the existence and importance of long waves
> are as follows.

(1)   The long waves belong really to the same complex
      dynamic process in which the intermediate cycles of
      the capitalistic economy with their principal phases
      of upswing and depression run their course. These
      intermediate cycles, however, secure a certain stamp
      from the very existence of the long waves. Our
      investigation demonstrates that during the rise of the
      long waves, years of prosperity are more numerous,

whereas years of depression predominate during the downswing.

(2) During the recession of the long waves, agriculture, as a rule, suffers especially pronounced and long depression. This was what happened after the Napoleonic Wars; it happened again from the beginning of the 1870s onward; and the same can be observed in the years after World War I.

(3) During the recession of the long waves, an especially large number of important discoveries and inventions in the technique of production and communication are made, which, however, are usually applied on a large scale only at the beginning of the next long upswing.

(4) At the beginning of a long upswing, gold production increases as a rule and the world market for goods is generally enlarged.

(5) It is during the period of the rise of the long waves, i.e., during the period of high tension in the expansion of economic forces, that, as a rule, the most disastrous and extensive wars and revolutions occur.

Kondratieff (1951, 34) concluded, "It is to be emphasized that we attribute to these recurring relationships an empirical character only, and that we do not by any means hold that they contain the explanation of the long waves."

In Kondratieff's discussions on the nature of long waves, he emphasized the relationship of gold to the long wave. He realized that gold is a commodity and has a cost of production. Once the economy has moved into the decline, the cost of production is at a low point. There is naturally going to be more gold production because gold will have its greatest purchasing power at the time it's cheapest to produce. Because of the complexity of gold and its pricing in a volatile economy, a chapter will discuss gold's relation to the long wave–especially the present winter season.

Kondratieff's (1951, 41-42) conclusions in his presentation on the long wave emphasize his increasing conviction of its existence while at the same time hinting of the question as to its origin:

> The objections to the regular cyclical character of the long waves, therefore, seem to be unconvincing. We believe ourselves justified in saying that the long waves, if existent at all, are a very important and essential factor in economic development, a factor the effects of which can be found in all the principal fields of social and economic life. Even granting the existence of long waves, one is, of course, not justified in believing that economic dynamics consist only in fluctuations around a certain lever. The course of economic activity represents beyond doubt a process of development, but this development obviously proceeds not only through intermediate waves but also through long ones. In alerting the existence of long waves and in denying that they arise out of random causes, we are also of the opinion that the long waves arise out of causes which are inherent in the essence of the capitalistic economy. This naturally leads to the question as to the nature of these causes.

In 1988, *National Affairs* (55) finally reported that, the day in 1926 when Kondratieff read his paper on long waves became "renowned in the history of world economic thinking." His work did not record the cycle's entire fall plateau season through the decade of the 1920s; however, the drastic global economic contraction and market crashes in the early 1930s were projected by his research.

In the late 1920s, Kondratieff had become one of the most well-known Soviet economists in the world. He was editor of a prominent economic journal and was an elected member of several scientific societies abroad. *National Affairs* reported that he was a member of the American Economic Association, the American Academy of Social Sciences, the Association for Agricultural Questions, various Russian sociological and statistical societies, and London's economic and statistical societies.

History has shown that most prophets are rejected in their native land. Nikolai Kondratieff proved to be no exception to this rule. Stalin enjoyed the idea of the eventual collapse of the free world's economy. However, there was much more to Kondratieff's theory. Quite obviously, the results of Kondratieff's research did not sit well with the Stalin regime, nor did his struggle for the introduction of market mechanisms and more independence in the Soviet agricultural system. Stalin was outraged with Kondratieff's prediction that the free market would come back stronger than ever, after being purged of its inefficiencies, debt, and excesses. Kondratieff was rewarded in the usual Stalin style with arrest and imprisonment in 1930. His work and research was banned in the Soviet Union.

After his arrest and imprisonment, Kondratieff became *persona non grata* in the Soviet Union. For all practical purposes, he vanished from the world scene, but his long wave theory remained. Much of his work was lost or destroyed. One of his books, written while he was in prison, has yet to be published. Kondratieff's death came only after the fulfillment of his prophecy of the inevitable downturn of Western economies, which took the disturbing form of the Great Depression.

It was only in the late 1980s that Kondratieff's name, work, and ideas began to circulate again in Soviet literature. As a 1988 *Forbes* article (Fuhrman, 34) reported, "Banned since 1930, Kondratieff's writings have begun to circulate freely again in the Soviet Union since this summer ... the Soviet Government has published, for the first time, a book of Kondratieff's essays. Kondratieff's prison writings are being sorted through. The economist's daughter, Elena, has been making public appearances in Moscow."

Most revealing are the fundamental changes the writings of Kondratieff have made in Russian economic thinking. Andrey Poletayev is the Russian economist leading the effort in the resurrection of Kondratieff's work. Poletayev told *Forbes* (Fuhrman 1988, 34), "Marx' theory of the inevitable decline of capitalism isn't accepted by any of the influential economists in the Soviet Union now ... There is also a transition in the highest levels ... toward accepting that the capitalist economies are self-regulating, not self-destructive."

The *Forbes* (Fuhrman, 35) article noted, as the Soviet Union was rapidly unraveling:

> In abandoning a bankrupt socialism, the Soviet rulers need a native prophet to justify new policies. They have found him in the long-dead Nikolai Kondratieff.... Nikolai Dimitriyevich Kondratieff is respectable again in the Soviet Union. Thanks to perestroika, the reputation of the famed originator of the Kondratieff long wave theory of economics has been rehabilitated.

Kondratieff clearly believed that the causes of the long wave are inherent within the capitalist free market system of human growth and development. The long wave appears to be an integral part of the capitalist system and is the market's way of cleaning out the impurities that will always build up. The buildup of debt and the overly speculative spirit as well as overproduction and inflation have to be purged from the system for it to get a fresh start.

Someone will invariably say, "Kondratieff wrote this theory in 1925. This is another time–the age of the microchip and fine-tuned monetary control. Surely you don't think we will see the full extent of the decline of the fourth long wave in the global economy?" But, we are clearly witnessing it now in the financial collapse of this long wave winter, and the full extent of the damage to be done during this winter season has yet to be determined.

The cycle Kondratieff wrote about–that hard evidence suggests exists–is beyond the reach of monetary control. No more than a meteorologist can control the path of a hurricane, can the Federal Reserve, the World Bank, or anyone else control the inevitable ebb and flow of human trade and the Kondratieff long wave.

Government fiscal policy and Federal Reserve monetary policy can potentially lessen the impact of a long wave decline with intelligent decision making, but they cannot change the inevitable. They are clearly pulling out all stops in an attempt to avert the deflation of the long wave winter season. Government and central banks around the world are now fighting the full onslaught of the Kondratieff winter season. Can the deflation be stopped? To what degree can it be resisted by aggressive monetary and fiscal policy?

It is true that the present is extremely different from when Kondratieff formulated his long wave theory. But are the differences of today truly deep in terms of the fundamental nature of what drives the global economy, or are they only surface differences that conceal the same long wave fundamentals? There are new tools being brought to the battle against the current global long wave. Are the new tools sufficient to overcome the long wave deflation? We will get our answer presently, in the closing years of this long wave winter season.

Chapter 3:

MODERN TIMES

"When business embarks on a rampage which does not help humanity to live and grow—when it pushes beyond this range of usefulness and overproduces human needs—or when it falls behind and outlives its usefulness—it runs into trouble of some kind. And when the business tree is crowded with these dead or dying branches, the tree as a whole begins to suffer. We run into a business depression or plunge into industrial war to shake the rotten branches down."

V.C. Kitchen

To appreciate Kondratieff's observations and the foundations of long wave theory, it is useful to briefly review highlights of the economic and financial history of the period to which long wave theory is applied. This exercise will provide solid long wave guideposts for the reader. Here we will examine chronologically some of' the key economic and financial events and developments in the four long wave cycles that have advanced and declined from 1789 to the present.

Lightner's thorough history of recessions and depressions was also utilized extensively in this chapter. This review is skewed toward U.S. history, although close examination of other capitalist nations will reveal developments with a similar seasonal long wave resonance in the same time frames.

Before examining the advance of the first long wave, which began in 1789, it is enlightening to examine some of the facts that indicate a long wave winter was in force and ending in the years just prior to 1789.

Following on the heels of the Revolutionary War, there was a brief time of prosperity and improving economic conditions. The relief of the end of conflict often brings spurts of economic activity. However, during the three years 1782, 1783, and 1784, after the war, conditions were prosperous. The jubilant feeling of victory brought optimism. There was also a great deal of money left in the country by the British and French armies. This post-war prosperity did not last long, however, ending with the depression of 1785-1789. Money quickly left the United States to pay for imported goods from Europe.

Remember that a key force of the long wave is prices. After the surge in post-war economic activity, which peaked in 1785, a sharp decline came in virtually all prices (i.e., deflation). This was likely the winter of the prior long wave, but there is not sufficient data to clearly identify a long wave. America was a nation hardly three years old when its people were introduced to the hard reality of the international power play of nation against nation in international commerce. Scarcely weaned, the United States was banned from trade in the British West Indies in 1784. Our young nation was elated by its newfound freedom. But it was short-lived; soon the bills had to be paid in international markets.

American merchants found themselves embarrassed when they had no money to cover credit purchases from overseas. The government was forced to beg for loans from foreign governments. Perhaps in its scope and scale, this crisis was greater than the Great Depression, relatively speaking. Benjamin Franklin couldn't get the money he asked for from France, because they were having problems as well. It clearly appears as though a long wave winter was in force and fortunately coming to an end in the late 1780s.

An indication that the years prior to 1789 were a long wave winter was that during this time the first protective tariffs against foreign competition were established by the new U.S. government. This trade war legacy haunts us today and plays an extremely important role in the long wave cycle, making it worse. It is important to point out that these tariffs came from the support of none other than the manufacturers, without concern for the consumer-a tradition still kept today.

Those who advocate protectionism due to trade deficits should note that America ran a trade deficit for 59 years after its freedom from England. The year 1840 was the first year we showed a surplus; the figures were $113,896,000 in exports and $107,142,000 in imports. We were insightful enough to see that profits made on the goods sold here were re-loaned and reinvested in America. Maybe we could learn more than a few political lessons from our founding fathers.

These were trying times. As European manufacturers, while selling their goods in America, were attempting to stifle start-up manufacturing in America. The historian Lightner (1922, 94) recorded a humorous account of the ends to which the British were willing to go to secure their markets:

> In 1787 a Philadelphia man came into possession of two carding and spinning machines which were supposed to save the labor of 120 men a day. These machines were purchased by an agent of a British manufacturer and shipped back to Liverpool, the object being to nip American manufacturing in the bud.

The depression of 1785 brought on conditions that spawned the first American insurrection in the form of Shay's Rebellion. This rebellion had 15,000 supporters. Being blessed with far more zeal than leadership, they were soon dispersed. Times were hard for our new nation, to say the least, but we were a nation with a vision. And a long wave winter was ending.

It is interesting to see that major financial changes come at the bottom of long wave declines when nations are in crisis. In the works for a few years, the U.S. government chartered the first bank of the United States in 1791. There was solid evidence in prices and interest rates of the beginning advance of the first long wave cycle. It would be safe to say that the world was entering a new era of international relations and economic development late in the 18th century.

The U.S. Constitution had gone into effect in 1789, which had granted government the right to coin money. Before long, the United States was back in business with an inflationary money system and growing economy. A long wave spring had begun.

This time period marks the beginning rise in international prices that peaked in 1814. This period represents the spring and summer advance of the first recorded long wave in the global economy.

Trade for the United States exploded in the early 1790s due to the war that broke out between France and England, which the rest of Europe was soon drawn into. During this period, America was master of the seas. Trade flourished for the new country. A large and steady demand of our agricultural produce by nations at war kept the shipping lanes busy from the states to the old world. Foreign trade was multiplied four times in the decade.

During the advance, the United States experienced a recession in 1808 and 1809 due to a well-intended, but disastrous, trade embargo by President Jefferson. This embargo was created in response to Napoleon's decrees against neutral trade. As an illustration of what trade wars can do to an economy, it is important to note that U.S. exports fell from $108,300,000 to $22,400,000 annually during this embargo. This was far greater proportionately and took place much more abruptly than any business decline in American history. When Jefferson gave in to pressure and lifted the embargo, business soon returned during this long wave advance. Recessions are brief during long wave advances.

The year 1812 found the U.S. once again at war with England. Washington was captured by the British on August 24, 1814, sending shock waves through global financial markets. We rebounded quickly after the war, which had been a humiliating draw at best, even with our excellent showing led by future president Jackson at the Battle of New Orleans.

An economic rebound in Europe did not last very long after the Napoleonic Wars had ended. Soon after the relief of the end of the war had passed, Europe was in the midst of a severe depression. Led by France, Europe entered the disinflationary fall season of the decline of the first long wave cycle between 1813 and 1815. The United States followed suit in the year 1818. It should be noted that the United States didn't enter the decline until a few years after most of Europe. There is often a number of years between nations moving into a new long wave season.

It is important to note that this period represents the beginning of the fall season of the long wave decline. This particular fall season was more severe than more recent fall seasons because the economy was almost entirely agriculturally based at the time. Agriculture suffers most during the long wave fall, ahead of the rest of the economy, which suffers more in the long wave winter season. When an economy is less dependent on its agriculture, it is reasonable to expect that the fall season will be milder and winter will be more severe. This appears to be the case in the present long wave.

There had been a general expansion of business for the decades leading up to this period of decline. In light of long wave theory, the reasons for this decline, as presented by Lightner (1922, 117-118), are fascinating: "A depression had to come for several reasons: first, as a reflection of European troubles; second, a stoppage of overproduction; and third, to get money on a better basis." The comparison of the global conditions of this first long wave declining period with the situation in the current long wave winter is all too obvious. Even with a clear understanding of the long wave cycle theory and its predictable outcome, the similarities provide remarkable insight.

News spread across the American states in 1818 that the banks were in critical condition. It seems that the central bank of the United States–the project of Alexander Hamilton, before being silenced by Aaron Burr–had created serious trouble in the economy. The inflationary tendencies of the bank had run full course. Banks couldn't return the gold that had been deposited for the simple reason that they had lent out far more money than there was gold to back up. Attempts to shore up the system failed and the banks greatly restricted their loans. Credits and loans to business and agriculture were curtailed.

This period marks the first widespread financial panic in American history. In 1819, a depression was well underway. Banks began to fail and shut their doors. Globally the picture was much the same, as Europe had led the way into the depression and economic downturn a few years earlier.

After rising since 1789, Lightner noted that "the four years between 1817 and 1821 the holders of property in the United States were supposed to have suffered a depreciation of nearly $800 million" in long wave decline deflation. "General bankruptcy spread its darkness over the land; many of the wealthiest families in America were reduced to poverty." In Europe, the story was the same. Average working men and their families suffered for want of bread, let alone meat. Development was abandoned. Scenes of national distress ensued.

We see a number of recessions on the way to the bottom of the first long wave decline. The year 1825 saw the collapse of cotton prices in England first, then the subsequent collapse of banks in New Orleans. Note that the long wave decline doesn't come all at one time or hit only one location; it is spread out over a number of years and starts at different times in different countries. The New Orleans crisis lasted only a few months and order was soon restored. A recession from 1837 to 1839 was due almost entirely to banking speculation and crop failures. There was a brief period of inflation before U.S. wholesale prices dropped to their lowest points of the cycle in the late 1830s to mid-1840s.

The bottom of the first long wave decline of Kondratieff's research came during the early to mid-1840s. The economy began to expand after this bottom as the next long wave advance got underway. There was a recession in 1847 that was short-lived due to the discovery of gold in California, which restored enthusiasm to all financial markets and confidence in general. The period between 1837 and 1857 is considered the "Golden Age" in U.S. history due to the great gold discoveries. Gold has always taken on new importance at the bottom of the long wave decline.

Observing history, we see that recessions during long wave advances are short, whereas recessions or depressions during long wave declines are longer. The United States suffered another brief recession in 1857. The amount of money in circulation during this period had risen greatly, including both gold and bank notes. Speculation both in land and industrial development increased drastically.

The Golden Age had seen enormous advances in the accumulation of wealth in this country and was accompanied by an increase in many prices. Records show that, during the period 1850-1857, President Buchanan calculated the production of gold in the United States at $400 million. This same period had seen a doubling of banks in the country and an explosion of railroad construction. The United States had seven-ninths of the world's railroad mileage. Clearly, the second long wave advance identified by Kondratieff was in full swing.

Investors and the public were investing in inflated future expectations. Excessive optimism ruled the minds of investors. There are incredible stories about banking conditions during this time.

One account tells of a bank examiner as he traveled through the Midwest. The banks knew his travel plans and had the same gold coin follow him around to be whisked in the back door of the banks he visited and quickly deposited in the vault. There was a vast amount of fraud and circulation of bad bank notes. It makes you think of many of the shenanigans that went on recently in the U.S. and global banking system.

The *Nichols' Bank Note Reporter* carried 5,400 descriptions of false money in 1858. This crisis and panic was due to speculation and overexpansion of credit in a long wave summer season. Prices were rising due to the enormous output of gold from California and Australia. However, it is generally accepted that a single incident pricked the bubble.

The Ohio Life Insurance Company had $5 million tied up in railroad loans. Their New York agent defaulted, causing the failure of the company with large liabilities. The dominos were set in motion and one institution after another followed suit. Many eastern railroads failed. In 1857, the United States witnessed almost 5,000 corporate failures. It was one of the more severe recessions during a long wave summer advance and is comparable to the 1973-1974 recession and banking crisis.

The resilience of the U.S. economy and the long wave advance helped the United States make a quick comeback from the recession in 1857. By 1860, things were back to normal with businesses. Prices were on the rise, in tune with the long wave pattern of an advance.

The first half of the year 1860 saw business running as usual, but as the election drew near, the storm clouds began to form on the horizon. Business began to slow as a result of heightened tension in both the North and South. November saw the election of Abraham Lincoln, and business came to near standstill awaiting the action he would take.

On December 20, 1860, the secession of South Carolina from the Union, proved to be the beginning of wild confusion in financial markets. "Bankers and financiers the country over perceived the gravity of the situation. They feared that the nation's trade would collapse and the whole framework of our political and financial system would be in danger," according to Lightner (1922, 149-150).

The lines were soon drawn in the economic heat of a long wave summer. In 1861, the South stopped payment on all financial obligations to the North. It is estimated that the amount of southern indebtedness to the North was $2 billion. The war was filled with economic and financial uncertainty. When peace came in 1865, the nation was relieved of the stress of war. Business in the North revived very quickly, but the South was held responsible for repaying many debts it had assumed to finance the war. The South was in deep depression for a number of years. In time, the wheels of commerce began to roll as the preserved union reentered the world market.

The United States saw a peak in prices in 1864 due to war demands, while European prices climbed until 1873. The long wave summer in the United States had ended and the fall had begun. In Europe, a long wave summer lingered. This marks the period of the shift in the second long wave from summer to fall.

The United States faced a small recession in 1869 due mainly to speculation in gold. September 24, 1869 was known as "Black Friday" in the United States, due to the crash in the gold market. (This crash is comparable to the gold price crash in the early 1980s, when the early global disinflation got started.) European prices held up longer. There were a number of failures during this time, but the panic soon passed and business went back to normal.

There had been a steady global advance in the long wave since the mid-1840s. We see this advance beginning to peak internationally in the early to mid-1870s, with world prices at their highest levels since the early 1800s. The mid-1870s to the mid-1880s represent the global fall season plateau of the second long wave cycle that Kondratieff discovered.

Economic expansion and contraction were increasingly being seen on an international basis at this point. A global economy was emerging. The effects were sobering.

Lightner (1922, 160) observed that internationally:

> Every line of industry had been stimulated beyond its needs in anticipation of still greater profits. Borrowers went heavily into debt, paying high rates of interest, to develop new industrial enterprises with the inevitable consequences of overproduction. The depression of 1873 was marked by failures and bankruptcy of many banks and business houses all over the country. This was a worldwide depression. It began in Vienna in May, 1873, spreading through Europe, particularly to London, England, Germany, Italy, Russia and South America. Although it was said to begin in Vienna, London was the real leader in terms of this period representing the peak of the British Empire.

The global recession/depression of 1873-1878 (the equivalent of the global 1980-1981 recession) marked the beginning of the fall plateau phase of the second long wave cycle decline. In the United States, there were over 20,000 business failures and money loss of a billion dollars. Over three million people lost their jobs. Internationally, prices began to slide at this time and did not reach their bottom until the end of the long wave winter season in 1896.

During the fall and winter seasons of the second long wave decline, there were recessions recorded in the year 1873, 1878,

1884, and 1889. The years 1893 to 1895 brought an acute recession/depression that proved to be the force that bottomed the second long wave cycle reviewed in Kondratieff's research.

The industrialization of the world made this recession in the 1890s unusually difficult, with large amounts of people being thrown out of work in industrialized regions. This brought on severely depressed conditions that would not have had as severe effects on a population that wasn't centralized for industrial output. During this time, great industrial centers were emerging in the Northeast of the United States that were extremely vulnerable to recessions. However, coming out of this setback, America and the world were in an advancing upswing of the long wave that would see the international marketplace reach such levels as were never before dreamed possible.

A new long wave advance and spring season, the third revealed in Kondratieff's research, began in the late 1890s. International finance witnessed the dawn of a new era of growth and prosperity. Even World War I proved to slow the advance of the new world economy for only a short season. Of course, the war had drastic effects on European industry, but they revived fairly quickly.

The upswing of the third long wave was noted by a number of brief recessions. A recession in 1903 was attributed to the U.S. monetary policy initiated in 1896. There was a large drop in stocks on all the exchanges, but the industrial machinery of the Western world soon pulled us through and had us on the move again in a long wave advance.

The United States suffered a slight financial panic in 1907 that was used as the impetus to bring about the passage of the Federal Reserve Act. With the outbreak of World War I in 1914, international financial markets were in confusion and every stock exchange in the world was closed. Financial markets soon regained stability, but business was hampered by the war.

Large amounts of gold were recalled from the United States that were owed to Europe; but as we began to export war material, the gold flowed back. The panic brought by the war caused a recession in the United States. This recession was brief for America as orders began pouring in from Europe in 1915.

You will note that war tends to come during the advance of the long wave.

In 1920-1921 we had the fall recession that kicked off the fall season of the third long wave and the resulting disinflation it caused. Commodity prices dropped significantly in the first few years of the decade, and then held up until 1929, when the bottom fell out of world prices. The United States had 50 percent of the world's gold in its vaults in 1920. This gave us the feeling of security. The recession of 1920-1921 was marked by no runs on banks or major failures in the U.S. corporate community. Business slowed, but was soon back to normal and building steam as the United States moved with speculative vengeance into the roaring 1920s and another fall season of the long wave.

The 1920s was a classic long wave fall season. Interest rates were falling during the 1920s. Deregulation of financial markets and other industries was a great theme during the 1920s (a tune played again in the 1980s and 1990s). The 1920s created the illusion of a prospering global economy, while fundamental problems were beginning to develop. There was virtually no inflation and in many areas there was actually some deflation—just as in fall seasons in the 19th century. The stock market was surging as overexpansion of industry left nowhere else for money to go but into financial markets and speculation.

Agriculture was in a severe depression in the 1920s, as in the other long wave fall season plateaus. Virtually every industry was fighting for protection in a world economy that was overproducing everything. The close observer saw many disturbing signs as the roaring 1920s approached the close of a decade of disinflationary good times.

It was now time for one of the most severe long wave winter seasons on record. Many theories surround the worldwide depression that began in the early 1930s and threw the world into more than a decade of industrial decline and stagnation. There are, however, a few facts accepted by everyone, such as prices had begun to decline in 1920, which undermined bank loans backing industrial outlays and expansion. Other facts were that the entire economy was clearly overproducing most goods in the late 1920s. Companies that hadn't already realized they were pouring money into a bottomless hole by expanding in a deflating economy began to slow or end expansion in 1928. In June of 1929, industrial expansion, production, and output peaked and began to decline. Corporate and personal debt had built up just as it had by the 1810s and 1870s. The comparisons with today's crisis are all to clear.

There was only one place for prices to go with no buying power behind industry or the individual. Stock markets had such momentum and speculative force that it was late October before the markets came to the realization that there was no economy underneath them to match the price level of stocks, as seen in 2000 and again with the double top in 2007 during this long wave transition to the winter season.

You can't help but think of the *Roadrunner* cartoon in which the coyote runs off the road and keeps running in midair for some time before he finally stops, looks down and realizes he left solid ground some time back. At this point, he proceeds to fall into a deep canyon.

The free fall that inevitably came in stocks and economic activity during the long wave winter of the 1930s brought destruction to the world economy that could never have been imagined. Many have the tendency to equate the Depression with the crash, but the crash was only a symptom of the underlying problem. The market crash and the Depression would be comparable to an uncontrollable sneeze at the outset of pneumonia. The economy had taken its long wave course and was to see a slowing of activity, not thinking to ask the permission of equity markets.

As the long wave winter continued its downward momentum, the global banking order collapsed in 1933. Unemployment reached as high as 25 percent of the working population in the United States as the industrial complex continued its demise. World trade was cut in half during the early 1930s due to the foolish protectionism of the nations of the world who failed to see their interdependence with one another. The Smoot-Hawley tariffs almost single-handedly wiped out world trade as nations turned inward to solve their growing problems. World trade dropped sharply, exacerbating the global problems of overproduction.

The seriousness and depth of the third long wave decline has come to be known as the Great Depression. The Great Depression is attributed to isolationism in world markets and a hesitancy of the business community in the fear and memory of what we had just been through. It should be noted that the United States suffered a serious setback in 1937-1938. The long wave winter season completed its decline after World War II came to an end in 1949.

The spring season of a new long wave was trying to begin in the years following the war. There was a slight decline in output beginning in March 1945, but by November things picked up. We saw another slight setback into 1948-1949 that now clearly marks the bottom of the long wave on inflation adjusted and average investment return charts.

The latest long wave advance didn't begin until 1949. As noted earlier, Bob Prechter of Elliot Wave International is credited as the first to recognize this date. Interest rates and prices bottomed in this time frame. We saw slight recessions in 1958 and 1961, but these were soon forgotten as the economy continued to expand in the long wave upswing. The global economy moved from the spring season to the summer season of the advance around 1966. The height of U.S. involvement in Vietnam brought recession in 1968 because of the large drain on national resources—as well as the time being one of national worry and anxiety.

The inflationary heat of the long wave summer gave us the energy crisis in 1973, as well as a business recession, but this recession was followed by exploding prices and high inflation. Many wholesale prices fell in the 1973-1974 recession. There are some observers who argue that this marked the end of the long wave advance and the beginning of the fall season. The bulk of the evidence, however, indicates this was not the case. Prices continued to rise and the economy continued to expand at a good clip after the 1973-1974 recession. Prices and, importantly, interest rates, the price of money, didn't peak until the 1980-1981 recession when gold and silver prices spiked up before a fall.

The recession of 1980-1981, which broke the back of inflation and consequently high interest rates, marked the end of the long wave cycle advance and summer season and the beginning of the speculative disinflationary fall season. We saw a peak and the beginning of a massive decline in commodity prices in the early 1980s, just as we had in 1920. The fall season is a time of a declining rate of growth in capital outlays.

It is clear that prices for raw materials and commodities in the fourth long wave peaked from 1980 to 1981, as the long wave summer turned to fall, just as the third cycle peaked in 1920 to 1921. The Japanese stock market peak in December 1989 appears to have been the first early sign of the beginning of the global shift from the fall to the long wave winter season, as disinflation turned to deflation in Japan. Now the entire global economy and all stock markets have joined in as the long wave decline runs full cycle and winter season is in full swing. It appears that the fall season, apart from Japan, lasted from 1981 to 2000 in some equity markets. The 2007 top was short of the 2000 top on an inflation adjusted basis. Evidence suggests we are now in a long wave winter season that should end in the years directly ahead.

The growing strength of the world economy and the power wielded by bodies such as the Federal Reserve Board appears to have lengthened the advance of the current long wave. This lengthier advance creates more volatile global markets in the last few years of the fall season leading to the beginning of winter. This phenomenon has led to an accelerated decline because of the height that debt and prices were able to reach.

The heights of debt and prices in the current long wave were unprecedented and are leading to a sharp decline and global economic winter. Some estimates put total debt in the U.S. economy at over 50 trillion dollars. Much of this debt is expected to be purged from the system in this long wave winter season in one way or another. Excessive amounts of debt created high prices and overproduction of products and services in virtually every industry, form banking services to housing to automobiles to toasters. We are in a classic long wave winter where these excesses must be wrung from the system in a devastating economic contraction.

Participants and leadership in the global economy once again do not recognize the familiar trends and the inevitable passing of the long wave economic seasons. The die is cast. As a result, the world will suffer. Intermediate planning is not enough for the long wave forces at work. Policies that do not consider the long wave implications will make matters worse, but it is not expected that politicians will consider the long wave since it is longer than the election cycle.

The depth of the Great Depression was the result of bad government policy. A long wave cycle decline is inevitable in a market economy, while a severe depression is the work of misguided politicians and bad policy. The greatest mistake the U.S. government is currently making is not allowing bad debts to go bad. Bankruptcy courts and judges should be allowed to purge the system of bad debt. Instead, the government is stepping in and forcing taxpayers to back the bad debt at all levels. This debt will be a major drag on the economy for years and will weaken the coming long wave advance.

The long wave can be distorted for a time, but in the long run, the long wave always works through its seasons of global economic ebb and flow. We must learn from past mistakes and use such knowledge to our advantage. The biggest lessons of the 1930s are that reducing taxes and avoiding protectionism should be priorities. Temporarily government spending is necessary as depression threatens, but should be reversed as soon as possible. Unfortunately, decades of overspending will limit government spending during this long wave winter.

Saddling taxpayers with all the bad debts of Wall Street and the banking system is not a lesson learned from the 1930s. Forcing taxpayers to pay billions in bonuses to those who created all the bad debt that collapsed the global financial system is not wisdom gleaned from the 1930s debacle. It is simply political buffoonery. It will make this crisis far worse than it has to be and the populist backlash will likely make history.

The U.S. Federal Reserve did learn a few things from the long wave winter mistakes of the Great Depression. Chairman Bernanke studied them in detail. Bernanke has responded to the crisis with the most aggressive monetary stimulus policy in history. It would be far better if prior policy had not made this long wave winter crisis so severe. The clear objective of recent monetary policy is to stop the deflationary debt collapse of this long wave winter season. It is difficult for advocates of free markets to observe such excessive central bank intervention, but the magnitude of the global crisis required some intervention. The world did look into the abyss, and the darkness of the abyss is still lurking, and will be a threat until the next long wave advance begins.

Central bank intervention around the world must be reversed as soon as possible to restore market integrity. Bernanke and other central bankers must find the will and the way to let the bad banks fail and clear trillions of dollars of bad debt out of the global system before this long wave winter comes to an end. They cannot just inflate the debt away. Deflation remains this long wave winter's likely outcome. It is expected that there will be far less deflation and, therefore, less debt collapse than there would have been without central bank action.

Watch central bank policy around the world closely during the remainder of this long wave winter season. Central bank actions to prevent deflation during this long wave winter are expected to lead to far more inflation during the next long wave advance. It is important to note that we are much closer to the next long wave advance than we were in the 1930s. There is a risk the U.S. Federal Reserve and other central banks around the world will overreact, creating excessive inflation during the coming long wave spring season.

Chapter 4:

SYSTEM DYNAMICS AT MIT

"Traditional mainstream academic economics, by trying to be a science, has failed to answer major questions about real-life economic behavior... A system dynamics model, as a general theory of economic behavior, now endogenously generates business cycles, Kuznets cycles, the economic long wave, and growth. The economic model provides the theory, thus far missing from economics, for the Great Depression of the 1930s and how such episodes can recur 50 to 70 years apart."

Jay W. Forrester

"Very much of what we call the progress of today consists in getting rid of false ideas, false conceptions of things, and in taking a point of view that enables us to see the principles, ideas and things in right relation to each other."

William D. Hoard

Dr. Jay W. Forrester has literally revolutionized the world with his inventions in the computer field. In addition, Forrester's System Dynamics Group at the Massachusetts Institute of Technology (MIT) provides some of the most convincing evidence available for the long wave. Forrester's research has silenced many skeptics and raised the discussion of the long wave theory to a new level internationally. The System Dynamics Group will likely be leaders in long wave research in coming years.

Inventing random access memory (RAM), the brain of all computers, is only one of many of Dr. Forrester's contributions to the world. But when the history books are written, his contribution in the creation of the System Dynamics Model at MIT may well be seen as his greatest accomplishment. Forrester's development of the computer-simulated model known as the System Dynamics Model, earlier known as the National Model

(NM), and the research it has initiated in the long wave, is a stunning and historic achievement.

When Kondratieff discovered long waves in the economy in the 1920s, he was looking at historical economic and price data. From the reams of data he collected, he observed the emergence of the long wave cycle. The System Dynamics Group at MIT conducts research using the basic structure of interdependent systems, such as ongoing economic, political, and financial relationships that make up economic activity. The program seeks to project characteristic behavior in the development of complex systems.

Forrester expanded the use of powerful computers to create simulated models. After great success with his earlier smaller-scale models of urban development, Dr. Forrester created the System Dynamics Model in the early 1970s. The object of the System Dynamics Model was to project the future direction of the national economy due to a myriad of interrelated relationships and processes.

The System Dynamics Model is a computer simulation of our national economy. The System Dynamics Model utilizes computers to project the future based on the outcome of current economic, financial, business, and political decision-making processes. It is important to note that old data are not used in the model. The System Dynamics Model is based on current decision making and relationships that produce spontaneous events. Forrester was looking for the future trends that relationships create by their interaction.

When Dr. Forrester first fired up his computer-generated System Dynamics Model, it naturally created and projected an approximate long wave boom and bust in the economy. He was not expecting this. The model did not look at the past. It projected that the economy will naturally produce a long wave due to "current" complex relationships and decisions being made.

When Dr. Forrester looked closer at the future projected by the System Dynamics Model he found that production, prices, and debt got out of control and created long wave periods of not just prosperity and but inevitable depression. The long wave cycle is created due to the everyday decision-making processes in the highest circles of business, government, and finance and their trickle down effect on the entire system. The elements that generated the boom and bust in Dr. Forrester's System Dynamics Model are the same ones Kondratieff had discovered. They are the same forces outlined and to be controlled in the Levitical law passage of the Jubilee.

Forrester's most recent thinking is available in his Plenary Address at the International System Dynamic Conference in New York, on July 21, 2003. The following is the salient abstract from that address:

Traditional mainstream academic economics, by trying to be a science, has failed to answer major questions about real-life economic behavior. Economics should become a systems profession, such as management, engineering, and medicine. By closely observing the structures and policies in business and government, simulation models can be constructed to answer questions about business cycles, causes of major depressions, inflation, monetary policy, and the validity of descriptive economic theories. A system dynamics model, as a general theory of economic behavior, now endogenously generates business cycles, Kuznets cycles, the economic long wave, and growth. A model is a theory of the behavior that it generates. The economic model provides the theory, thus far missing from economics, for the Great Depression of the 1930s and how such episodes can recur 50 to 70 years apart. Simpler system dynamics models can become the vehicle for a relevant and exciting pre-college economics education.

In his 2003 speech Forrester delved into the topic of recurring major depressions and made key observations relevant to the current debt crisis. Only in 2008 did we begin to hear widespread comparison of the current crisis with the Great Depression. Forrester highlighted Bernanke's interest in the

Great Depression in this 2003 speech, before Bernanke began his term as Chairman of the Federal Reserve in February 2006. It would be appropriate if Congress would enquire of Bernanke his current views on the System Dynamics Model at MIT, and its evidence for a systemic cause of depressions:

> There have been major depressions greatly exceeding the severity of ordinary business cycles, around the 1830s, the 1890s, and during the Great Depression of the 1930s. Economic theory has offered no convincing and generally accepted explanation for such major economic dislocations. According to one writer, 'To understand the Great Depression is the Holy Grail of macroeconomics." [Note: II Bernanke, Ben S., 1994. The Macroeconomics of the Great Depression: A Comparative Approach. *National Bureau of Economic Research* (Working Paper No. 4814), 1-53.]
>
> The Great Depression of the 1930s is usually seen as an unfortunately severe ordinary business cycle. In mainstream academic economics there is little acknowledgement that the major depressions could be a dynamic mode that is separate from business cycles. Such rejection of a long economic fluctuation probably results from there being no systemic theory that could explain depression episodes that are decades apart.

It is hard to explain why mainstream economists have been so slow to consider the evidence for the long wave, other than the necessity to focus on short term developments. Recent history may cause economists to reconsider the potential for a systemic cause of depressions. Forrester recognized the problem of mainstream economic appreciation for the evidence for the long wave in his 2003 speech:

> However, outside the mainstream economic theory, a substantial body of literature exists with observations and hypotheses about a behavior usually known as the

Kondratieff cycle, or economic long wave. Historical data has been analyzed to show widely spaced deep economic downturns but the data analysis methods have been highly criticized and mostly ignored. Most economists deny the existence of a systemic cause for depressions. Among the few who do believe there is such a phenomenon, most adopt a unitary explanation, that is, picking a single cause such as when wars occurred, when gold was discovered, or when new inventions replaced the old technology. All such efforts to explain the major depressions have been hampered by absence of a coordinated theory of how a fluctuating economic activity with peaks spaced 50 years and more apart could be generated.

We come now to a system dynamics model that does generate economic depressions many decades apart. A model is a theory that explains the behavior created by the model. The structure of the model and the policies in it are clearly the reasons for the behavior that results from the interactions of the parts of the modeled system. Whether or not the model can be accepted as a theory describing the real world depends on the plausibility of the model. Confidence in such a model depends on whether or not the structure of the model can be identified in the real world, how similar the model behavior is to the kind of behavior that has been observed, and how well changes in model policies result in changes in behavior that are reasonable and that have been observed in actual economies. After many years of model development and comparison with numerous aspects of historical economic behavior, I believe that the model will pass an acceptable range of confidence tests. [Note: Sterman, John D., 1986. The Economic Long wave: Theory and Evidence. *System Dynamics Review* 2 (2), 87-125.]

This is not the place to go into detail about the model and its simulations, but a few examples will give a glimpse of what can be done. I am starting a book that will contain a disk with the complete model and will show computer simulations of behavior and the effects of policy alternatives.

One of the most important observations made by Forrester in his 2003 speech is the impact of aggressively liberal monetary policy on extending the length of the long wave, and the smaller business cycles. The impact on the long wave of loose money is simulated with the System Dynamics Model. The aggressive fiscal and monetary policies of the 1990s and 2000s, bought us a few more years of economic growth, but the price tag for those years may be in the trillions of dollars.

It should be noted that the evidence from the System Dynamics Model clearly indicates that Bernanke is being required to manage a problem created by prior aggressive Federal Reserve monetary policy that over stimulated the economy. However, it should be appreciated that Federal Reserve policy is typically reacting to the problems created by overly aggressive fiscal policy (i.e., excessive government spending that distorts financial markets and makes the Federal Reserve job difficult, if not impossible).

Bernanke should be given credit for the job he is doing to manage a financial mess he did not create. Bernanke's knowledge of prior systemic crisis makes him the ideal Federal Reserve Chairman at this time in history, but he would benefit from the insights provided by the System Dynamics Model and the long wave. Forrester does a great job of describing the impact of lower interest rates on the long wave that is now in crisis mode.

Several powerful feedback loops contribute to the economic long wave, or Kondratieff cycle by linking together:

- Overinvestment in capital plant
- Excess borrowing to build the excess equipment and buildings
- Monetary policies that extend the expansion and promote the excesses

- Changes in real interest rates that accentuate the rise and collapse
- Increase and dissipation of growth expectations

As one of the powerful feedback loops driving an economic fluctuation of many decades between peaks, Figure 6 illustrates loops in which the monetary authority accentuates the long wave by holding down real interest rates during the expansion phase and thereby increasing the excesses of debt and overbuilding.

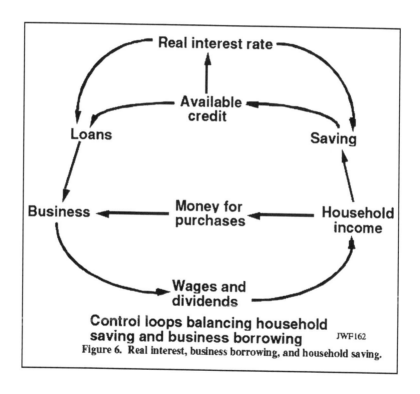

Control loops balancing household saving and business borrowing JWF162

Figure 6. Real interest, business borrowing, and household saving.

Real interest equals nominal bank interest minus inflation. By holding down bank interest and allowing inflation, especially inflation in asset values such as equities and real estate, the monetary authority maintains a low real interest during the long wave expansion. Low real interest encourages business to borrow and expand, encourages increase in asset prices, but also discourages household saving. As a result of more loans and less saving, the monetary authority must make available expanding credit to hold down the bank interest rate.

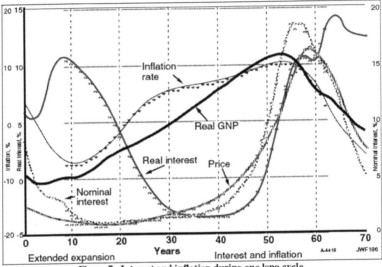

Figure 7. Interest and inflation during one long cycle.

Figure 7 is a computer simulation over a cycle of the long wave for a model without growth in population or technology. It shows the very low, even negative, real interest during the expansion phase of real GNP. But as the peak is approached, debt becomes burdensome, production capacity outruns demand, and competition drives down prices. Inflation becomes deflation, meaning negative inflation, causing a rise in real interest. At the peak of the long wave, capital plant is excessive and the real interest rate has risen, which together make additional investment unattractive and drive down new capital spending. In the present U.S. economy, the collapse in capital investment is especially evident in those companies that supply equipment to the telecommunications industry.

Several years ago Japan fell into a typical long wave depression brought about by excessive credit and an extreme bubble in real estate prices. It has yet to default on the resulting debts and awaits the eventual depreciation of buildings and capital plant.

Peaks of the long wave are often considered to be some 50 years apart. However, about 70 years have now elapsed since the Great Depression of the 1930s. An explanation appears to lie in some simulations we have made in which an aggressively liberal monetary policy was introduced a decade before the peak would have otherwise occurred. It appears that expansive credit, as we have had in the United States, can extend the peak and delay the downturn for two decades or more.

Here Forrester relates his initial surprise at discovering the long wave in the System Dynamics Model. He was not aware of the long wave literature, but his model produced the clear result of a long wave when two major sectors of the economy meet for business:

In my experience, modeling has often revealed behavior that was unexpected, and for which there was no prior reference mode, but which was then found to exist in the real system. Such was our introduction to the Kondratieff cycle. I was not aware of the literature, mostly in European sources, about the possibility of a large, long-period fluctuation in economic activity. But, as soon as we coupled a capital-producing sector to a goods sector in the model, we observed a large-amplitude instability with an interval of several decades between peaks.

When such unexpected behavior occurs in a model, one should start by looking for errors in the model. However, as a model is improved, there is a rising chance that unexpected behavior is revealing something about the real system. After careful examination of the model behavior, the causes of the long-period oscillation seemed reasonable and we were led to the related literature, the controversies, and the contradictory explanations. The explanations of the long wave in the literature seem contradictory only because they lack the context of a unifying systemic theory. In light of the behavior we see in the model, the literature is a replay of the fable of the four blind men and the elephant in which each feels and identifies a different structure. Most of the economic long wave literature contains correct fragments when one realizes that each writer is looking at a different part of a complex behavior that has multiple manifestations.

A review of some of Forrester's prior publications and appearances remains highly relevant to recent developments. Addressing the Joint Economic Committee of Congress in the 1980s, Dr. Forrester tried to convince the politicians in Washington of the consequences of his research and the dangers faced by the global economy. Congress was clearly warned to pay heed to the long wave evidence. If they had listened then, maybe the magnitude of the crisis we face now could have been avoided. It should be noted that, in 1984, we had just made the transition from an overheated long wave summer of inflation into the long wave fall season of corporate efficiency, which may explain why Forrester's warnings fell on deaf ears. Forrester (1984, 1) introduced the idea of long waves to Congress with the following statement:

> The long wave consists of rising economic activity for two or three decades, then a broad peak some ten years wide, and then a rapid drop into a major depression that can persist for a decade. After the depression, another long-term recovery starts.

The System Dynamics Model at the System Dynamics Group at MIT is a groundbreaking approach to studying the economy.

Some of Forrester's earlier thinking is relevant. Forrester's (1984, 1) research using the System Dynamics Model caused him to make the following observations about his work and the long wave to the members of the joint committee:

> Some of us at MIT have been drawn into considering the economic long wave through our work on the System Dynamics National Model. The National Model differs substantially from the more familiar econometric models. The National Model is built up from the operating policies within corporations and government, rather than from macroeconomic theory. It is derived from management policies as observed in the practical working world, rather than from a statistical time series representing aggregate economic behavior.

It is clear that Forrester's (1984, 1-2) research was coming at the subject matter of economic expansion and contraction from a totally different angle than Kondratieff's research. Forrester continued his address to the committee with the following evidence:

> The National Model generates, from interactions within its internal policies, the same patterns of change that have been observed in real life. The Model exhibits short-term business cycles of three-to-seven years' duration. Under the appropriate circumstances, it manifests stagflation and reveals the cause of simultaneously rising unemployment and inflation. Also, from the interactions within the private sector and government, the National Model produces an economic long wave, or Kondratieff cycle, of 45 to 60 years between peaks. The National Model provides for the first time a coherent theory to explain how a major rising and falling economic pattern spanning half a century can be systematically and internally created within an economy.

Forrester (1984, 2) went on to explain to the joint committee some of the basic characteristics of this remarkable cycle:

> The long wave is an alternating over- and under-accumulation of capital plants. In Western industrial economies, capital investment has been concentrated in periods of economic excitement lasting about three decades. Such periods of aggressive new construction have been interrupted by major depressions occurring in the 1820s, 1890s, and 1930s. Now, after the expansion of the last several decades, we are probably entering another such economic downturn. Along with the overbuilding of capital plants go rising prices, leveling out of productivity, speculation in physical assets, rising unemployment, and accumulating debts. Debts, which were taken on during expansion with the expectation of rising prices and profits, become burdensome when profits decline and interest rates remain high. Banks must write off uncollectible loans. Speculatively elevated land prices must re-adjust downward to come into balance with salaries and wages."

In considering Forrester's observations, it is obvious that the latest long wave spring advance began in the late-1940s. The spring and summer advance lasted during the 1950s, 1960s, and 1970s. The 1980s were the beginning of the fall season after the real economic peak in economic growth rates. The 1990s were the transition from a long wave fall season to the long wave winter season, but loose fiscal and monetary policy juiced the economy with the Internet bubble, and then the housing bubble that ran into 2006. Now we are witnessing the accelerating global decline predicted by Kondratieff and projected by the simulation of the System Dynamics Model. The debt liquidation phase is upon us. Please note that these are my interpretations of where we are in the long wave and I do not seek to imply that anyone quoted or the System Dynamics Group at MIT agrees with my particular interpretation of the current long wave evidence. I would encourage you to support the System Dynamics Group and seek out their current literature as it becomes available on the long wave.

John D. Sterman (1985, 6) in the System Dynamics Group at MIT in a working paper, entitled "The Long Wave: Theory and Evidence," put forward the following thoughts on the origin of the long wave:

> The long wave is characterized by successive waves of overexpansion and collapse of the economy, particularly the capital-producing sector. Overexpansion means an increase in the capacity to produce and in the production of plant, equipment, and goods relative to the amount needed to replace worn-out units and provide for growth over the long run. Overexpansion is undesirable because, eventually, production and employment must be cut back below normal to reduce the excess.

I encourage you to reread this paragraph and consider how it applies to global automobile, computer, and commercial real estate markets in the 1990s and early 2000s. There is only one solution to the excessive production in virtually all areas of the global economy: A severe economic decline is inevitable. The cutbacks, bankruptcies and mergers in these three industries alone tell the long wave story of decline all too well. How many new makes of cars were introduced in the 1980s and 1990s and new production plants opened?

Sterman's (1985, 1) observations of the System Dynamics Model and the long wave show just how extensively it affects our lives:

> Though the model focuses primarily on economic forces, the theory emerging from the NM is not monocausal; it relates capital investment; employment, wages, and workforce participation; inflation and interest rates; aggregate demand; monetary and fiscal policy; innovation and productivity; and even political values. The NM is unique among recent theories of the

long wave in that it views the long wave as a syndrome consisting of interrelated symptoms and springing from the interactions of many factors. The NM integrates diverse hypotheses about the genesis of the long wave. The NM also provides an analytical framework in which alternative theories can be tested in a rigorous and reproducible manner.

The most insightful and practical research and analysis of the long wave and what can be done to curtail its effects on business and financial markets will likely take place at MIT in the System Dynamics Group. When the global economy has suffered enough long wave booms and busts, we may see the program at MIT called upon to play a role in the corporate and government decision-making process to avoid the extremes of the long wave. We can always hope that our national leaders and those from other nations will realize the value of the work done by Forrester, Sterman, and many others and will call upon the program and its experts for advice.

Forrester (1984, 8) ended his address to the Joint Economic Committee of Congress with the following observations, which can now be viewed as prophetic observations as government officials have recently looked into the abyss of a global financial meltdown and are scrambling in the search of solutions as we face the greatest financial crisis since the Great Depression:

> Social, political and economic innovations are needed to reduce the hazards that lie ahead and to accentuate the strengths we now have. But can we be sure of choosing policies that will make the best of the situation? Too often, laws passed at times of crisis are either ineffective, counter-productive, or too late.

The System Dynamics Model seems to say that the old ways of doing things in the private sector and in Washington will perpetuate the severe boom and bust of the long wave. Forrester (1984,8) touched on this when he said:

Intuition and political compromise are not an adequate basis for dealing with the complexity of our economic system. New approaches that can explain more realistically how private sector policies and governmental laws interact are needed. One such approach is the System Dynamics National Model from which I have been drawing insights. If we are to cope in the best possible way with growing economic stresses, there should be a national priority for quickly achieving a much better understanding of economic behavior.

Long before the cold war was pronounced over, the Soviet Union had dissolved and the global economy had hit the skids. Dr. Forrester (1984, 8) made these observations in his address before the joint committee:

We should reexamine our national priorities. The internal economic threat to the country is now far greater than the external military threat. Even so, the country does not strive for economic understanding with the forcefulness and adequate funding that are established patterns for military research. It is time that seeking a better understanding of economic behavior should receive attention in keeping with its importance. Several major projects should be established, each with the goals of reaching within three years an improved understanding of how to avoid those policies that would make matters worse and of finding the few high leveraged policies that will take advantage of existing national economic strengths.

Dr. Forrester's advice has yet to be followed, even as our domestic economy, along with the global economy, heads into the latest long wave decline. The Year of Jubilee, like Forrester's idea of finding new ways of dealing with long wave economic forces, was meant to protect the economy from the natural internal tendencies of extreme in a free market economy.

I agree with Dr. Forrester that we can find ways and take steps that would greatly reduce the pain of the long wave cycle, but I believe it will always exist in some form in a free market economy. The long wave cycle runs deeper than economic and political statistics and decision making. It is part of the psychological learning curve in the arrival and passing of new generations of individuals that make up our society. Each new generation is destined to learn its own lessons.

The Year of Jubilee was a time of celebration for the new economy that would begin after a year of economic corrections and adjustments. My own optimism for the future is reinforced by Forrester's (1984, 9) views below. However, since these observations, he has demonstrated with the System Dynamics Model that this long wave may have been extended by a decade or two from aggressive monetary policies and artificially low interest rates. We now appear to have waded–if not plunged–into the swamp of economic difficulties. The wrong choices were made that now require correction:

> A bright new economy lies ahead, but it begins about a decade from now. There is a swamp of economic difficulties to cross before reaching the rising ground on the other side. Many choices can be made in moving from here to there. Those choices will affect how smoothly we make the transition from the old economy to the new economy. If we simply react to pressures as they arise, we will continue to be dominated by forces for which we are unprepared. On the other hand, by coming to a better understanding of how economic forces are being created, we can begin to shape policies for a more desirable transition into the new economy.

If we are ever as a nation or global economy going to learn to deal with the causes and consequences of the long wave, it is very likely that such breakthroughs will come from research on the System Dynamics Model within the System Dynamics Group at MIT. If you believe that, your company, foundation or government could benefit from the work and research done at MIT by the System Dynamics Group, I encourage you to arrange to support the program. A number of individuals, international companies, foundations, and governments are sponsors of the System Dynamics Model research program. Allegheny Corporation, Citicorp Investment Management, Kollmorgen, Digital Equipment and Merrill Lynch are just a few of the corporate supporters of the program. Intelligent corporate leaders are using the System Dynamics Model to consider their own plans for the future.

Sponsors' tax deductible contributions range from a yearly $10,000 for participation in research to $100,000 for firms who wish deep involvement in the various aspects of the program. You can receive additional information on the System Dynamics Model program by visiting (http://scripts.mit.edu/~sdg/) or by writing: System Dynamics Group, Sloan School of Management, Massachusetts Institute of Technology, Cambridge, Massachusetts 02139.

Chapter 5:

ECONOMIC FIELD THEORY

"... he conceived and developed the nature of the field and established the reality of the field as the underlying reality of all spatio-temporal phenomena."

T.F. Torrance, On James Clerk Maxwell

"Maxwell's equations are laws representing the structure of the field .... All space is the scene of these laws and not, as for mechanical laws, only points in which matter or charges are present."

Albert Einstein

"If men could remove cycles from the world they would destroy themselves. Fortunately men have no such powers. But they are indelibly convinced they do, which is why cycles will work forever."

PQ Wall

The extended implications of the evidence produced by the System Dynamics Model at MIT are pointing market cycle research into a new area of potential scientific inquiry. It would appear that interactions of parts of the model produce the structural manifestations of the model in the real world, i.e. long waves. The model appears to generate a field of economic and financial activity of sorts. To the extent that human behavior drives interactions of the parts of the model, then the possibility of the long wave and other cycles being manifestation of fields of human action must be explored.

In this regard, examining 20th-century developments in the hard sciences for insight into business cycles is shaping up an important exercise for any study of long wave the smaller market cycles. A possible scientific explanation of long waves in both the U.S. economy and the global economy comes from a fairly advanced scientific perspective. The concept of business cycles, long waves in particular, being the manifestation of interconnected fields of financial, economic, and political activity (i.e., human action) must be briefly explored.

The term "fields," as used here can be defined as a specific range in space and time of interconnected phenomena. This definition of fields is analogous to the concept of business cycles. Economic activity is certainly an interconnected phenomenon as demonstrated by the System Dynamics Model at MIT. But naturally occurring fields of interconnected activity are far more accepted as the explanation for observable phenomena in the hard sciences. This is particularly true in the area of electromagnetic and quantum fields in physics and morphic fields in advanced theories in microbiology.

The bridge between the application of field theory, so commonly accepted in the hard sciences, to long waves or economic cycles in the social sciences has yet to be fully constructed. However, it is important to note at the outset that economic cycles are, at their hearts, social cycles. Economic activity is a manifestation of social action, or, as the case may sometimes be, social inaction. Arguments presented in this chapter specifically, and in this book in general, should be seen as a rough draft for one possible bridge between the social sciences and the hard sciences.

Field theory warrants detailed consideration as the debate on long waves and their origins continue. The work and writings of financial analyst PQ Wall, and what may prove to be some of his br' akthrough applications of the principle of fields in the har   nces to fields of disequilibrium in political/economic
was my first introduction to the relationship
science fields and the long wave or what could be
les. Credit for many of the ideas presented here
' (1993). Others invariably have and will make
ns to the eventual acceptance or rejection

An introduction to some of the basic premises of field theory applied to long wave theory is a reasonable goal. Here I merely present the argument that there appears to be a relationship between the interconnected nature of the long wave and field theory.

A review of field theory along with long waves is in line with the injunction of Paul Samuelson (1947) in his book *Foundations of Economic Analysis*. He asserted that physics is the science for economics to imitate. However, Samuelson appears to have had in mind physics based on objective-oriented Newtonian mechanical physics, which were actually displaced before his observations were written. Samuelson believed in the Keynesian approach of objectively determining macroeconomic values and imbalances in the system and controlling them with government's institutional intervention. Samuelson believed Keynes's perpetual boom was achievable through the mechanical intervention efforts of government institutions.

Samuelson was evidently not aware that Newtonian theory had been displaced by electromagnetic field theory and then quantum field theory, which pushed physics out of the realm of objective mechanical laws, or points of action, into the realm of subjective fields of influence.

This same displacement of mechanical physical concepts of cell development by field theory has occurred in advanced microbiology. James Lovelock and Rupert Sheldrake have postulated a radical change in how we view the development of living biological life forms. They have discovered what they call "morphic fields," working alongside DNA codes, which, PQ Wall noted (1993, 2), are "shaping both development and behavior of living things."

The cyclical development of interconnected activity over what appear to be the predictable spans of the regular business cycle and the long wave resembles the notion of observable fields of interdependent development in the flows or movements of energy and matter and the development of living organisms. The implications of field theory for the social science of international political economy, if applicable, are no less radical than they were for the hard sciences of electromagnetics, physics, and biology.

The possibilities, as further evidence will indicate, appear to be the opposite of the mechanical understanding and intervention Samuelson intended to endorse. It is, of course, conceivable that there is no link between fields discovered in the hard sciences and those that appear to be evident in the long wave, but such remarkable coincidences are doubtful. Certainly, drawing such parallels could be a misguided premature proposition, but the possibilities should at least be open for discussion. They should be explored and debated in light of the evidence for what appear to be naturally occurring long waves displaying interconnected field-like characteristics.

A mechanical approach to economic intervention could have been implemented with scientific authority when mechanical Newtonian foundations ruled the science of physics. The world was believed to be mechanical. Mechanical analysis and solutions to social ills were, therefore, logical. However, electromagnetic field theory and quantum field-theory have removed much of the objective measurability of physical phenomena. This is due to the logical consequences of basic field theory characteristics.

In electromagnetic field theory, Newtonian mechanics were undermined as the complete explanation for physical action. In quantum theory, the notion of discontinuous as opposed to continuous release and absorption of energy that manifests itself in fields made the causes of physical phenomena unmeasurable in many respects. Sure the size of the fields produced in terms of time and space can be measured, but what cannot be measured is precisely how and why the deviations of the fields occur based on intrinsic actions and facts or a measured breakdown of component parts. Institutional economics have yet to catch up with modern physics in terms of what makes or doesn't make things happen in the physical universe.

In his book on James Clerk Maxwell's formulation of the theory of the electromagnetic field, T.F. Torrance (Maxwell 1982, 23-24) writes:

Clerk Maxwell 'created for the first time a field theory which was independently testable against Newtonian force theories.' He created a situation in which the dominance of Newtonian mechanics over the whole spectrum of physical science was called into question and decisive steps were taken in the direction of a non-mechanical thoroughly relational understanding of the intelligible connections immanent in the universe ... Clerk Maxwell's work was of profound conceptual importance ... he conceived and developed the nature of the field and established the reality of the field as the underlying reality of all spatio-temporal phenomena. At this point we cannot do better than let Einstein himself speak. 'The formulation of these equations is the most important event in physics since Newton's time, not only because of their wealth of content, but also because they form a pattern for a new type of law .... Maxwell's equations are laws representing the structure of the field .... All space is the scene of these laws and not, as for mechanical laws, only points in which matter or charges are present.'

Fields are here suggested to be interconnected activity in space and time—a sort of ebb and flow discovered in the physical universe. The parameters of these fields can be observed, but the fields themselves are an inherently dynamic part of the system. The fields appear to be guided by external degrees of freedom that are somehow separate from the internal forces at work. The proposition put forward here is that long waves in the global economy, as observed by Kondratieff in historical data and projected by the System Dynamics Model at MIT, and all that they entail, are indeed spatio-temporal phenomena. That is to say they exist in space and time.

The clear implication, if the global economy is categorized as a spatio-temporal phenomenon, as it surely must be in numerous, if not all respects, is that the underlying reality of our global economic system is that of a field of interconnected human activity. It cannot be logically argued that social activity, both economic and political, is not a spatio-temporal phenomena. The formation and activity of the global economy resembles the development of a living organism.

What a number of theorists in the hard sciences have observed is that the development of life appears to resemble more of a mind than a machine. Economic and political activity, indeed all social activity, occurs in space and time. Maxwell and Einstein's work would appear to suggest that this activity, due to its spatio-temporal characteristics, must be part of a field of one form or another. The obvious implication here is that the long wave is the representation of one such social field.

The further implication is that Maxwell's work on the electromagnetic field and its impact on light was the foundation of that part of Einstein's work that led to relativity theory. Relativity in turn led to the formulation of quantum field theory. These discoveries produce a major problem for the institutional mechanical tools of government interventionism. One observation concerning the problem of objective measurement in quantum physics relative to fields was expressed by Aharonov and Petersen (1971, 138) in Quantum Theory and Beyond, who concluded:

> ... it is not surprising that the relativistic constraint on interactions imposes limitations on measurements in the quantum domain. For example, to measure the momentum of a field according to the canonical method one would need an interaction proportional to the momentum and to some external degree of freedom belonging to the apparatus.

Free market thinker, Friedrick August von Hayek, noted that the expected deviations for calculations in the international economic structure cannot be known; in the same way, there are also limits on measurements of the field in the quantum domain. The bottom line of the new physics for the policy makers is that this suggests that any measurement of an economic phenomenon that occurs in space and time in terms of determining value for wages or prices appears to be truly relational or subjective, in the deepest scientific sense. It is truly a relative exercise, relative to the ever-changing structure of the global economy, as literally trillions of decisions by billions of individuals are perpetually changing the allocation and use of their material, physical, and mental resources in the international system. Bottom line, the social system is interconnected and dynamic, just like the quantum field.

What this logic suggests is that Hayek was correct about the danger of a scientific approach to economics when all the data is not, and apparently cannot, be known. Following this argument to its completion, a statistical and objective calculation of what the minimum wage, prices, or the interest rate should be presents a serious problem, unless one ignores the fact that Newtonian mechanics no longer represents the complete equation for measurement of spatio-temporal phenomena. If so, one bases decisions on simplistic and potentially incorrect assumptions of value regardless of the consequences. The result is the distortion of the global economy or the field of interconnected activity in the national or international system.

A.S. Eddington (Dewey and Dakin, 8) presents the argument for such a subjective approach to the world and, therefore, policy and planning in *The Nature of the Physical World*:

> The quantum physicist does not fill the atom with gadgets for directing its future behavior, as the classical physicist would have done; he fills it with gadgets determining the odds on its future behavior. He studies the art of the bookmaker, not the trainer.

Government interventionists believe that economic problems and social ills just need institutional gadgets for correction. Field theory says such programmable gadgets cannot be accurate, and, therefore, cannot be effective. The action and impact of the gadgets that make up the global economy can be observed, as seen in long waves, but not controlled and directed since their values within the dynamic field cannot be completely measured. The implication is that the entire field itself can be observed but not measured and directed internally, at least not successfully over time.

Newton's view of the universe was mechanical. The arguments in support of aggressive fiscal and monetary policy to manage the economy were based on this concept of mechanical monetary tools for redressing imbalances. The more fully-developed "scientific" arsenal of economic statistics emerged with Mitchell's institutionalism in the 1920s and 1930s. It was presumed that objective scientific data reinforced arguments for fiscal policy and monetary policy for desired economic and, therefore, social results.

Scientifically based economic institutionalism received a theoretical boost with the publication of Paul Samuelson's arguments in 1947 and many other Keynesians who believed in what they called the new economics. This was just a few years after Bretton Woods launched the international institutions that could be used for the intervention and application of the new economics of Keynesianism. The monetary and bureaucratic mechanics could go to work.

Government institutional activity clearly represents what are asserted to be objective rather than subjective perspectives of value in the international system. The approach was clearly appealing to anyone with Newtonian scientific leanings. But if Samuelson is to be taken at his word, then the study of political economy must consider the relevance and implications of quantum field theory.

Government institutionalism believes it can objectively and scientifically figure out, regulate, and know both economic causes of events and the economic values that should exist in the system. This includes minimum wage, car gas mileage and tariffs. The idea that economic events and solutions to problems are mechanical and can be known objectively clearly leads to mechanical solutions. Keynesians believe that solutions to social problems can be applied objectively with solid planning through institutional frameworks of analysis and intervention. They use limited knowledge and call it objective fact to dictate policy they claim is scientifically grounded.

With the disequilibrium that emerged with economic crisis in the overheated long wave summer of the 1970s and the crisis as the long wave winter that began in the late 1990s, it became increasingly clear that Keynesian-based decisions had not been as scientifically grounded as presumed. All the data had not been considered in the government's equations. The economic projectiles did not fly according to even the best laid mechanical plans. Other forces must have been at work-forces significant enough to produce severe crisis and uncoordinated economic activity. The idea of social development occurring in an interconnected field, in which the optimum level of values cannot be known objectively and, therefore, manipulated effectively by government, appears to be more relevant than ever, and field theory may well offer some insights. The fact may be–and this is the first long wave in which it will be put to the test on a grand scale–that government intervention actually exacerbates the extremes of the field. Now that we are deep in the global crisis, $10 trillion in government intervention may mute aspects of the crisis, but the crisis has reached this scale precisely because of government intervention and creeping state capitalism that has distorted the economy and financial markets.

If the application of field theory is a valid concept, there appear to be interrelationships in the fields that are incalculable and so complex as to be unknowable. The give-and-take within the fields of the global economy produces recognizable long wave patterns of international system development. Adam Smith clearly stated that the natural price prevailed at a specific time and place. By implication, the next moment, in the same or a different place, natural price or value could change. This dynamic characteristic of price-imputed value is due to the continual emergence of new product and service uses, substitutions, discoveries, and technologies, which must be incorporated into values. What's more, the information that informs the market as to these changes may be late, biased, or simply bad. Disequilibrium is to be expected in prices.

Smith never addresses the matter of price in terms of definitive equilibrium, but in terms of what more closely resembles disequilibrium. Smith's arguments suggest that market prices and thus the market is dynamic.

Field theory suggest that even in a pure unencumbered market system there would be a natural cyclical expansion and contraction tendency in all interconnected fields, which defines the parameters of the field. This is a reflection of the disequilibrium forces of market price in search of natural price, in other words, the search for value. The search appears to lead the system into regular recurring patterns of not only 3-to-5-year business and market cycles, but 50-to-70-year long waves.

The case that long wave theory makes is certainly relevant to the general observations of field theory. The international system appears to have a natural, even predictable, tendency for perpetual, although regular, disequilibrium. From a more distant perspective, this could certainly be seen as a very broad equilibrium.

Price in all markets is always searching for, but never finding, equilibrium. This process of perpetual disequilibrium appears to produce interconnected, field-like characteristics. This is clearly opposed to the classical notion of a system that does, or could if given a chance, tend toward equilibrium.

The final answer to the question of whether the field theory accepted in the hard sciences is related to what appears to be regularly recurring long waves and the smaller cycles in the social sciences may still be some time away. However, the question certainly deserves to be asked and discussed. Long wave cycles, if they exist–and the evidence is impressive–are certainly interconnected social phenomenon taking place in a specific range of space and time. Cycles are clearly fields of human action. The intraday low print in a major market like the S&P 500, is the demarcation of division between fields of human action. The current global crisis is a field of human action–some of it good, some of it not so good–occurring in space and time. This observation is irrefutable.

Our work suggests that some of the fields in the international political economy, and markets which drive it, can be discovered using what we term as Theory 144 Analytics. In our work we seek to discover and track these fields, which manifest themselves in various cycle relationships, in price and time.

Chapter 6:

THE GLOBAL ECONOMY

"There can be economy only where there is efficiency."

Benjamin Disraeli

"The future of nations cannot be frozen . . . cannot be foreseen. History is a story of growth, decay and change. If no provisions, no allowance is made for change by peaceful means, it will come anyway–and with violence."

Herbert Hoover

Every long wave expansion has witnessed an increase in the interconnectedness of the global economy. The most recent long wave advance was no exception. The advent of technology, information systems, satellite communications and the Internet has radically changed the world and connected it in remarkable ways. While prior editions of this book predicted the advent of 24-hour-a-day markets and trading, they are now a reality. Financial markets are now truly global. What happens in one country has an immediate impact on markets and prices in others.

In April of 2009 the International Monetary Fund (IMF) warned of growing parallels with the current global crisis and the Great Depression. The IMF highlighted the increasing global nature of the economy and the impact on the current crisis:

However, while the credit boom in the 1920s was largely specific to the United States, the boom during 2004-2007 was global, with the increased leverage and risk-taking in advanced economies and many emerging economies. Moreover, levels of integration are now much higher than during the inter-war period, so United States financial shocks have a larger impact on global financial systems than in the 1930s... Moreover, declining activity is beginning to create feedback effects that affect the solvency of financial intermediaries, which risks of debt deflation have increased.

Clearly, we are now living in an interconnected, global economy. When long wave forces are unleashed they have immediate ramifications that are felt in the financial markets of every nation. This is being born out acutely in the current global long wave systemic crisis. This is the first long wave winter season where global dissemination of information is instantaneous.

The interconnectedness of the global economy has been building to its present debt crisis crescendo. Before the 19th century, what happened in one country or region typically didn't have a very large impact on what went on in neighboring states. There was a time when one region or country could have been in economic turmoil and its neighbors might not even have known of its plight.

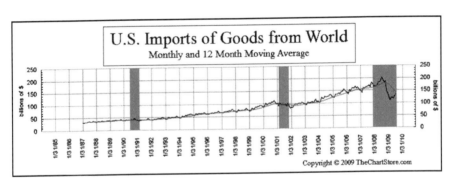

Chart 6.1 Imports of Goods to the U.S.

The tulip fiasco in Holland in 1635 didn't have a great effect on market conditions in London. Portugal's loss of a major trade expedition to hurricanes wouldn't have affected the markets in Frankfurt, Germany, in 1675. China's large, public investments in the Great Wall had no repercussions on Barbarian trade in Europe. Particular areas and regions in the world were independent economic entities, economic organisms that could get sick or die off without a large impact on other parts of the world. In the late 1700s, this independence began to change.

The close of the 18th century saw the distinct beginnings of the emergence of an interdependent global economy. The trend toward a truly global economy gathered momentum over the past 200 years. Over recent years we have seen international ownership, foreign investment, financial exchange activity, and, therefore, global interdependence exploding to record heights.

An all-important piece in the world economic puzzle was the rise of the international banking system late in the 18th century. Before this new era, nations were as a rule financed from within for their various governmental and business activities, whether public works or military conquests. The international banking community emerged as a sovereign, able to make or break governments and guide the destinies of nations by a simple yes or no to requests for financing. Trade and commerce were financed through the network of the international private banks, which were intertwined with increasingly powerful central banks.

Observing the global economic organism, we must label the flow of funds controlled by the international private banks and central bank of the world as the blood that flows through the veins of the global system. When the international banking system is in crisis, the entire system is threatened. The expansion and contraction of global banking and money supplies are a major component in the long wave.

We have no choice in the realm of international trade but to pay our bills, secure a line of credit in the international banking system, or dip into the till at the International Monetary Fund. Global relationships, which benefit all of us, also come with strains and new tensions that are not always easily resolved. This is evidenced by the fact that armed conflict among nations has increased rather than decreased since the long wave emerged. The long wave appears to be superimposed on our international economic relationships.

The global economy operates with accounting standards, although the standards occasionally have been bent and twisted. Governments may rise and fall, but the business records are still being kept. To play in the international economic arena as a sovereign state, you must play according to the rules of international finance.

Kondratieff observed that the long wave cycle was a global capitalist phenomenon. The cycle passes through all capitalist economies of the globe fairly simultaneously, although evidence indicates there may have been long wave cycles before the advent of capitalism.

A number of obvious forces have shaped the emergence of a global economy over the past 200 years, but as mentioned earlier, there are two major ones: innovation in transportation and advances in communications.

Shipping evolved from limited, often unseaworthy, sailing ships to vessels carrying vast amounts of goods to virtually any place in the world. Canals from the Suez to Panama opened up trade lanes for enhanced efficiencies in international commerce. Railroads, on the cutting edge of world industrialization, brought the trade of the continents to the major world ports. Water transportation became more dependable and affordable for tourist and official travelers alike. From Hong Kong to New York, from Bombay to Rotterdam, and from Rio de Janeiro to Cape Town, the states and continents of the world became dependent on each other for the flow of goods.

During the 1920s, the stage was set for global interdependence to accelerate a great deal. Charles A. Lindbergh made history by flying across the Atlantic from New York to Paris in 1927. This marked the beginning of a great explosion in the already growing business alliances between Europe and America. Air travel began to take off and made the world even more susceptible to international economic dealings and financial relationships. The consequences of the global interdependence in the 1930s are remembered by everyone who experienced or studied the period.

The second major force of this new global economy could be placed on a pedestal. It is the advance by leaps and bounds that has come in communications. In scarcely a century, the economic centers of the world went from communication by pigeons, when they flew where they were supposed to, to instantaneous communication and information by satellite. The impact and consequences in the movements of markets is overpowering and almost unimaginable.

In more recent years, the advent of computers and satellite communications systems, along with sweeping transportation innovations have precipitated the new economic reality. What is the new reality? It is simply that all nations play a role and are an integral part of an interdependent global economy.

When word went out that the U.S. government would not step in and save Lehman Brothers, as they had Bear Stearns in 2008, hundreds of billions of dollars in value were wiped out from global markets in hours and trillions of dollars in value were wiped out in days. Half a millennium earlier, America did not even exist and England was still looking over its shoulder in fear of an invasion from barbarians.

With global markets open 24-hours-a–day, most investments are traded on a 24-hour basis. News that affects markets is known immediately throughout the world, due to our advances in communications. These advances have done a great deal to increase the number of banking transactions on an international basis, and stimulate world trade. International orders are being processed in a fraction of the time it took a few years ago, because of the financial links through new communications technologies that allow same-day order execution from virtually any location on the globe.

In the 1995 edition, I noted that no one knows what will happen when these new global financial links are forced to unravel in an international crisis. Late in 2008 we discovered what would happen, when the interconnected international financial system broke down. Financial and government authorities were said to have "looked into the abyss." Trillions of dollars in rescue funds began to flow to stop the descent into the abyss, but the ultimate outcome is still unknown and the abyss is still within the realm of possibility.

Nassim Nicholas Taleb, author of *Black Swan*, noted the importance of the emergence of an integrated global economy during this financial crisis when he was quoted in a May 2009 *Bloomberg* article by Shiyin Chen and Liza Lin:

> The current global crisis is "vastly worse" than the 1930s because financial systems and economies have become more interdependent... "This is the most difficult period of humanity that we're going through today because governments have no control," Taleb, 49, told a conference in Singapore today. "Navigating the world is much harder than in the 1930s."

Another key element in the emergence of the global economic organism is the multinational corporation. Many of these giants have a gross national product larger than that of dozens of smaller nations totaled together. They command vast empires on which the sun never sets. For years, we tended to think that the control of a company resided in one nation. Not so for the multinational. These companies are owned by residents of almost every nation in the world.

This goes for the biggest companies, such as IBM, Exxon, and Archer Daniels Midland. Foreign-based multinationals are in the same situation. Virtually all major European and Japanese car builders have plants in America that hire Americans and sell to Americans as well as build cars for export out of America back to their own countries. Virtually all other industries have experienced the same expansion of global relationships. Most basic products, such as cars and computers, are made with parts and materials from dozens of different countries. These trends are causing the people and economies of the world to be tied together more closely than ever.

Companies that have chosen not to join the international trend will eventually be put out of business if they haven't already failed. In a general sense, there is no longer such a thing as a domestic economy. You would be hard-pressed to find any company that is not in some way affected by the global economy. The multinational has, perhaps more than any other element, forced national government into the global economic organism.

Having a formidable interest in every corner of the world, the large multinational must have a vehicle to express and/or guarantee its interest. This job has often been taken up by governments. It has even been rumored that governments have been toppled in line with the desires of the multinationals. They form a network in global commerce that tightens the bonds of the global economy.

Energy needs came hand in hand with industrialization, so treaties and pacts between and among nations began to emerge based on access to energy markets. Alliances and trading partnerships were formed from every corner of the world due to the demand for black gold-oil. Certain regions had an abundance of energy but no climate for agriculture, so marriages were made and strategic interests were solidified by the fate of nature.

In recent years, there has been an enormous increase in foreign investment and ownership in the U.S. Total assets in the United States owned by foreigners rose from just over $100 billion in 1970 to several trillion in the 1990s. The three major components of this investment are in treasury securities, direct investment, and corporate stocks. It was noted in a Reuters' article by Nick Carey that Grant Thornton reported total assets of foreign owned U.S. companies increased to $9.2 trillion in 2005. In early 2009, over $3 trillion in U.S. treasuries were owned by foreign entities.

Agriculture is an all-important element in the rise of the global economy. The superfarm is changing the way the world feeds itself and is making many nations vulnerable to major difficulties in the event of an unhealthy climate of world trade.

Energy is another case in point. The U.S., China, Japan and much of Western Europe are depending on the oil fields of the volatile Middle East. Another example of interdependence in the world community is South Africa. Because South Africa is the major producer of a number of strategic metals used in the U.S. defense complex, the Pentagon and the CIA closely watch developments on the southern tip of Africa, thousands of miles away from American shores.

The last few decades of this latest advance and especially the latest long wave advance saw more extensive links in the global economy than ever before. More so than at any time in history, every nation of the globe is a player in one form or another in the global long wave. What happens in Japan, Germany, Russia, Mexico, China, England and even much smaller countries affects the United States and the world, and is incorporated into the sum of human action and therefore market action on a daily basis.

The reality of our present predicament in a truly global economy brings us to a number of sobering conclusions. There is no such creature as an independent economic nation. We are all bound by the global economy; thus, our fate is linked by the global system.

A small, developing nation can send shock waves throughout the world financial markets by defaulting on its obligation to pay its creditors. An oil tanker struck in the Persian Gulf in regional hostilities or an explosion at an Indonesian refinery can send oil prices up on world markets. Above all, the downturn in a few key capitalist nations can bring the global economy to its knees.

Of course, this works both ways. We enjoyed a long wave expansion and advancing global economy from the late 1940s to 1990s. We are now in the midst of a long wave winter that brings falling prices, an international increase in bankruptcy, a global real-estate depression, a global banking crisis, and a worldwide business contraction. Even though the long wave winter tends to begin in one leading speculative nation of the advance, such as the U.S. in the 1930s and Japan in the 1990s, the long wave is still a global phenomenon. The fact that the ties in the global economy are stronger than ever means that during this long wave winter solution the crisis may well take on global dimensions never before dreamed possible.

The 1995 edition of this book read, "There is the possibility of a global New Deal being the solution offered by a consortium of leading governments such as the G-7 financial powers, including the United States, Great Britain, France, Germany, Japan, Canada, and Italy, or the Group of Ten, which would add Belgium, the Netherlands, and Sweden to the list. There is also a great chance that governments will not be able to work together due to internal pressures caused by a long wave winter crisis." Working on this chapter for this new edition in April 2009 as the global crisis deepened during this long wave winter, it was a bit of a surreal experience, as at the G-20 meeting in London a Global New Deal of $2 trillion was pitched, which was quickly shot down by Germany's Chancellor Angela Merkel. The G-20 settled on a mere $1 Trillion dollar commitment to seek to jump start the global economy.

The global economy and the spread of capitalism to new markets is an essential aspect of the ebb and flow of the global long wave. The greatest long wave force currently at work to ignite the next long wave advance is that over 2.5 billion people in Brazil, Russia, India and China, known as the BRIC countries, are beginning to participate in the global economy. When you add Eastern Europe, South America and other countries in Asia the emerging force of these markets is the most potent long wave force at work. The remarkable economic force of a natural long wave expansion of capitalism into these new markets should not be underestimated. However, these BRIC economies are now making the shift from export driven economies to advanced economies to sufficient domestic demand to drive long-term growth, and this shift will take years, not months. Domestic growth of these new markets will become export growth of more advanced economies.

At the beginning of the last long wave in 1949, markets for capitalism were shrinking as the Soviet Union seized much of Eastern Europe, and China had succumbed to communism. Today these are all new and growing markets with phenomenal growth potential that could pull North America and Europe out of their long wave slumps and into the next long wave advance. However, it is likely that necessary long wave adjustments due to global debt, production and prices will offset the power of these rising new markets for a few more years, when the next long wave will be unleashed with astonishing force.

In the new era of a truly global economy, there is increasingly an interlinking and regular rhythm to the booms and busts in the international system. In evaluating the present situation, we have to come to a simple, yet telling, conclusion: as participants in the global economy, we are all riding the present long wave together!

PART II
THE SIGNS

Chapter 7:

PSYCHOLOGY

"I can calculate the motions of the heavenly bodies, but not the madness of people."

Isaac Newton

Laissez-faire economics, the supremacy of individual capitalism and entrepreneurism, was the rage of the 1980s and 1990s. The quest for acquiring the almighty dollar as a measure of one's worth was at levels not reached since the 1920s. There was a mood in the air that said, "Give me an ounce of opportunity and nothing in the world can keep me from cutting out my piece of the pie."

Social and psychological forces similar to those prevalent in the United States were also evident in Europe and Asia. Basically, globally we were in a historically upbeat mood in the 1980s and 1990s. Since the market top in 2000, and the following top in the real estate bubble, like the 1930s, we are now seeing a society that is far more subdued and introspective. The trend appears to be accelerating.

In this chapter, we will observe that public mood may well be a primary force in driving the long wave. It may be a leading long wave indicator. The 1980s and 1990s were amazingly similar in social mood and political policy to the 1920s. Therefore, the period we now find ourselves in may be similar to the prevalent depressing mood of the 1930s. The psychological and social aspects of long wave theory are the sum of personal experiences. Observers of popular psychology should remove themselves from the long wave winter season drama as it is unfolding presently and observe how the popular mood is leading human action.

Competition was king in the 1980s and 1990s. From airlines to banking to trucking, government was cutting the strings and letting the capitalist nature take its course. Conservative politics have long been the ticket of the free market and have endorsed the belief that the private sector can do far more to make society and the economy reach new heights of return and personal reward than can government intervention and meddling. Indeed they are right, but what is the other side of the coin? For each action, there is an equal and opposite reaction.

Does the success of a free market push human psychology to an extreme that takes a good thing beyond its healthy bounds? Does the inevitable reaction usher in a new era of regulation and government intervention? Could it be possible that human psychology plays an important role in the rise and fall of the long wave cycle? The evidence leans toward just such a hypothesis.

Due to the amount of data available and the fact that the decline known as the Great Depression occurred in the 20th century, it is weighed heavily in analysis of psychological implications of the long wave. However, more recent years are becoming just as instructive.

Though we can trace liberal and conservative political and social movements running in conjunction with the long wave for the past 200 years, the Great Depression tells us far more about what to expect in the latest long wave decline because of its closer approximation and resemblance to current times. Indeed, we are already seeing mass psychology lurch away from the embrace of *laissez-fair* and into the embrace of government intervention.

The yuppie generation that was the driving force in the 1980s and 1990s had no memory of the pain of the Depression in the 1930s. Instead, they had the idea stuck in their heads of a fairly pain-free, riskless society. They were the engine driving a new breed of speculators and risk takers in global markets. Their only experience was with rising global stock markets and real-estate values. I have long enjoyed the political philosophy of Englishman Jeremy Bentham, who is quoted by Dick Stoken in an article on the Kondratieff Cycle and its effects on social psychology in the February 1980 issue of *The Futurist*, which is all the more relevant today.

Bentham (Stoken 1980) said, "Nature has placed man under the governance of two sovereign masters, pain and pleasure. It is for them alone to point out what we shall do." This thought conjures up the vision of humanity as a great pendulum swinging back and forth within the economic long wave. Individuals first find their economic freedom and after taking it to a painful extreme, swing back to a stifling protectionist stance, turning control back to government as a force beyond themselves. Few are able to rise above the mood of the masses and remove themselves from the spirit of the times.

In the 1980s and 1990s, the most respected person on the block was the one with the newest, most expensive car and the fanciest clothes. In the early 2000s, the mood change of a long wave decline was already becoming obvious. Now the person with the used, functional car and moderate lifestyle is the more respected. The expensive shopping malls have been replaced in popularity by price-cutting Wal-Mart stores.

In the 1980s and 1990s, living "beyond our means" was in. Living frugally, working harder, and saving for the future are trends accelerating today. When this decline reaches its worst years, frugality will practically become a religion. Will the capital formation of such an attitude of thrift and hard work help the economy move forward in the next advance? You can bet it will!

When individuals find themselves a few rungs higher on the ladder of financial success and are more economically independent, as happens at the end of a long wave advance, he or she tends to become a freewheeler, willing to try something new, willing to step a little closer to the edge of uncertainty for just a little more financial gain. Think of the red hot Internet stock market and real estate bubble. This individual can have little effect on the direction of the global economy and history of the world as a lone actor, but when whole nations are experiencing this phenomenon in unison, as happened in the 1920s and the 1980s and 1990s, the history of humanity is hanging in the balance.

Fifty-plus years are sufficient time to drain pessimistic and cautious blood out of the mainstream of economic activity. We tend to forget the stories our parents and grandparents told us about food and unemployment lines. Visions of the Great Depression had no place in the consciousness of those in a

position to potentially see it coming again in recent decades-
therefore they took no action to lessen the impact of dangerous
trends.

In his article, Stoken (1980) said:

> When people perceive less risk they put more trust in
> their own powers. They become more adventurous and
> more willing to take chances. Because they are now being
> directed by a different set of underlying assumptions
> than during a downswing, they do things they would not
> have done during hard times. Economic success leads
> people to believe they now have control over their own
> destiny, with the power to solve their own and society's
> problems. They idealize existence and become less
> tolerant of injustice. (14-17)

When the trend of optimism and its manifestation in
speculation have run full course, the long wave peaks and begins
its decline. The psyche of society takes on a new character, and
humanity is not so confident in its ability and power to overcome
obstacles. Unbridled capitalism loses its luster and falls from its
pedestal. The dreams and aspirations of the proponents of a
poorly executed *laissez-faire* system are shattered, providing the
pain necessary to begin the swing of the pendulum back to a
sedated view of the system.

Going further, Stoken (1980) said:

> On the one hand, a long period of prosperity and
> affluence produces increases in assets, wages, social
> mobility and the standard of living that exceed people's
> expectations, causing them to be pleasantly surprised. A
> depression on the other hand, has an untoward effect
> on jobs, wages and asset values. People unexpectedly
> see their goals frustrated and this serves as a lesson of
> pain. Pain produces a definite psychological change
> in most people. They become motivated to avoid
> pain and to seek security. In a risky world people feel

helpless, lose faith in their own powers and become very cautious and unwilling to take chances. To protect themselves and ward off danger, they bond together into groups.

To modify behavior in the direction of group unity, there must be rules and social restraints as well as the acceptance of some kind of authority. Naturally the mood at such a time runs against individualistic capitalism, with its free markets and emphasis on competition. (14-17)

We can see this clearly in the growth of the unions in the 1940s and the 1950s as the pain of the Depression was fresh on the minds of people all over the world, yet as this generation grew older and the economy was in good shape, we saw unions struggling for survival. If history holds true, unions will once again be on the rise and membership will be booming soon after the world economy enters its next advance and a more sober society gets back to work in a new economy.

As a cautious and risk-averse generation becomes the rule in the decline, a slow change occurs: A few individuals step out from the group and buck the trend. These new leaders come from within industry and companies as well as in the form of lone rangers. They are the inventors and the innovators that are, through their bold and aggressive natures, going to lead the world out of its mesmerized risk-averse state of decline and into the next advance of the long wave cycle. During the last years of the long wave advance, you tend to find everyone and his brother jumping on the entrepreneurial bandwagon, as everything is looking up and everyone is prospering in an advancing economy. A large majority are parasites looking for a quick buck at the expense of someone else. The true entrepreneur emerges when the chips are down and the economy is in a decline. These are the entrepreneurs who have the "right stuff." The impostors will be flushed out with the downturn.

In the upswing, moral and ethical restraints are replaced by more permissive and rebellious attitudes. Discipline and authority are lost concepts and the younger generation grows up with a carefree, easy-come-easy-go attitude, to the frustration of parents who have worked hard for their places in society.

Perhaps herein lays one of the clues to the imminent demise of the economy at the end of the advance. For this generation has a misconception of hard work and the value of a hard-earned dollar, yen, pound, euro, yuan, and so on. Good economic instincts are learned, not hereditary. While the parents of this new generation were working to provide their children with something more of the good life, the children's value systems lost touch with notions of hard work, thrift, and sacrifice. Yet these children have grown up to be the managers of Wall Street and other major industries in the 1980s and 1990s, and into the early 2000s. Their way of assuming the world owes them a living is most popular in the long wave fall season and early winter seasons of the long wave as speculation runs rampant.

As the world economy begins to decline, conservative politics take a back seat to sweeping liberal political plans and government's re-involvement in the private sector. The Great Depression saw government taking the driver's seat in business, trying to steer the economy clear of the carnage created and left by what was thought to be mistakes of the free market of the 1920s. In fact, it was only a natural shakeout, separating the sheep from the goats, and government should have stayed out of business. The new psychology of the decline pleads for big brother's help, as we have seen on Wall Street in this crisis. Since government was already in charge to a greater degree this time around, we are seeing the counter current of a revolt against government in some regards during this long wave winter season.

The psychology that moves the long wave is affected enormously by the broad-based move toward a more spiritual worldview as the decline deepens. Religion becomes more important. We are told in scriptures that Christ came to save the meek, the poor, and the humble; all three categories have exploding populations during the economic downturn of a long wave winter season.

When things are looking good and the economy is on the upswing, individuals look within for their strength. We see positive thinking and get-rich quick seminars on the increase. We witnessed this in the 1980s and 1990s. These seminars are very similar to the self-help programs of the 1920s. But as the tide turns and the chips are down, the average person, although they are introspective, doesn't look within for strength, but looks to secure institutions, such as government and church. My view is that the turn toward church can be greatly positive.

The 1920s had its version of the sexual revolution. Stoken (1980) speaks of how women just after receiving the vote did away with the conventions of the Victorian period. Women began drinking and smoking in public. Skirt lengths rose to the knee. Other changes were taking place:

> There was a proliferation of sex magazines, which were gobbled up by a public obsessed with the subject. People liberated themselves from the restraints of Puritanism. There was a vast increase in the divorce rate which rose from 8.8 for every 100 marriages in 1920 to 16.5 for every 100 marriages in 1928. (14-17)

All these psychological changes took years to penetrate the mainstream of society and emerge as the current social norms. Like a great wave moving through history, the long wave is the interconnected sum of a broad array of social forces.

Again, I must quote Stoken (1980) with his gifted perception into the psychology of the wave as he follows the social revolution into the downturn:

> Initially, few people expect that a depression is going to last a long time. Most people think it is a cyclical contraction rather than a major change in the economy. The first sign that people no longer see the world in risk-free rose-colored terms often occurs with a subtle change in the relationship between the sexes. At the outset of the Great Depression, women lowered their skirts, dressed more conservatively, began to wear white gloves and became more respectful of a meal ticket. The

sexual code was no longer flaunted so flagrantly. There was less ado about sex, while glamour and romance came into their own. The deepening depression shattered the assumptions of a relatively risk-free world that had dominated the mood of the 1920s. People became more cautious. Hedonistic behavior subsided and there was less tolerance of deviant social behavior. The younger generation became more respectful of their parents and less scornful of the old traditional values. The music slowed down. Marriage and the family became more highly prized as social institutions and the divorce rate fell. People stayed home and spent more time with their families. (14-17)

These trends are once again in play. Taking a broad view we see that the long wave is driven by political trends, morality, religion, and social mores. It is a staggering thought that a long wave that has run its course nearly four times since the formation of America can be seen in the divorce rate.

This chapter has emphasized America and how psychology has driven long wave developments and been reflected in society. But human nature is the same around the world, so this chapter was not meant to limit its scope to America only. The reactions here apply to any peoples being pulled in one direction or the other by the long wave, as can be observed in Japan, which is experiencing major psychological changes presently. Japan has led the way into the long wave winter season. Japanese psychology has led the way in this global long wave. The Japanese are continuing the trend of more sober expectations.

We cannot take lightly the history of the long wave and the potential force it has been shown to generate. This force could have an enormous impact on social and political change during the present decline–an impact relevant to national security and international stability. We can have at our disposal all the statistical data in the world, but if we cannot understand and perceive human nature and what human response will be in situations beyond our immediate control, our data will be of no use.

National and local elections are guided by the mood of the people and what they are looking for as a result of their psychological disposition at election time; thus, a knowledge and understanding of the long wave could be of enormous importance to would-be candidates. The platform necessary for election or reelection during the most critical time of the cycle would be closely related to the psychological impulses of the long wave and their influences on constituents. One could almost design a rough platform years in advance by the known impact of an economic decline. The advent of the long wave winter season was clearly evident in the elections of 2008.

So the long wave is partially measured and is fulfilled by the psychological impulses of the population of the globe. It is a sobering thought that psychological tendencies reflected by the long wave guide the destiny of nations. Many of the latest trends are already evident as the global economy has weakened and nations begin to enter the decline. A more sober view of the world and the economy began emerging in recent years. The full psychological effects on the economic binge of the latest long wave advance and speculative fall season will not be realized until the cycle reaches bottom in the years ahead. The effect of fear and frustration will be magnified tenfold before the cycle has completed its purifying and painful decline.

After looking at the ups and downs of human psychology in the expansion and contraction of the long wave, we gain a new respect for Jeremy Bentham and his view of humans being guided by the two masters of pain and pleasure. There is no doubt that society had swung far in the direction of pleasure in the most recent long wave advance and speculative fall season. The full effect of the pain is yet to come as the pendulum completes its full swing in the opposite direction.

Chapter 8:

WAR

"War is an ugly thing, but not the ugliest of things. The decayed and degraded state of moral and patriotic feeling which thinks that nothing is worth war is much worse. The person who has nothing for which he is willing to fight, nothing which is more important than his own personal safety, is a miserable creature and has no chance of being free unless made and kept so by the exertions of better men than himself."

John Stuart Mill

"I know not with what weapons World War III will be fought, but World War IV will be fought with sticks and stones."

Albert Einstein

"A wise prince should never remain idle in peaceful times, but industriously make good use of them, so that when fortune changes she may find him prepared to resist her blows, and to prevail in adversity."

Machiavelli

This review of war is not an attempt to make the case that war guides the long wave, but just the opposite. War is guided by the same social forces that produce other long wave manifestations. War, like the long wave itself, appears to most often be the result of fundamental shifts in the economic structure of the international system. Evidence indicates that military conflict is far more likely during the economic expansion phases of the long wave advance. This chapter will examine wars as they fit into and provide evidence of the four long wave cycles from 1789 to the present.

Since records have been kept, men have been in conflict and at war. There are several periods during which the conflict has not been as widespread and destructive, but basically all of history has seen war. However, an interesting pattern begins to emerge as we take a closer look, especially over the past 200 years of long wave history.

As the economies of individual nations begin expanding and growing they tend to become competition for each other for raw materials. Interaction between national economies is similar to individual action. When an individual begins to get established economically and to reach certain levels of success, he or she begins looking about to see what the next venture might be. In time a country needs more raw materials, capital and markets. Thus, as times are good, output is increasing, internally the economic outlook is stable and the domestic population is comfortable, national leaders begin to get restless and look beyond their borders to see where and how they may expand their economy and influence.

The nation, just like the individual, will invariably step on someone's foot; and that nation, just like the individual, will retaliate. It may be a dispute over scarce resources and raw materials or a conflict over markets. It may just be a restless leader seeking to expand his influence or use his military arsenal and new weaponry.

We will take a look only at the history of armed conflict since 1789–the beginning of the upswing of the first long wave. A telling fact is that almost the only time great powers were at war in modern times was during spring and summer upswings in the long wave cycle. Great powers typically do not do battle during long wave fall and winter seasons. World War II was an exception, clearly a very big exception. We must consider what "a great power" is in order to draw such a conclusion.

Jack Levy's book, *War in the Modern Great Power System* (1983, 16), assisted me a great deal in considering the relationship between the long wave and war. Some of my material in the review of war, as well as the following quote, is taken from that work:

A Great Power is defined here as a state that plays a major role in international politics with respect to security-related issues. The Great Powers can be differentiated from other states by their military power, their interests, their behavior in general and interactions with other Powers, other Powers perception of them and some formal criteria ... Most importantly, a Great Power possesses a high level of military capabilities relative to other states. At a minimum, it has relative self-sufficiency with respect to military security. Great Powers are basically invulnerable to military threats by non-Powers and need only fear other Great Powers.

The first of the long wave cycles began its advance around 1789 and peaked around 1815. Our first major conflicts of this period were the French Revolutionary Wars from 1792 until 1802. The storming of the Bastille on July 14, 1789 marked the beginning of France's transition from a monarchy to a democratic nation. The coalition had its difficult moments as it went through its reconstruction period from 1789 to 1791. The new constitution collapsed in 1792 and the new legislative assembly declared war on Austria on April 20, 1792, accusing them of counterrevolutionary agitation. The Reign of Terror (1793-94) was during this period. This marked the beginning of 10 years of war fought from the Caribbean to the Indian Ocean, though most of the conflict was in the Low Countries, the Rhineland and Lombardy.

During this first upswing of the long wave, Western nations were emerging and beginning to lay the groundwork for the capitalist nations that would dominate the world to the present day. Early conflicts in the first advance set the stage in France for Napoleon. The internal French Revolutionary Wars saw the death of some 700,000 in battle, while the expansionary Napoleonic Wars can be attributed close to two million deaths.

Napoleon Bonaparte proclaimed himself emperor of France in 1804 and waged war throughout Europe until 1815. The object of the allies of the nations of Europe was to stop French expansion. Napoleon was finally defeated by the Duke of Wellington at the

Battle of Waterloo on June 18, 1815. The Napoleonic Wars were by far the most costly conflicts during the first upswing.

Other wars that deserve mention during this period are the Russo-Turkish War and the War of 1812. In the latter, America settled its independence from Britain once and for all, though not as quickly and decisively as it would have liked. The war lasted until January 1815 when General Andrew Jackson won a decisive victory at New Orleans. A surging nationalism swept America after that victory, in which the British lost over 2,000 men and the Americans lost only 100.

Around the year 1815, the first long wave began its decline and continued until the 1840s. This close to 30-year period was virtually war free, with the exception of the Franco-Spanish War, which lasted from April to August 1823 and was the result of France trying to interfere with the liberal revolution going on in Spain.

Another conflict was the 1827 defeat of a Russian-British-French fleet at Navarino Bay by a Turkish-Egyptian fleet. This embarrassing defeat caused Russia to declare war in 1827 and came to be known as the Russo-Turkish War. During this conflict, Russia launched an invasion of Bulgaria. Turkey was forced to sign the treaty of Adrianople in 1829, which recognized Greek independence. The treaty also gave Russia a majority of the Black Sea's Caucasian coast.

The remainder of this first long wave downturn seemed to scarcely produce a fist fight, so reserved were nations during this time of economic contraction. There appears to be a clear pattern of more conflict during the period Kondratieff labeled as the long wave advance and far less during the decline in the first long wave.

The second long wave began in the 1840s. As we enter the upswing of the second long wave and the economics of the nations of the world begin to expand, we again see an enormous increase in both the number of wars and their severity. The first incident of this period was the Austro-Sardinian War in 1849, which cost close to 6,000 lives. This same year saw the First

Schleswig-Holstein War as well as the Roman Republic War; both were no more than brief skirmishes.

The next battle of this second upswing came in 1852 and was the first major confrontation since Napoleon's defeat: the Crimean War. Russia's desire to see the Ottoman Empire destroyed was the chief cause of this war. France, England, Prussia, and Austria joined to fend off the aggression of Russia in the Crimean region. They were successful, but at the expense of 500,000 lives. The Treaty of Paris on March 30, 1856 guaranteed independence to the citizens of the Ottoman Empire. One of the good things that came out of the Crimean War was the work and leadership of Florence Nightingale, by whose work army hospitals and nurses came into existence.

The year 1856 also saw the Anglo-Persian War, which lasted only four months and cost fewer than 1,000 lives. In 1859, the region that is now Italy began struggling for its economic independence. This led to the War of Italian Unification. All the major powers of Europe had interest to one degree or another in this area. But under the leadership of Garibaldi, the Italians fought for their freedom and established Rome as the capital of their new nation. The first national Italian Parliament met on February 1861 and Victor Emmanuel II became king.

By far the bloodiest war of the upswing in the second long wave was the American Civil War from 1861-1865. The death toll, according to many estimates, exceeded 500,000. Not only was the slavery issue settled, but so was the issue of where the industrial strength of the United States would lie for a hundred years to come. The war was, in many respects, over conflicting economic interests of the North and South during this time of rapid economic expansion.

Napoleon III was responsible for a number of French ventures during this period, one of which was the Franco-Mexican War, lasting from 1862 until 1867, in which some 8,000 died. The French army had put Maximilian on the Mexican throne, but his troops and the native Mexican forces were able to overthrow him.

The unification of Italy caused developments to the north that were settled by the Austro-Prussian War. Italy was defeated at Sadowa on July 3, 1866, Venetia was ceded to Italy as a result.

The final major confrontation of this second upswing in the long wave came in the Franco-Prussian War (1870-1871) in which 200,000 died. France lost, and its government was left in shambles for attempting to avert the unification of Germany.

The second long wave began to peak and turn down in 1873, and for almost 30 years the world economy slipped into an economic decline of previously unknown proportion. During this period, the world was in a state of peace it had not known since the days of the Roman Empire. Two brief conflicts marked this period. One was the Russo-Turkish War (1877-1878), which culminated with the treaty of Berlin (July 13, 1878). This conflict saw 120,000 men lose their lives. The other conflict during this time was the Sino-French War which took place from 1884 to 1885 and cost 2,100 lives.

The year 1896 saw the bottom of the second decline of the long wave cycle. The pattern was once again clear, with more war during the advance than during the decline.

The beginning of the third advance of the long wave came in the mid-1890s. When nations began expanding their economies, war was not long in coming. The first war of the period came in 1904 with the Russo-Japanese War. Apparently Russia was exerting too much control and influence in Manchuria and Korea, causing the Japanese to get restless. Negotiations failed and Japan attacked the Russians in Port Arthur, Manchuria on February 8, 1904, without a declaration of war. Japan had far superior organization and leadership, as well as shorter supply lines, and was able to deliver a final blow by destroying the Russian Baltic fleet at Tsushima (May 27-28, 1905). President Roosevelt arranged a peace conference at Portsmouth, New Hampshire on August 5, 1905. Japan was granted its wishes in the region, but only after 45,000 men lost their lives.

The next conflict during this third upswing was the Italo-Turkish War (1911–1912). During this campaign the Italians were able to annex Libya at the price of some 6,000 lives. And of course the next war was "the war to end all wars," World War I (1914-1918). For the first time in history, the entire world—or so it seemed—was at war. The death and destruction were unimaginable. Close to 30 million lives were lost and the total cost of the war was over $180 billion.

The last confrontation of this third upswing came in the form of the Russian Revolution. Nicholas II abdicated the throne on March 15, 1917 and, for a brief time, Russia was a democracy. But on October 23, 1917, the Bolsheviks, who were the most extreme of revolutionaries, seized power. Thus the emergence of the Union of Soviet Socialist Republics took place. Surprisingly, there was not a great deal of bloodshed in the initial revolution; the bloodshed came in the form of internal purging later on.

The long wave peaked shortly after the close of the First World War, plateaued throughout the 1920s, and then fell dramatically in 1929 and the early 1930s. This period, from the early 1920s into the 1940s, was the third decline in the long wave. The world was once again fairly peaceful during most of this time of economic decline. The only wars to speak of during this time were the Manchurian War and the Italy-Ethiopian War in which a combined total of some 14,000 lives were lost.

The Sino-Japanese War began on July 7, 1937. Its causes were deeply rooted, but it broke out over a minor clash of Chinese and Japanese soldiers on Marco Polo Bridge near Peking. What followed was a bloody Far East war that was to merge four years later with World War II.

Again, typically, wars among major powers do not occur during long wave winter seasons. But World War II has shown that one madman, in this case Adolf Hitler, can have an impact on the long wave cycle. His ruthless aggression brought the entire world into war. It is estimated that some 20 million lives were lost and the cost in property and monetary damages so vast, it would be futile to attempt to estimate it. World War II may also be partially due to the depth of the long wave decline, which created great global tension and trade wars and spilled over into great political stresses. It should also be noted that the worst years of the global depression were over before World Ware II began.

The Russo-Finnish War fought in 1939 and 1940 could be listed with World War II, but was somewhat of a separate conflict and cost some 16,000 lives. The Communist Revolution in China came to a close during this period. While no one can be sure of the death toll, it was certainly in the millions. The pattern in this third long wave appears to follow the trend established for the cycle except for the big problem of World War II.

From soon after the end of World War II until 1980, we were in the advance of the fourth long wave cycle. Let's consider the wars that occurred during this period.

The Korean War (1950-1953) was the first military stance taken by the United Nations as it joined against Communist aggression at a price of over one million lives.

The Russo-Hungarian War of 1956 cost some 7,000 lives and Hungarian hopes of more political and economic freedom.

The Vietnam War (1962-1973), which cost 56,000 American lives, and the Iran-Iraq War which started in 1979 and cost 500,000-plus lives are both wars that can be attributed to the fourth advance of the long wave. The advance of the fourth long wave, which lasted from the late 1940s to 1981, appears to have been a less severe period for wars than were other long wave advances. Of course, the fourth decline of the long wave, or at least the beginning of the fall season, began with the 1981 recession.

The Gulf War, during the decline, was not a war among great powers. Iraq could not produce its own weaponry. Virtually all of Iraq's weapons were bought and imported from great powers such as the former Soviet Union, France, and the United States. The United States displayed an impressive arsenal of military might, technology, and ability, even if Iraq could not be labeled a great power. The present Iraq War, or Second Gulf War, is once again not a war among great powers. It should be noted again that WWII was the only instance of a war between great powers during a long wave decline.

In review of this chapter, a startling fact emerges, one that goes a long way to enforce the argument in favor of the existence of a long wave. This fact concerns the total losses of life in the wars that have ravaged the world during the period from 1789 to the present. During long wave downswings–except for WWII, which I readily concede is a massive exception–we have seen only several hundred thousand deaths from armed conflict, while during long wave upswings, there have been in excess of 30 million deaths due to war.

The evidence speaks for itself. The world is far more likely to see war during advances of the long wave than during declines. In recent years all the great powers have been too concerned with their internal problems to get involved with foreign entanglements. Britain, Russia, France, Germany, Japan, China, Canada, Italy and others are spending their time and energy dealing with problems in their national economies. China is in better shape than most. Unemployment, slow or negative economic growth, financial crisis, banking problems, and real-estate collapses are all keeping governments busy within their own borders.

Once the problems of recessions and depression are worked through and internal conflicts are straightened out, things will be different. When the nations and economies of the globe move into a new long wave economic advance, internal tensions will subside and will not be so critical and all consuming. Nations will once again begin to look with envy beyond their borders at raw materials, labor, and markets. China and Russia may be potential leading aggressors during the next advance due to their growing economic strength and need for raw materials.

We should have a fairly peaceful world in terms of resource conflicts until the next long wave advance begins, at which time we can expect to see a rise in armed conflict, even between great powers. Terrorist-driven conflicts are another matter.

Once the global decline of this long wave winter flushes most of the excesses out of the global system, conflict between Great Powers could come sooner rather than later in the next advance. As the BRIC countries of Brazil, Russia, India and China grow rapidly in the next long wave advance, there will be a booming demand for raw materials, and increasing stresses between the countries that require and compete for those raw materials.

We will not likely enjoy total peace during these final years of this long wave winter, as evidenced with the Iraq War and war in Afghanistan. There will inevitably be a few clashes and conflicts; however, there will likely be no major conflict between great powers. There will be small wars and eruptions on hostile borders during the long wave decline.

All in all, the willingness or lack thereof of Great Powers to wage war sheds a revealing light on the long wave advance and decline. The relationship of war to the long wave should be studied closely moving forward in order to understand and gain insight into the nature of the long wave and how it expresses itself in international affairs.

Chapter 9:

BANKING AND THE LONG WAVE

"Every generation needs a new revolution."

Thomas Jefferson

"The ultimate effect of shielding men from the effects of folly is to fill the world with fools."

Herbert Spencer

The underlying premise of this book is that the long wave winter in the global economy produces the modern day version of the year of the ancient Jubilee of debt forgiveness. The banking business is primarily about issuing debt or loans as capital to borrowers for what the banker hopes are viable businesses (i.e., they produce sufficient cash flow in the future to pay their bills and their debts). The business of banking, both commercial and central banking, has what appears to be the natural tendency to inject too much debt into the global economy prior to a long wave winter season. In short, the future cash flows of the individuals, businesses and governments that are required to repay the loans are over estimated, they come up short.

In April 2009 the IMF released a new report projecting that the global writedowns "losses" of financial assets will reach $4.1 trillion by the end of 2010, and that $2.5 trillion of this is on the balance sheets of global banks, with $2.7 trillion at U.S. institutions. These projected writedowns may well rise again as this long wave winter continues. Clearly, there was too much debt created in the global economy, requiring a global Jubilee in the form of a long wave winter season of writedowns. However, if the debts are merely transferred to taxpayers, U.S. and others, the Jubilee has not occurred and the debt will produce a massive drag on the global recovery and the next long wave advance.

Banking is historically a conservative business. Part of the reason it is conservative by nature is because it experiences the greatest pain in a long wave winter season. Banking grows accustomed to lending money to the industries and businesses that drive the global economy during a long wave advance.

As the long wave matures, they lend too much money and feed the overproduction of all industries. The conservative bankers that created the stable institutions and remember the pain of the last winter season, when they were young, retire during the long wave fall season. The young and restless are taking over the banking system. During the long wave fall and winter season, there is an overproduction of banking services, like the overproduction of other industries like cars, refrigerators and houses. An oversupply of bankers is over-lending to the old ideas of a fading long wave.

Banks need the new economy of a long wave advance with new viable inventions and industries that require capital. The problem is that during the long wave winter these businesses and industries have not yet gotten underway. They are still in the lab, so to speak. It takes a long wave winter to force the necessity of invention and creation of these businesses, which banking can then supply with capital to produce the requisite cash flows to pay their loans.

It is, therefore, to be expected that of all industries a long wave debt crisis, a deflationary debt bust will have the most significant and revolutionary impact on the banking business. This has proven to be the case in every long wave decline for over 200 years. This long wave winter season is no different.

Earlier editions of this book predicted that a deflationary debt bust would bring the global banking system to its knees and usher in massive changes to global commercial banking and central banking. Even in the early 1990s the banking system in the United States was showing signs of stress; when the full history of this era is written, the view is likely to be that, even then, the capital base and loan portfolios of the global banking system had grown far weaker than during the long wave spring and summer season of 1949 to 1981. In the early 1990s the Japanese economy and banking system had already begun to exhibit major long wave problems (i.e., loans to businesses with bad assumptions of assets value and the ability to generate cash flows). However, with creative bookkeeping encouraged by Uncle Sam, a good spread in interest rates, and financing for bailouts, we managed to keep the U.S. banking system rolling from one bubble to another in the 1990s and early 2000s as a long wave fall season turned into winter.

Major problems had been building under the surface for years. Many of the loans made during the long wave speculative fall season that end up funding overproduction in industries that are past their prime go bad during the long wave winter. Loans made during a long wave winter season are far more suspect than at any other time; subprime lending could not have happened at a worse time in terms of the long wave. As noted earlier, in a Jubilee system, you would not make 20 year loans ten years before a Jubilee of debt forgiveness. Projected growth patterns and asset price trends calculated during a long wave advance and speculative fall season just don't hold. The assets that collateralize the loans are found to be substantially overvalued as the global debt deflation kicks in. The banking system is destabilized.

Banks must make solid loans to private industry and individuals collateralized by assets that do not fall in value in order to be viable for the long term. A beneficial interest-rate spread can create only a temporary bailout for banks. In the 1990s banks borrowed from the public at low relative rates with CDs and savings accounts and lent to governments at higher rates by buying government debt and funding the incredible deficits. This created temporary bank profits and the illusion that the fundamental banking problems of the 1980s and 1990s had gone away. This is being tried again now during this global crisis. It is really an unfair tax. Those prudent enough to keep their powder dry are paid virtually nothing on their deposits. The Internet and real estate asset price bubbles were on top of this trend. The long wave decline fundamentals of a debt deflation finally came to bear on the global banking system in recent years.

There are many reasons for the banking crisis, but when they are boiled down to the basics, we see the fundamental forces of the economic long wave at work. The solid long wave expansion provided healthy loans for the banking system. But there is a group mentality that expects trends to last forever. When major trends reverse with the long wave, most banks and business people are taken by surprise. When the long wave is combined with government trying to protect the people from the consequences of bad or shady business ventures, instead of letting the market and justice systems purge the foolish and guilty, the result is disaster.

The days of banking, as we have grown accustomed to them, are always numbered heading into a global long wave winter season. Every long wave decline has seen major changes and restructuring take place in the international banking system. The 1930s saw major changes and the removal of gold as the basis to the dollar. The long wave decline of the 1870s and 1880s saw constant restructuring of the banking system and was marked by persistent banking failures. Banking failures and restructuring in the long wave decline of the 1820s and 1830s were commonplace. These major changes don't come due to great new ideas springing spontaneously from government and the banking industry. The banking system eventually comes to the end of the line. Changes come because crisis, failure, and chaos demand them. The bankers and the bureaucrats have no choice. The latest long wave decline and winter season is no different.

For years the bad loans that accumulated during the latest long wave fall and winter season in the form of real-estate debt, consumer debt, corporate debt, and Third World debt were being reshuffled faster, and with more sleight of hand, than a deck of cards in a back-room poker game. The safer money was in the poker game, however, because poker players at least knew the risks better than those who expected trends to last forever.

When you reach the end of the speculative fall season and plateau of the long wave, all types of debts are at unprecedented levels–this includes personal, corporate, and government debt, both municipal and federal. In early 1993, as Japan was the first nation to enter this long wave decline, Japan had $10 trillion in interest-bearing debt and another $8 trillion in derivatives. Tracy Herrick in *The Money Analyst*, pointed out that this amounted to $6 for every $1 of gross domestic product. The U.S. banking system got as leveraged as Japan with the housing bubble, CDOs and other derivatives. It doesn't take a great deal of thought to realize that the game being played, as in past long waves, has got to come to an end.

Bankers came out of the Great Depression feeling very conservative, as did everyone else. Interest rates were low and the industrial corporate world was expanding, providing safe havens for the banker's abundance of free cash. And free cash it was, as the humble public would never ask for such a thing as interest on demand deposits. So the bankers found themselves in a position that was hard to beat. Asset values were rising, so few loans went bad; borrowers were conservative; and investors were scared of stocks and other financial instruments, so they kept their money in the banks and accepted low returns.

In the latter years of this long wave, the public became more demanding. The generation that had experienced the Depression was growing older, and a new generation was taking over. They began putting money in liquid investments that appreciated the value of a dollar and that were willing to pay customers handsomely for their considerable deposits. The bankers, on the other hand, figured they were doing the public a favor by opening their doors from 10:00 AM until 2:00 PM. Banks were slow in understanding the gravity of the shift in consumer demand–a shift in long wave psychology. The thrifts and savings and loans had cut deeply into the banks' bottom line before the bankers had begun to seek solutions to the growing problem. This newfound competition, coupled with rising interest rates and inflation on an upward trend– typical in the upswing of the long wave–forced bankers to evaluate their situation closely and use a bit more creativity in their financial dealings. They became more aggressive.

One of the ways of increasing business came when a number of big banks struck on the idea of making high-yielding loans to the developing Third World. Bankers have an acute tendency toward the herding instinct, so when the giants, such as Chase and Chemical, began lending to the Third World, the entire world banking community assumed it was a good idea. The loans were good for a while and interest payments were made. However, Third World debts were the first of the loans made in the last long wave advance to begin plaguing the system.

Billions in loans were rolled over. Banks are beginning to realize the loans aren't worth what they assumed. Billions were packaged and dumped on the World Bank so the world's taxpayers could pay for the banker's mistakes.

A nation is sovereign and lives a perpetual existence (its citizens hope), unlike a corporation, which can turn bottom up and vanish when times get bad. This perception seemed to play a major role in the thinking of the world bankers during the late 1960s and 1970s, as they somehow could not perceive a nation or state becoming insolvent. But sovereignty cannot be expected to take the place of solvency.

With a bunch of Western bankers in pin-striped suits waving billions of dollars in their faces, the leaders of the Third World were more than happy to oblige and take the money. This is not to say that the leaders of the Third World were forced to take the loans and thus were not responsible for the situation. They were very much responsible. They were well aware of the amount of debt they were taking on and what the limits were of the countries they ruled. What they were not aware of was the shifting tide of the world economy and the havoc played by depressed economic conditions on a nation that must sell its raw materials on the world market to pay its massive loans. The fact of the matter is that billions of dollars lent to the Third World were uncollectible and written off the books of banks.

Three body punches will bring the international banking system into submission during the latest long wave decline. The Third World debt crisis was the first punch to be landed on the international banking system–a powerful punch that weakened the entire system. The second punch is proving to be even more devastating: the collapse of residential and commercial real-estate prices, with Japan the global leader and the U.S. now following suit. The big money-center banks were primarily affected by the Third World debt crisis. Real-estate deflation is affecting almost all banks globally. The third punch, which will most likely be the knockout punch for the banking system as we know it, will be default and failure of consumer and corporate loans. When the full force of the third punch has landed, a soft breeze will be sufficient to send the global banking system to the mat. This third punch is now landing, which will be the final blow to the international banking system.

Like all other components of the economy in the long wave the banking system overestimated the future. This overestimation of business expansion and future growth and the belief in ever-rising prices coaxed banks into overexpansion of loans to segments of the economy that were peaking and headed for decline. You can't blame the bankers. Not everyone looks at the economy from a long wave perspective. The bankers didn't know that agriculture, oil, real estate, and eventually consumer spending were going to enter a long wave decline. The overexpansion that brings overproduction and falling prices is the key to understand the problems faced by the banks.

Corporations are currently in debt-to-equity situations and debt-to-working-capital and debt-to-available-cash positions that have not been seen since the Great Depression. If that's not bad enough, the individual consumer is in far worse financial condition than prior to or during the Great Depression.

There invariably comes a time when the corporation, individuals and even governments have borrowed beyond their limit. This tends to happen at the end of the fall season of the long wave–the late 1920s and now once again–causing spending to come to a screeching halt. Since government makes the rules, it can be more flexible in its spending habits as the long wave runs its course. The U.S. government was actually in good shape when the Great Depression began. But presently, the U.S. government is in terrible financial shape and this time around,

Uncle Sam will not have the borrowing power available to ease the pain. Government spending will increasingly be blocked by political pressure and populist backlash. The amount of spending required to counter the forces of a long wave winter will not be tolerated and the long wave will take its course.

When individuals, corporations, and governments have borrowed beyond their ability to pay and cannot borrow more to pay off interest and loans, the game is over. The assets they have borrowed against fall in value. The credit binge begins to contract and unravel. This accelerates the deflation of the long wave decline pulling the rug out from under the market value of the loans made by the banks. As the assets backing the loans fall in price and become worthless, the banking system plunges over the edge. The financial house of cards created during the upswing comes tumbling down.

These long wave forces are at work to varying degrees throughout the global economy in the current global crisis. Today, there is so much slack in the economy, with industry operating far below capacity, that large increases in the money supply still don't inflate prices. Capacity utilization just dropped under 70% in the United States and is dropping around the globe. This capacity was funded with debt from the banking system. Industry scrambles to fill increases in demand and is forced to keep prices low to attract new business. Prices are incapable of moving up to any sustainable extent when the economy is operating at far below capacity. Long wave deflation rules the day.

What clearly happened to the money created by the banking system during the fall season is that it went pouring into financial assets, where it encouraged and fueled financial market inflation and bull markets throughout the world. The banking system was creating paper millionaires in the stock market with financial inflation. The central banks of the world are at a loss to understand why their loose money policies have not ignited inflation to any substantial degree, because they do not recognize the forces at work in the long wave. The fact is that the only way one can come to a clear understanding of the global crisis situation we are facing is by taking the all-encompassing view revealed by long wave theory.

Deflationary pressures build as the long wave takes its course in the fall and winter season. No monetary manipulation is able to stop the inevitable. As the amount of world debt in all sectors continues to mount and the sliding values of commodities, capital outlays, and capital expansion become evident, the market value of bank assets fall. This puts banks in a squeeze. We are now seeing the underlying value of loan portfolios collapse with falling asset values during the current long wave winter.

If you lent $1 million dollars on a building that is now worth $500,000, you have a problem. Clearly $500,000 of the value of the asset is gone–poof!–evaporated in a Jubilee winter deflation. The problem, it must be recognized, is in the books of the bank. You can apply this concept to almost all bank loans. Falling asset values are undermining and will continue to undermine the foundation of the entire banking structure. If you understand this basic principal of the long wave, you understand why banks are in deep trouble during the long wave winter season. This fall in asset values must be recognized and written off. If it is just reshuffled and transferred to taxpayers, it will still be a drag on the system.

Where are the nations, corporations, and individuals who can afford to take on the credit the government wants them to create during this long wave winter season? The global economy has not yet generated the new businesses that can produce cash flows from the deployment of such capital. The idea that central bank action can stop deflation is simply invalid. Falling prices that undermine bank loans and the global banking system are inevitable. My conviction remains that the central banks will prove to be impotent in trying to avoid the inevitable long wave outcome of deflation and an extended Jubilee debt purge.

The over-production in all industries creates price competition to capture markets. When the world is over producing and prices are falling, there eventually emerges a lack of borrowing. The world is producing more than it needs. It doesn't matter how low interest rates go. Demand of loans dries up and banks can't make sufficient amounts of solid loans. World prices slide in this competitive market. The loans that backed the production, based on higher prices, go bad as prices fall. Banks are squeezed.

Nations, companies, and individuals will eventually simply not be able to afford any more spending on borrowed money. Eventually, there is not enough spending to support bank loans that finance production. Because of the continued and increasing weakness in demand across the board, prices will tumble further. It is a vicious downward spiral. The slowdown will force layoffs and firings, slowing demand and spending even further. Bank loans become weaker and weaker. As the long wave declines, the prices of raw materials, wholesale goods, commodities, consumer goods, and real estate collapse.

We have seen drops in raw material and commodities prices. The forces generating these drops will soon be seen throughout all industries and the entire global economy. Falling prices spread to real estate, wholesale prices, and consumer prices. The effect of falling prices will snowball into the bottom of the long wave decline. First it is disinflation, but as the decline accelerates, we see deflation across the hoard. Deflation means only one thing for the banking community: troubled loans.

The natural turning in the long wave is fueled by an important component in our global economy and the chief means by which much debt owed to the banks is being repaid: the price of oil and other forms of energy. Many global businesses and national governments repay bank loans with oil revenues. If prices fall low enough, oil-exporting Third World nations and the businesses that drill the oil will not even be able to pay interest. Many of the oil-producing countries have debts that must be repaid with oil revenues. Repayment of foreign loans is only a small part of the picture when it comes to the effect of oil on the economy and the banking system. All goods are shipped by some means: rail, ship, truck, or air. If oil prices plunge, the prices of delivering goods also drop significantly. A drop in the price of oil will also force down the price of other competing energy sources, including coal and natural gas. Oil by products are used in the production of many products, such as cars, tires, computers, televisions, plastics; the list could go on and on. Oil and its by products of gasoline and diesel fuel affect the price of almost every economic and business activity you can think of.

The brief run up of commodity prices into mid-2008 was a temporary financial market liquidity and speculation driven phenomenon. Oil has fallen from $150 as of this edition. Falling oil prices accelerate price declines of virtually every other product and industry. Falling prices (i.e., falling oil prices) undermine bank loans. The Gulf War was fought because Saddam Hussein wanted to stop Kuwait from cutting prices on oil and undermining Iraq's markets. Far from keeping oil prices low, the Gulf War boosted prices for several years–by taking Kuwaiti's production out of the market along with Iraq's. The deflationary acceleration of the latest long wave decline would probably have come sooner if it hadn't been for the Gulf War.

A major banking collapse has come with the decline of every long wave since 1789 and each collapse has been followed by major changes in the financial system of the world. The Great Depression and the banking collapse of 1933 saw the world come off the gold standard. The 1930s crisis also prompted more power granted to the Federal Reserve System and an overall centralization of banking in the United States and the world. Government backed banking deposit insurance was introduced in the Great Depression. This time around, we may return to gold playing a role in our currency.

It is my contention that, if government had reduced its role in banking in the 1930s, the banking system would have taken care of itself. The bad banks would have been purged from the system and depositors would have been wiser and more cautious next time. The Depression would have been far shorter and it wouldn't have taken World War II to get the economy and people back to work. Our economy would likely be far more advanced and developed than it is today had the market been allowed to clean the slate. Instead, we got a promise from government that they would protect us from foolish banking practices by guaranteeing everyone's deposits. It should be noted that there are, of course, many economists, market analysts and students of the Depression, who disagree with this assessment.

Governments and central banks have now stepped in to attempt to rescue the global banking system from the disastrous use of too much leverage again as the global economy has entered another long wave winter season. Ambrose Evans-Prichard in a January 2009 article in the UK *Telegraph* recognizes that they may not succeed:

> Taken together, the rescues may make the difference between global recession and a deeper slump that causes mass unemployment and social turmoil, perhaps destroying the open global order we take for granted. We can only guess.
>
> There is no guarantee that the measures will succeed. The vast scale of government borrowing may exhaust the stock of global capital. Markets are already beginning to question the credit-worthiness of sovereign states. The Fed may find it harder than it thinks to disengage from colossal intervention in the bond markets.

Readers will have gathered by now that long wave theory and my interpretation of it does not fall into the Austrian School of economic thought and analysis. The Austrian School basically defines itself by blaming central banking, fiat money and government intervention for every financial problem and economic cycle. The Austrian school dismisses long waves, because long wave theory suggests they are a natural aspect of free market expansion and contraction, independent of fiscal and monetary policy. Although I tend to favor some Austrian libertarian thinking on the value of human freedom and the remarkable power of human action, I do not believe the combination of central banking and fiat money is the root of all evil.

The Austrian School regularly and repeatedly attacks central banking and fiat money. They believe that these two components are the cause of all business cycles–be they small cycles or major economic disruptions. They fail to recognize that central banks are given the thankless task of managing the monetary system when the politicians manage fiscal policy like drunken sailors. Managing monetary policy in an environment of constantly rising government deficits is a virtually impossible task. Government intervention in the economy and many industries increases the difficulty. My views on central banking and fiat money have clearly changed over the years and each new edition of this book.

Although I have great respect for their libertarian views and positions on human freedom, it has become clear to me that the Austrian school has an oversimplified view of business cycles, recessions and depressions. They essentially reduce business cycles to central bank policy, fiat money and government intervention. Granted, these things play an important role, however, since the Austrian School dismisses long wave theory, they do not have a system of theoretical thought that represents how the global economy and international finance actually functions. They do not understand the role of the long wave in the expansion, growth, survival and global dominance of free market capitalism.

Even if the Austrian School could achieve their goals of abolishing central banking and fiat money in exchange for money only backed in gold or other commodity, their theories would then be discredited because powerful economic cycles would still exist and shatter their deficient theories on business cycles. There is a great deal of irony in the fact that many world-systems theorists with socialist and neo-Marxist leanings actually understand the dynamics of free market capitalism and its global expansion better than most Austrian School economists.

Central banking and fiat money have major weaknesses. However, if government deficits were reduced and the role of government in the economy was reduced, the Federal Reserve could do a far more effective job at managing stable monetary policy. There is a great danger during this long wave winter season that the Federal Reserve loses its independence and becomes politicized. This should be fought across the board. The Federal Reserve must maintain its independence. If politicians have undue influence on the Federal Reserve they will always attempt to force the Federal Reserve to monetize the debt in an attempt to inflate their way out of debt and create more debt.

Any long wave discussion of banking of necessity requires a discussion of currency and consideration of what the future holds, both during this long wave winter crisis and beyond it, for both national and international currency. Prior editions of this book speculated on the potential rise of a new international digital gold currency system, a currency that has the potential to produce phenomenal growth, stability and opportunity for the global economy in the years ahead. The emergence of just such a gold based currency and its implications are increasingly clear.

This long wave winter season is loaded with potential in terms of new technological development, with a major impact on banking and currencies. We are in the midst of massive technological change with far reaching implications. The advent of certain technologies, specifically the Internet and object-oriented programming, is creating a new force for powerful growth and stability in the global economy. The Internet is one of those technologies that is going to have major implications for positive change and drive growth during the next long wave advance, specifically regarding new currency options.

It is clear that there is a need for international free market capitalism to provide a check on government spending and bad monetary policy. International commerce needs an alternative to unstable fiat money due to government mismanagement of budgets and economic policy. The solution has already been created. Technology–including the Internet and data systems– along with safe and secure vaults and trusted management have created international currency that is very similar to the currency system advocated by America's founding fathers in the U.S. Constitution. Digital Gold Currency (DGC) is effectively a pure 100% gold currency on account for the account holder. It is on the rise and is the natural free market demand driven international currency solution offered as a result of market forces seeking stable currency. It is international free market capitalism at its best and a clear sign of the rise of The Great Republic.

DGC provides an option for individuals, investors, local and national companies, global multinational corporations and even governments to avoid and escape the destructive deficit spending tendency of governments and the resulting monetary instability. DGC as a pure gold currency will be, by its very nature, constantly providing feedback on how the world's fiat currencies and their sponsoring governments are doing, based on the exchange rate of those currencies into gold (i.e., DGC).

It is my contention that some national governments may create their own DGC systems, either as their only currency, or to operate in parallel with their fiat currencies. The U.S. is a good candidate for such a parallel currency system that could actually strengthen the U.S. dollar as the world fiat reserve currency. It would be great for the economy, producing jobs and growth in the mining industry and many other industries. The key to a successful DGC will be trust. Governments will have to establish constitutional amendments that establish a right of citizens to own such accounts or they will open them in countries that do provide such guarantees.

DGC will not replace international central and commercial banking as we know it, but will provide a global system of checks and balances that will force government budgets under control. The market driven forces of DGC will provide a more manageable environment for central and commercial banking. Governments that do not control their budgets and entitlement programs will discover that DGC will mercilessly punish their currencies. This positive market based response to a market need that is emerging in this long wave winter is addressed more fully in the chapter on DGC.

Central banking and fiat money will dominate national and global commercial banking activity in the years to come, but they will have growing competition from DGC. In order to force a reduction in the size of government and a reduction in deficits, government-sponsored fiat money and central banking need healthy competition to provide the market with the necessary options to do its job and mitigate risk for investors and global commercial interests.

During the final years of this long wave winter season the key theme to creating a stable global banking system will be debt deleveraging. Debt levels must be drastically reduced and banking system equity must be increased. New international regulations will require a reduction in leverage and an increase in bank equity. In order to achieve these goals there will likely be a major conversion of debt to equity in many forms during this long wave winter.

The global banking system has begun the process of rebuilding balance sheets. Unfortunately a major way they are doing this is by paying almost no interest on deposits, while earning higher interest on loans to borrowers. This reduced income for depositors is part of the long wave winter of consumers with reduced income and buying power, decreasing economic demand for goods and services and forcing depositors to take risk they shouldn't take in search of yield in a long wave winter.

Long wave banking system deleveraging is a multi-year process and only began with the global financial crash and crisis in 2008; it will not be complete until 2012 and beyond. Banking system and other deleveraging is deflationary. There will be ongoing crisis and banking failures during this process; systemic crisis remains a risk until this long wave winter season gives way to a global long wave spring and the powerful force of a new long wave advance.

Chapter 10:

A TIME FOR TRADE WARS

"Patriotism is usually stronger than class hatred, and always stronger than internationalism."

George Orwell

"No nation was ever ruined by trade."

Benjamin Franklin

"A self-contained nation is a backward nation, with large numbers of people either permanently out of work, or very poorly paid in purchasing power. A nation which trades freely with all the world, selling to others those commodities which it can best produce, and buying from others those commodities which others can best produce, is by far the best conditioned nation for all practical purposes."

Walter Parker

"Underlying most arguments against the free market is a lack of belief in freedom itself."

Milton Friedman

The current long wave winter season is expected by this author to be less severe than the long wave winter of the 1930s Great Depression. One reason for this is that we are closer to the end of this current long wave than during the Great Depression in the 1930s. The economy is now far more globally integrated and closer to a new long wave advance. Increased globalization and the spread of capitalism will help pull the global economy out of this long wave winter season.

Critical to understanding the dynamics of the current long wave is recognition that the BRIC countries of Brazil, Russia, India and China, and many other smaller countries, have only relatively recently fully embraced market economies. They will play a major role in pulling the world out of this long wave as their domestic economies begin to develop and grow. They are and will demand more foreign goods produced in the United States and other markets. This will help the U.S. rebalance from an over weighted consumer to a high end product producer economy.

There is, however, one caveat to this more optimistic assessment. If protectionist forces are not checked and trade wars erupt, all bets are off. The impact on global trade of increased protectionism and trade wars would be catastrophic, and what could prove to be a mild long wave winter season this time around could plunge into a global depression.

Unfortunately, protectionism and the tendency for trade conflicts, which had been percolating under the surface since the transition from the long wave summer to the fall season in the early 1980s, are suddenly growing rapidly stronger since the global economy took a sharp dive with the global financial crisis of this long wave winter season.

Jeff Berman, Group News Editor for *Supply Chain Management Review*, reported in April 2009 that, since late 2008, 17 of the G20 member nations have implemented nearly 50 measures restricting trade that have dramatic implications for global supply chains. Protectionism and trade war pressures are clearly brewing and may boil over.

The Wall Street Journal reported that President Obama took office with strong backing from antitrade labor unions, which are now calling on Obama to act to stop imports that are costing U.S. jobs in targeted industries. This highlights the political and economic forces that are at odds during a long wave winter season. China is deeply concerned about the U.S. government imposing import taxes on foreign companies to cover carbon contained in products shipped to the United States, but, to date, it appears that the Obama administration is not supporting this form of protectionism, but will be under increasing pressure to act on an environmental agenda, which helped get President Obama elected.

Forces pushing for protectionism, tariffs and subsidies are rising fast in the current global crisis. Ian Bremmer in his article, "State Capitalism Comes of Age" in the May/June 2009 issue of *Foreign Affairs*, made the following observations regarding the rising forces of protectionism:

> Protectionism begets protectionism, and subsidies beget subsidies. The Doha Round of world trade talks in 2008 failed in part because of the United States' and the European Union's insistence on continued high agricultural tariffs and China's and India's desire to protect both their farmers and some of their still-nascent industries, which cannot yet compete on their own. The Doha stalemate has already costs hundreds of billions of dollars in potentially increased global trade.
>
> Other protectionist initiatives have begun to weigh on global commerce. China has reinstated tax relief for certain exporters. Russia has limited foreign investment in 42 "strategic sectors" and imposed new duties on imported cars, pork, and poultry. Indonesia has imposed import tariffs and licensing restrictions on over 500 types of foreign products. India has added a 20 percent levy on soybean oil imports. Argentina and Brazil are publicly considering new tariffs on imported textiles and wine. South Korea refuses to drop its trade barriers against U.S. auto imports. France has announced the creation of a state fund to protect domestic companies from foreign takeover.

Those who understand the free market system know that the global market system works best when the consumer is granted freedom to choose. Free access is crucial if consumer decision making is expected to produce smooth operating markets. The consumer must be the central force and pivotal element of the market system. The consumer, free of constraints, creates the economic phenomenon of demand. Industry, free of restraints or props, responds with the economic phenomenon of supply. Protectionist sentiment injected into the system is a poison. It eventually produces trade conflict and, in time, trade wars. Trade wars distort both supply-and-demand, creating inefficiency, waste, and stagnation in the global system.

Unfortunately, protectionism is a distinct characteristic of long wave declines. History has shown that during the long wave decline, there are always periods of abrupt decline in the volume of global trade. This has proven to be the case in all three long wave declines of the past 200 years. The latest long wave decline will likely prove to be no different.

Trade deserves close attention in relation to the long wave so that we may gain an understanding of the nature of this disturbing interruption in commerce among nations.

Since the peak of the long wave advance in the early 1980s, calls for protectionism and demands for trade barriers have been a part of the regular political discourse and popular debate. This is typical in a long wave decline after there has been a transition from the summer season to the fall season, as occurred in the 1981-82 recession. Since the turn to the fall season of this long wave there has been what appear to be breakthroughs in global trade: the North American Free Trade Agreement (NAFTA) and the General Agreement on Tariffs and Trade (GATT). During the election, Obama promised to renegotiate NAFTA, but backed down on this after the election. If he stands by this position, it will spell trouble for global trade and indicate this long wave decline will be far deeper than it has to be.

Even with progress on trade deals, just under the surface, protectionist sentiment has continued to stew. As predicted in previous editions of this book, trade agreements have come under a great deal of pressure and criticism as this long wave decline and winter season has progressed and may very well collapse due to the long wave forces at work. Protectionist pressure that builds in a long wave fall season invariably erupts into crisis in a long wave winter season. This is what we are seeing now.

Long wave domestic economic problems exacerbate international trade relationships. The 1920s were experiencing many of the same protectionist pressures of the 1980s and 1990s. This was also the case during fall season of the 1870s, not to mention the conditions in the years just before and following Napoleon's defeat in 1815 in Europe. The old country was being swamped by goods from America and protectionism produced trade conflict.

For a better understanding of what is in store for global trade in the years ahead, we need to review what occurs throughout the stages of a complete long wave in relation to trade. Just what are the forces that lead to protectionist sentiment, trade conflict, and global trade wars?

When the global economy comes out of a long wave decline and winter season into a new advance, interest rates are low, and the world economy has been flushed of its burdensome debt. Global overcapacity of industry has been removed by corporate failures and bankruptcy.

Labor is cheap in the spring season of the long wave and laborers are willing to put in a hard day's work. They have learned to appreciate holding a job after long periods of unemployment and worry. Employees are willing to sacrifice to get their company and the economy rolling after experiencing the pain of the hard times during the decline.

A key to understanding why global markets tend to open up in the long wave spring and summer season advance is that there are new industries driving the economy. New inventions and technology are being introduced to global markets. These breakthroughs create new young industries in communications, transportation, and other areas. As these new industries are too young to be overproducing or stepping on each other's feet, there is plenty of room in the market for everyone.

Producers have been streamlined and made more efficient during the decline and are willing to support the tearing down of tariffs and barriers prohibiting international trade. Interest rates and wages are low. As prices begin to pick up in the spring season advance, profits are on the rise. Global tensions in the long wave advance come from the need for access to raw materials rather than from overcapacity and overproduction in every industry.

Demand for new and old goods is on the rise as economies pick up in anticipation of better days to come. But the world is still cautious during the spring phase of the new advance. Companies are still risk averse. In the spring season of the advance, companies will not take the chance of expanding production of their goods beyond what they know for sure the markets will sustain. Managers and owners still remember the damage done in the decline to companies that overshot the needs of the marketplace.

At this point of the long wave, the world is slowly moving into a state of recovery and renewed optimism about the future. World prices begin to rise more rapidly and the economy picks up steam. Prices begin to rise slowly as the demand for products is on the rise.

During the spring season, there is no reason to seek protection because business is cautious enough that goods are not overproduced and there is plenty of growing demand. The 1950s and early 1960s were such a spring season of the long wave. Competition was not intense. In a long wave advance, companies are eager to peddle their wares in foreign markets and give others the right to do the same. Protectionist sentiment is almost nonexistent.

As the spring season becomes a long wave summer, the global marketplace is once again demanding an ever-increasing amount of products. However, the global economy is not yet producing more goods than markets can comfortably absorb. In fact, in the summer season there tend to be shortages, which produces inflation and coaxes existing producers to expand production and new producers to enter markets.

Producers in many industries, such as electronics and computers, didn't exist in the 1920s and 1930s when other industries were overproducing. When these new industries began during the latest spring and summer seasons, there were more than enough markets for their products. In the 1980s and 1990s, they had reached maturity, and the competition affected the bottom line. They then began calling for protection from the competition as the global economy approached the long wave winter season of excess capacity utilization and overproduction.

The system is pushed too far when the global long wave advance has experienced several decades of growth with only a few, small recessions. Industry owners and managers believe a new era of eternal growth has emerged. There has been a turnover in leadership in the global economy, and the new blood does not remember the last major decline and depression. Time and general prosperity has the effect of draining most of the caution out of the system. Corporations, individuals, and governments become willing to pay more for the right to borrow money, not to mention borrow far greater amounts. Growth and profits are projected many years into the future based on the previous year's trends in growth and prices. It happens first in commodities and agriculture.

A classic example of the effect of the long wave advance on industry is the global oil industry. The industry geared up for the expansion of the 1950s, 1960s, and 1970s, and production capacity eventually far exceeded the world's need for oil. Production was based on rising expectations and not real economic needs of the global economy. A great deal of money was borrowed and used to expand refinery and production facilities in developing countries. Those facilities eventually aided in the overproduction of oil, thus forcing prices down and making those developing countries incapable of paying their loans. Domestic oil producers wanted protection from foreign producers and increased tariffs and taxes on oil imports.

When prices were rising and markets were growing, this protectionist pressure didn't develop. Eventually, supply outstripped demand. This same series of events occurred in numerous markets from textiles to agriculture to microchips. There was overcapitalization and too much production capacity created in virtually every industry during the upswing.

Interest rates climb throughout the upswing of the long wave, increasing the costs of capital. This drives all prices higher. Sales increase and business booms. The decision makers driving business and future expansion plans overestimate the future due to innate optimism and the overall economic expansion. These forces build to a climax or final blow off for economic expansion. This is what occurred in the late 1970s in commodities and agricultural products at the end of the long wave summer season.

Interest rates peak and then fall as the economy enters into the fall season where overproduction becomes the rule. Investment shifts in the fall season away from real economic expansion and into the financial markets.

Obviously, one of the most important aspects of the more competitive global marketplace of the long wave decline is the effect on trade among nations. Industry, fighting to survive its overexpansion which was financed with expensive debt, begins pressuring government for more protectionist legislation. Since the peak in the economic expansion in the early 1980s, the introduction of legislation for trade barriers and tariffs has been on the rise. This has not been confined to Washington, D.C. Every capital in the world has begun to feel the pressure. An extended long wave fall season and mild early winter postponed much of this pressure for protection.

The push for protection explodes in the winter season of the long wave decline as demand for goods by consumers in global markets shrink as economic activity collapses. Unfortunately, in a long wave winter, someone has to go out of business to bring the global system and supply-and-demand back into balance. This is where trade pressures really begin to grow. No company owner wants it to be her company and no politician wants it to be a company from his area, employing his constituents. No national leaders want it to be the companies from their country. But the inevitable trend is unstoppable.

The long wave would take its course with or without the element of trade barriers and trade wars emerging in the fall and winter season. However, it is still important to take a brief look at the forces and outcome of protectionist sentiment.

In a speech delivered to the America Society in New York City during the 1980s long wave fall season, David Peterson (1987,

230-231), the premier of Ontario, presented some startling thoughts on the tides of international trade. Here are a few highlights:

> We are all aware of the consequences incurred when the international trading system collapsed after the adoption of such measures as the Smoot-Hawley Tariff of 1930 and the British Tariff of 1932.
>
> The sudden surge of protectionism snapped a golden age of trade, cutting down assembly lines and creating soup lines, closing banks and foreclosing farms.
>
> The foundations of those protectionist trade walls bear a remarkable resemblance to trends we see today, more than a half-century later.
>
> The trade wars of the 20s and 30s were sparked by slow growth in demand for traditional goods and services; a sudden spread of technological knowledge which narrowed competitive gaps between nations; an abrupt decline in the need for raw materials; and rapid shifts in the balance of market power.
>
> The similarities to today's conditions remind me of the words of a great philosopher, Yogi Berra: "It's déjà vu all over again."

The same forces Peterson noted in the 1980s are the same trade pressures that have been contained during the fall and early winter of this long wave. The pressure for protection begins in raw materials and commodities and spreads to other areas of the economy. The pressure here late in the winter season will likely be more focused on consumer and finished goods which are being overproduced, such as tires. We are now close to a new long wave spring season and we need to avoid the calls for protectionism that will grow louder as this long wave winter lasts several more years. You can't really blame industry for wanting protection from foreign competition in a long wave decline. Profits drop as the economy enters the mature long wave phase of overproduction. Without looking at the long wave or the

System Dynamics Model at MIT, you could not have predicted the new era of disinflation/deflation and overproduction. Farmers, carmakers, shoe producers, computer makers, and dozens of others have legitimate complaints. They do face stiff competition and loss, but they are the ones overproducing. Why should consumers pay more for everything to cover up producers' mistakes and miscalculations?

A market economy has to decide whether it will side with the producer, who over calculated and has his or her neck on the financial cutting block, or the consumer, who just wants the best product at the best price. In a true market system, there would be no choice. The consumer would be king, and producers would be told to sink or swim on their own and not beg for legislative protection.

Companies fighting for protectionism believe consumers should be forced to pay the bill for their inefficiencies and lack of responsibility. Consumers took on more debt than they could handle and producers expanded beyond the needs of the global economy. In a free market, there must be punishment for economic mistakes. Otherwise, the economy gets confused and miscalculates even more dramatically. Much of the time, producers want consumers to pay more for goods to protect industries that actually belong in other countries for a more efficient market allocation of labor. Japan wants to protect its rice farmers, even though rice can be grown far more cheaply elsewhere in Asia and even in the bayous of Louisiana.

The fact is that the domestic economies are hurt by protectionism, not helped; but, more importantly, the brunt of this inefficiency falls on the consumer. The lifeblood of the economy is the discretionary income of the consumer and is the economic factor most threatened by protectionist policy. If decisions are based on what is best for the consumer, the economy always comes back faster from a decline. The only bright spot in the entire affair is that the new economy that emerges from the carnage of a long wave decline promises to be better for both consumers and industry.

The storm clouds of trade wars are forming on the horizon as they have in the past when we have moved into the advanced stages of a long wave decline and winter season. If trade wars are allowed to get under way in these final years of a long wave winter, this decline will be far deeper and darker than necessary, just as the Great Depression was far deeper and lengthier than it should have been, due to growing international trade isolationism. Built into protectionism are enormous hidden costs that stifle the economy. The Center for the Study of American Business at Washington University released a study in the 1980s that should deter the protectionist warlords, but that has not yet ended their special-interest financed blindness (Andres 1985). In one year in the 1980s, the American consumer paid foreign governments and foreign manufacturers more than $4 billion (adjusting for inflation) for textile and apparel quotas alone. Tack on another $19 billion for the tariffs—a tax we pay our government on the value of apparel entering this country—and the total comes to $23 billion—money that could have gone to revitalizing and spurring growth in our economy.

Remembering that for every action there is an equal and opposite reaction, we must consider what protectionism in Washington will bring in retaliation from Tokyo, Seoul, London, Beijing, and Taipei. In looking at the past, it would appear the reaction is often stronger than the action. For example, in the 1980s, when we restricted $55 million worth of cotton blouses from China, China retaliated by canceling $500 million worth of orders for American grain, a brilliant move by our farsighted Congress. This is an excellent example of how protection of one industry shifts the burden onto another. As one nation blocks trade, the nation that is hurt will surely retaliate and the entire world will suffer.

John Oliver Wilson (1985, 517-519), chief economist at Bank of America, has spoken of a repeat in history in the area of protectionism. Wilson's words are just as relevant today as the call for trade protection will grow loud in the next few years:

> This is not the first time in our history that the threat of trade war has erupted. And it is useful to briefly recall this history, for the lessons from the past can serve us

well in the present. In 1930, the United States passed the Smoot-Hawley Act which broadened tariff coverage to 25,000 products and provided for substantial increases in over 800 tariff rates. The reaction of the rest of the world was immediate. Widespread protests erupted. Tariffs were raised in a dozen major countries and they were targeted against American products. The League of Nations, which was working hard to halt the upward trend in tariffs, was powerless. The seeds of economic isolation had been deeply planted.

There is a risk that trade wars could be conducted by the three major trade blocks of Asia, Europe, and North America. We may see free trade within these blocks while the three blocks themselves engage in trade wars and protectionism.

A major trade conflict between the United States and some trading partners may be inevitable. The new Democratic Congress is more protectionist oriented than any in recent memory. At some point in the final years of this long wave winter, the Obama administration may be forced, due to political pressure, to move toward protectionism. Such a move could progress into a full-scale trade war. Other nations will invariably be drawn into this conflict. Throughout history, trade wars have often become shooting wars. Hopefully, this will not be the case in any conflict between the United States and our trading partners.

When the world plunges deeper into the long wave decline and barriers are thrown up everywhere to protect ailing industries that have expanded beyond world demand for their goods with expensive debt, the situation could force major changes. Let us hope that leadership emerges that can take a trade crisis during this long wave winter to produce sweeping positive changes in the form of new free trade agreements for the global trading system. It is possible that we maintain free and open markets and go in the direction of greater free trade for the next long wave advance, since we are only a few years away.

There is no doubt that the economic conditions and forces that brought about the protectionism and trade wars of the last three long wave cycle declines exist in the global economy today. Unfortunately, the more severe the global trade conflicts become in the years ahead, the deeper the long wave winter is likely to be.

Chapter 11:

TECHNOLOGY AND INVENTION

"Truth as old as the hills is bound up in the Latin proverb, 'Necessity is the mother of invention.' It is surprising what a man can do when he has to, and how little most men will do when they don't have to."

Walter Linn

The greatest life-changing inventions and ideas, typically conceived in a long wave decline's fall and winter season, bear their economic fruit when fully capitalized in the next long wave advance. The electric light, cotton gin, steam engine, and automobile were all products developed during long wave declines and fully capitalized during the ensuing advances. Winter is a time of hibernation, reflection, and planning. In spring, the best laid plans begin to bear fruit.

Kondratieff began his review of long wave theory by stressing that capitalist economies progress in a cyclical pattern and not in a linear or constantly advancing manner. He concluded that this cyclical pattern is always progressing to new heights. Each new cycle of the long wave starts out further along in the development of the global economy. Great technological advances help a civilization move into new phases of growth.

The development of new technologies and the introduction of new inventions play a major role in the character of the long wave. If it were not for innovation, the long wave would just continue to turn over in one place and society would make no real progress toward higher standards of living and better ways of doing things.

There has been a great deal of speculation and discussion about how new inventions and technology contribute to the rise and fall of the economy. Kondratieff's research showed that there was an increase in the number of inventions during a decline because people were looking for more efficient and effective means of production to get their particular industry moving in a profitable direction. Kondratieff emphasized heavily the effect of inventions in the areas of communications and transportation on the long wave.

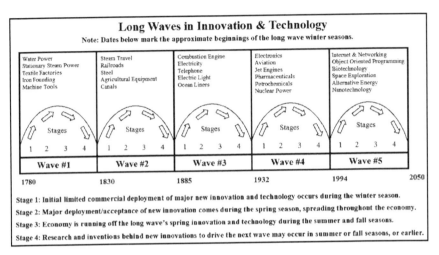

Chart 11.1 Long Waves in Innovation & Technology

There is the possibility that during hard times we tend to be more thinking and contemplative creatures and thus spend more time considering our predicament and making plans to better our condition. Unemployment is also a motivator. Many who don't get hired create their own jobs and form new companies. It is difficult to study the effect of invention on the long wave due to the complexity of both the inventing process and the implementation of new ideas.

The problem with just totaling the number of inventions during the decline and comparing it to the total during the upswing is that inventions have different qualities and characteristics and fall into different categories. Some inventions are in the capital goods area and are developed in an effort to minimize the cost of producing consumer products; these inventions are usually developed in research and development (R&D) departments of industry and government. Other inventions are in the area of consumer goods and new retail products aimed at improving the life of the general public rather than efficiency in industry. These inventions come from government research, including military and space research, and the private sector, both the freelance inventor and the R&D of industry.

For the past 200 years, there has been a steady increase in the number of inventions each year, while it would seem through the research of a number of individuals, including Kondratieff, that some of the more important inventions that had enormous economic impact were developed during major economic declines.

Gerhard Mensch assembled important evidence that clusters of basic innovations occurred in the 1820s, the 1880s, and the 1930s, exactly during stagnating long waves. Economic history, in turn, confirms that the investment outlays for the first massive applications of these basic innovations generally occurred 10 years later, after the turn from the depressive long wave to the expansionist long wave had already taken place.

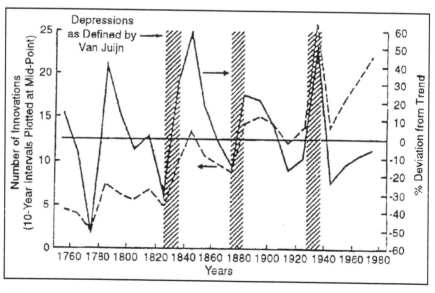

11.2 Surges in Major Innovations Worldwide (Hochgraf 1983)

The time of the actual invention is not as important to understanding the dynamics of long waves as understanding the economic forces causing capital to flow. The greatest capital flows into the new innovations come so they are integrated into the accelerated upswing of growth and expansion.

Ernest Mandel (1980, 41), a long wave theorist of Marxist inclinations, pointed out that J. Schmookler (1966) "has tried to prove that the patent cycle is closely related to the business cycle in general and does not precede or anticipate it." This is to say that the actual use of new inventions will increase with the advance of the long wave and decrease with its decline.

Mandel continues (1980, 41):

> Although the argumentation seems convincing, it does not distinguish between qualitatively different types of patents and thus it cannot provide an answer to the question we pose. What is decisive is the phenomenon of patents permitting radical innovations, not the patent cycle in general.

It is easy enough to understand that everyday-type patents are facilitated by major developments that increase communications and transportation.

John D. Sterman (1985, 21-22), of the System Dynamics Group at MIT, made the following insightful observations about technological innovation and the long wave cycle.

> In contrast to the innovation theories of the long wave, the National Model suggests a long wave theory of innovation better describes the situation. The NM shows how fundamental physical processes in the economy can create the long wave without any variation in innovation rates. The bunching of innovations can thus be explained as the result of entrainment of the innovation process by the long wave (Graham and Senge 1980, 283-84): 'The long wave creates a shifting historical context for the implementation of new inventions. Midway into a capital expansion, opportunities for applying new inventions that require new types of capital become poor. The nation is already committed to a particular mix of technologies,

and the environment greatly favors improvement innovations over basic innovations. During a long wave downturn, basic innovation opportunities gradually improve, as old capital embodying the technologies of the preceding buildup depreciates. Near the trough of the wave, there are great opportunities for creating new capital embodying radical new technologies. The old capital base is obsolescent, bureaucracies that thwarted basic innovation have weakened, many companies committed to producing old types of capital are bankrupt, and traditional methods are no longer sacrosanct.' Though innovation is not necessary to explain the long wave, there is little doubt that each long wave seems to be built around a particular ensemble of basic technologies, including particular forms of energy, transport, communications, and materials. These ensembles evolve synergistically and, like species in an ecosystem, compete against other candidates for a limited number of available niches.

Sterman's observations indicate the great impact of technology and innovation on the economy and the long wave. Lower interest rates and wages, as well as cheaper raw materials, greatly increase the profit picture as the economy enters a new advance, thus creating more investment capital and an overall more favorable environment for the implementation of the new technology.

When the financial markets reach their peak at the end of the fall season and as winter begins, industry is caught in a squeeze. The slowdown of investment in expansion is profound. When the general overexpansion and overcapitalization of industry with expensive debt begins to take its toll and the buying power of the world is eroded, prices tumble. When prices fall below what it costs to produce, the screws clearly tighten on the economy.

For a while, companies still operate to cover fixed costs, but soon prices drop too far and companies begin shutting their doors. Unemployment and bankruptcies reach new highs and the entire economy slows. As we move deeper into the decline and the companies that make it through the first years of the decline are no longer expanding, a buildup of capital begins. Interest rates, wages and payrolls fall. Costs fall. The profit picture begins to improve, yet companies with the newfound tendencies toward risk aversion are extremely slow to expand or spend money on major outlays.

A natural place for the investment of the company's excess capital during this time is in R&D. This new research expenditure coupled with the psychological factor of seeking solutions during hard times breeds new products that can help pull the world out of its economic slumber and into the next upswing of the cycle. When the old ways crumble, it frees us to see in new ways.

Kondratieff concentrated heavily on inventions in transportation and communications and their impact on the expansion of the long wave. Transportation and communications are extremely important fields of development in that they have a triple effect on growth during the expansion period of the long wave. First, they create new industries of their own for investment and profit. Second, they generate more trade among nations and continents and, in effect, stimulate the development of the global economy. Third, stimulus to world trade helps to encourage development and capitalization of other less important inventions and products that are not necessarily in the fields of communications or transportation.

The act of inventing, the process of development and the implementation of inventions are all part of what we consider the growth of technology. It is said that humanity is now doubling its knowledge of the universe every few years. This increase in knowledge and the explosion of technology that accompanies it is opening all sorts of avenues for business and science. These new avenues are creating wonderful opportunities to build a better world and are providing for the possibility of a more peaceful coexistence among nations.

Kondratieff and others have explained, and we have seen in this chapter, that communications and transportation are the technology leaders in pulling the economy out of the contraction and into the expansion.

This discussion of technology and invention related to the long wave is not just theoretical. It can be applied in a practical manner to business and investment decisions. Globally this long wave made its turn from fall to winter in the recession of 1994 for the economy and for financial markets at the market top in 2000. In the U.S., loose monetary policy and aggressive fiscal policy has clouded this seasonal transition with the Internet and housing sector bubble years driven by accommodative monetary policy. The emergence of new participants, such as the BRIC countries, into international capitalism have also distorted this turn with temporary better returns on capital in new periphery countries. In the late-1990s, it was clear that the emergence and use of the Internet was a communication technology that was experiencing its initial commercial deployment during the long wave winter season. The next generation of the Internet will bring even more changes during the coming long wave spring season.

Based on the fact that the Internet was clearly a long wave communication technology, this author became founder and CEO of an Internet-based medical research and marketing services company, focused on the life sciences industry. The business plan was to use the Internet to bring efficiencies and scalability to health care marketing research and life science product communications. The company was successful and served 19 of the top 20 global life science companies with research and marketing services.

Part of the development strategy included identifying computer code and programming technology innovation that would be the driver of Internet deployment, both during this winter season and in the coming spring season of the long wave. To be successful in the long run, technology must be accepted and incorporated as the standard. This can be viewed as the commoditization of technology for long wave deployment.

The computer code and programming innovation that was identified clearly as having the potential to become a global standard is known as object-oriented programming. Microsoft is playing a major role in the acceptance of object-oriented programming with the creation of the .Net infrastructure and extensive object-oriented programming tools for corporate

IT requirements. The company deployed a loosely coupled distributed object model platform that is remarkably flexible and scalable. We were fortunate to have a vice president of technology that had worked with one of the originators of object-oriented programming code in the 1980s. The distributed object model based platform created executes complex research and marketing tasks with large numbers of participants.

The platform deployed can interact with thousands of physicians in real time. Older technology would take hundreds of people and thousands of hours of labor. The platform includes a virtual life sciences product detailing and sampling platform. Ongoing upgrades to the distributed object model platform has the company well positioned for this long wave winter and prepared for the next long wave advance. This example demonstrates a practical application of long wave development in communications, in this case object-oriented technology platforms, for executing complex business tasks and corporate development.

Object-oriented programming (OOP) and resulting object model infrastructures will dominate IT in the next spring season of the long wave. OOP is becoming imbedded during the long wave winter as companies seek to create efficiencies and scalability to improve profits. Object-oriented programming combined with the Internet and other networks will usher in changes to how virtually every industry does business in the years ahead. It has already begun, but you have seen nothing yet. The changes to come are even bigger and more far reaching. An interesting aspect to OOP is the degree to which it allows the virtual world to replicate and imitate real world relationships, and, therefore, organize information and manage the real world problems. No industry will be untouched by OOP combined with networks in the long wave advance to come.

The field of nanotechnology is creating major innovations and technology that will drive the coming long wave advance across many industries. Nanotechnology seeks to control matter on the atomic and molecular level. Nanomedicine is the medical application of nanotechnology. Nanomedicine is exploring the use of the self-organizing properties of lipids on the molecular level for life sciences applications. Drug delivery systems are using nanotechnology to deliver compounds into the body with more effective disease targeting.

My current entrepreneurial endeavor is ALP Life Sciences, LLC, which is conducting research in the area of applied lipid polymorphism. ALP is pursuing a promising medical application using the self-organizing properties of lipids. It is a unique application of nanomedicine with potential for diagnostics and treatment of lipid disorders and inflammatory diseases, including arthritis, heart disease and cancer. Whereas most lipid nanotechnology research is utilizing lipid self-organization for compound delivery systems, ALP is exploring lipid self organization properties for the potential removal of unwanted compounds from the body, including liver triglyceride deposits and arachidonic acid eicosanoids.

It is also clear that during this winter season the next phase of space exploration is also beginning to emerge. New technologies are now being developed and some deployed that will be applied to a new space race. Great competition will likely exist in space exploration between the U.S., China, Russia and the EU during the coming long wave advance. The new space race will likely involve both public and private space exploration and travel.

Space flight falls into the innovation category of transportation and will also be accompanied by breakthroughs in communications. We will see great advances in all areas of space exploration in the years ahead. Space flight may be almost as common in the next peak of the long wave cycle as air flight is today. The construction of additional space stations and moon bases during the next advance will create hundreds of new ideas, products, and manufacturing processes. Before the next long wave advance is over, it is likely that millions of jobs will be created as a direct result of advances in space technology. Space travel developments will help propel us into the next long wave advance. Governments should encourage space and other technologies as the next long wave advance drivers.

Alternative energy is no doubt emerging during this long wave decline as a major force for the next long wave advance. Solar, wind, fuel cells, shale, new and safer nuclear, and many others will provide a huge boost to the global economy in addition to shifting our dependence away from the old technology of oil. However, new technology in oil exploration will also see to it that we have the oil supplies required as we shift to new forms of energy.

Biotechnology and genetic engineering will open new frontiers for industry. Artificial intelligence and the use of a new generation of robotics will bring numerous avenues of growth to the economy. Magnetically levitated trains will drastically change ground transportation. New batteries will be invented that will make widespread use of electric cars common during the next advance.

These examples demonstrate that the economic long wave is an observable and functional phenomenon in innovation and technology that can be used to drive business decision making. Commitments made to technology during the winter season are the engines of growth during the next long wave advance. There are real world applications for pursuing anticipated long wave developments in innovation and technology for new product development and, therefore, business strategy. Many are using the long wave to look ahead and plan without being fully aware of the long wave implications and impact.

The collapse of computer prices in this long wave decline is leading to their widest possible use in all types of research and engineering. A whole wave of new technology and products will be traced to the mass distribution of powerful computer systems that are being placed into the hands of almost anyone who wants them. The future is being created on computer systems in garages, home offices, offices, and in the research departments of major corporations. New products, processes, and materials are being developed during this decline and will propel us into the next long wave advance.

But first we must survive the challenging, yet stimulating decline, during which the impurities and inefficiencies that have built up over past decades will be purged from the system. The result will be a prospering and expanding global economy built on pooled and individual talent that was challenged to survive during this long wave winter season, and stepped up to the challenge.

We have come to see that technology and invention do indeed play a major role in the rise and fall of the long wave in the global economy. It is important to remember that without a severe decline that shakes the system and its participants, creating new ideas, many of the new advances of the next long wave economic expansion would never come about. Necessity is indeed the mother of invention, and will force the changes that must be made to insure our future success.

Chapter 12:

ON POLITICS

"I hate all bungling as I do sin, but particularly bungling in politics, which leads to the misery and ruin of many thousands and millions of people."

Goethe

"I place economy among the first and most important virtues, and public debt as the greatest of dangers to be feared.... To preserve our independence, we must not let our rulers load us with perpetual debt.... We must make our choice between economy and liberty or profusion and servitude.... If we run into such debts, we must be taxed in our meat and drink, in our necessities and our comforts, in our labors and in our amusement.... If we can prevent Government from wasting the labors of the people, under the pretense of caring for them, they will be happy."

Thomas Jefferson

"It only stands to reason that where there's sacrifice, there's someone collecting the sacrificial offerings. Where there's service, there is someone being served. The man who speaks to you of sacrifice is speaking of slaves and masters, and intends to be the master."

Ayn Rand

Few would argue that what gave Franklin Roosevelt victory in 1932 was the pain of the Great Depression and his promise that government would take care of the people and bring the speculative and dangerous market forces under control. His promises to more closely regulate the banking industry and the financial markets, which were perceived as catalysts of the crash in 1929 and in turn the Great Depression, were major factors as well. Economic pain and the same call for government solutions can now also be said to have been the key driver in the election of President Obama. Conversely, few would question that Ronald Reagan's promise to get government off people's backs and to give industry more freedom in the marketplace through deregulation played a large role in his being elected in 1980 and reelected in 1984. There should be no doubt that the location of the economy within the long wave plays a major role in politics and who gets elected.

In his working paper at MIT, "The Economic Long Wave: Theory and Evidence," John D. Sterman (1985, 26) made the following observations on political and social values:

> Substantial evidence exists that political and social values in Western nations fluctuate with the period and phasing of the economic long wave (Namenwirth 1973, Weber 1981). Independent content analyses of political tracts in the U.S. and Great Britain revealed statistically significant 50-year value cycles in both countries which coincided with each other and with the phasing of the economic long wave. During periods of long wave expansion, material wants are satisfied, and social concerns turn to civil liberties, income distribution, and social justice. During the later phases of the expansion, foreign-policy concerns predominate. As the expansion gives way to decline, conservatism grows, and political attention returns to material needs. Economic policy takes center stage in legislative agendas. During the downturn, the accumulation of wealth becomes the overriding concern, at the expense of civil rights, equity, and the environment. The most dramatic example of this cycle is, of course, the rise of fascism in the 1920s and 1930s. The student rebellion of the 1960s and growing conservatism of the 1980s in many Western nations are also consistent with the current long wave cycle .... The variation of political values is primarily the result of entrainment by the economic cycle.

It would be foolish to try to link every world leader or U.S. president from George Washington to the present with the position of the economy relative to the long wave. The long wave theory does not attempt to do so. It is, however, possible to make such a link during the critical turning points of the cycle. These prove to be the most volatile periods for the economy and thus the most predictable periods in the struggle for power within the political system.

There are powerful forces at work in the years leading up to the long wave peak, during the fall season, and during the first few years as the economy slides into the long wave winter. The left had no chance for victory as we moved into the seeming prosperous and speculative laissez-faire climate of the long wave fall season.

In the late 1920s, Hoover was a president with a hands-on management style. Contrary to common belief, Hoover believed the government, rather than the market, should fix things. The fact is that Hoover and Roosevelt did a great deal to make the Depression far worse than it had to be. We will always have the long wave decline. We don't have to turn it into a devastating and lengthy depression. Many have argued that if government had gotten out of the way in the 1930s and let prices, wages, banking and business adjust naturally, the decline would have been far less severe.

I'm a bit hesitant to criticize President Roosevelt. Grandmother Barker, who is still alive and well for this third edition at the age of 94, never hesitates to inform me that I wouldn't be around if it hadn't been for President Roosevelt seeing to it that there was food on the table during the Depression, even though my grandfather never turned down a day's work. I like to think that free markets would have been more compensating of hard work, but you don't argue with your grandmother.

Paul Johnson (1991, 240) in his book *Modern* Times, had some fascinating insights into the economic events of the Great Depression and the political responses by Hoover and Roosevelt. Looking at an honest assessment of what occurred in the 1930s reveals the forces that were at work in the 1930s and reveals how things will have to be different this time around:

> The credit inflation petered out at the end of 1928. The economy went into decline, in consequence, six months later. The market collapse followed after a three-month delay. All this was to be expected; it was healthy; it ought to have been welcomed. It was the pattern of the nineteenth century and of the twentieth up to 1920-1921; capitalist 'normalcy'. A business recession and a stock-exchange drop were not only customary but necessary parts of the cycle of growth: they sorted out the sheep from the goats, liquidated the unhealthy elements in the economy and turned out the parasites; as J.K. Galbraith was to put it: 'One of the uses of depression is to expose what the auditors fail to find.' Business downturns serve essential purposes. They have to be sharp. But they need not be long because they are self-adjusting. All they require on the part of governments, the business community and the public is patience.

Many wrongly assume that Hoover maintained the *laissez-faire* policies of Harding and Coolidge up until his defeat by Roosevelt. The fact is that when the economy got weak and the market crashed, Hoover blinked. He turned to intervention early on in his administration. The idea of letting the free market heal itself was thrown out the window. Hoover was educated and trained as an engineer before he entered the political arena. He tried to use government to engineer the country out of the crisis-thereby exacerbating the economy's decline. Johnson (1991, 244) observed:

> When the magnitude of the crisis became apparent, Andrew Mellon, the Treasury Secretary, at last repudiated his interventionist philosophy and returned to strict *laissez-faire*. He told Hoover that administration policy should be to 'liquidate labor, liquidate stocks, liquidate

the farmers, liquidate real estate' and so 'purge the rottenness from the economy'. It was the only sensible advice Hoover received throughout his presidency. By allowing the Depression to rip, unsound business would quickly have been bankrupted and the sound would have survived.

The government's attempt to stop the Great Depression guaranteed its severity and longevity. The interventionist direction taken by Hoover has been the blueprint for government ever since. Ronald Reagan tried to change this, but his advisors got the best of him. Johnson's (1991, 244-245) account of Hoover's early action should be a lesson for getting government out of business this time around:

From the very start, therefore, Hoover agreed to take on the business cycle and stamp on it with all the resources of government. 'No president before has ever believed there was a government responsibility in such cases,' he wrote; ' ... there we had to pioneer a new field.' He resumed credit inflation, the Federal Reserve adding almost $300 million to credit in the last week of October 1929 alone. In November he held a series of conferences with industrial leaders in which he exacted from them solemn promises not to cut wages, even to increase them if possible–promises kept until 1932 .... It is true that Hoover ruled out direct relief and wherever possible he channeled government money through the banks rather than direct to businesses and individuals. But that he sought to use government cash to reflate the economy is beyond question. Coolidge's advice to angry farmers' delegations had been a bleak 'Take up religion.' Hoover's new Agricultural Marketing Act gave them $500 million of Federal money, increased by a further $100 million early in 1930. In 1931 he extended this to the economy as a whole with his Reconstruction Finance Corporation (RFC), as part of a nine point program of government intervention which he produced in December. More major public works were started in Hoover's four years than in the previous thirty.

Hoover was spending a pile of money to try and save the economy from depression, therefore, he decided government needed more revenue to continue pioneering his new government endeavors. It is difficult to believe that anyone could be so foolish as to think that any form of tax increase could help the economy when it is in decline. The deficit was drastically increasing in the early 1930s due to the explosion of government programs. Johnson (1991, 245) tells us how Hoover decided to pay for his doomed government ventures.

> ... the 1932 Revenue Act saw the greatest taxation increase in U.S. history in peacetime, with the rate on high incomes jumping from a quarter to 63 per cent. This made nonsense of Hoover's earlier tax cuts but by now Hoover had lost control of Congress and was not in a position to pursue a coherent fiscal policy.

Government intervention in the economy only makes matters worse. Recent protectionist sentiment should be viewed in the context of government engineering during the Hoover administration. Johnson (1991, 246) tells us the consequences of trade policy during the period:

> The final crisis came when America's protectionist policy boomeranged. The atrocious Smoot-Hawley Tariff of 1930, which sharply increased import duties, more than any other positive act of policy, spread the Depression to Europe. In the summer of 1931 the collapse of Austria's leading bank, the Credit Anstalt, pushed over a whole row of European dominoes ... and a series of debt-repudiations ensued. What remained of America's exports to Europe vanished, and her policy of foreign loans as a substitute for free trade collapsed.

Looking at the close of the Hoover era, Johnson (1991, 246) observed that, for all his effort, Hoover's policies did nothing to stop the Great Depression and, if anything, made it worse:

> By that time Hoover's interventionism had prolonged the Depression into its fourth year. The cumulative banking crisis had, in all probability, the deflationary effect which Hoover had struggled so hard and so foolishly to prevent, so that by the end of 1932 the very worst of the Depression was over. But the cataclysmic depth to which the economy had sunk in the meantime meant that recovery would be slow and feeble.

Looking at the transition from the Hoover to Roosevelt administrations, we see that there really was no significant difference in the policy of the two presidents. They were both planners and interventionists. Roosevelt went for direct relief, while Hoover distrusted this approach. Quoting Johnson (1991, 255):

> Roosevelt's legislation, for the most part, extended or tinkered with Hoover policies. The Emergency Banking Act and the Loans to Industry Act of June 1934 extended Hoover's RFC. The Home Owners' Loan Act (1932) extended a similar act of the year before. The Sale of Securities Act (1933), the Banking Acts (1933, 1935) and the Securities and Exchange Act (1934) merely continued Hoover's attempts to reform business methods.

Johnson (1991) concluded that the Hoover-Roosevelt interventionism was a continuum. By leading government involvement in the economy and markets, "they impeded a natural recovery brought about by deflation." Bush and Obama have taken their cues from Hoover-Roosevelt in terms of government intervention to stop the deflation.

An interesting note on politics and insight into the fact that Japan is the leader of this long wave decline is that, in 1992, in the midst of the collapse of the Japanese stock market, the Japanese government created the Securities and Exchange Surveillance Commission (SESC). This agency is modeled after the SEC, which was created by Roosevelt at the same point in the last long wave decline and along with the same political rhetoric of controlling the markets. And some say history doesn't repeat itself. At this writing we see that Japan has yet to recover and appears to be declining again along with the entire global economy.

The U.S. economy has never returned to the growth levels seen before the Great Depression and especially during the great economic advances of the 19th century. Since the Great Depression, government has continued as a yoke around the neck of the economy. While government and the public sector of the economy have grown, the private sector and the free market have shrunk relative to the total economy. Offering a smaller piece of the pie is not the way to feed a growing, more-demanding crowd.

The trend of bigger government doesn't have to continue. Indeed, all trends must come to an end. We have evolved into an interventionist system that doesn't come close to resembling the economic system envisioned by America's founding fathers. We saw the Soviet Union collapse due to the failure and folly of central planning and government intervention. For years the United States has been moving in the same direction.

As we go into this decline, the economic facts are different from those of the 1930s. Instead of having a balanced budget at the beginning of this decline, the government is drowning taxpayers in trillions of dollars of red ink.

Thus far the Obama administration appears to be taking its cues from the Roosevelt administration. In prior editions I questioned whether the public would go for another Roosevelt-style New Deal solution. However, most Americans have come to realize that with deficit spending the government is shortchanging their future, as well as the future of their children and grandchildren. The American people will pay down debt during the winter season and they will ultimately want their government to do the same thing. During this decline of the long wave, the political turmoil and demand for change in the United States will be greater than at any time since the Civil War, if not the American Revolution. We are already beginning to see signs of this overdue reality rock the system.

It may well be that the bulk of the American people are going to look for another way out before the next long wave advance gets fully underway. Recent elections are indicative of a new trend against the flow of power to Washington. Polls show that voters distrust the existing two-party political process more than at any time in history.

Typically under the two-party political system in America, the obvious tendency would be for the election of Republican presidents in the laissez-faire fall season phase of the long wave and the election of Democratic presidents during the winter. During a majority of the years of the long wave advance, it would be hard to predict the political party elected to power-since economic growth makes politics less important in the minds of the public.

Normal long wave political rules may not hold this time, due to public anger and distrust of Washington. The real standard of living of the middle-class family in America has fallen since the 1970s, even with two people working instead of one. The American people are angry with the deterioration of the situation and with government. This anger is not limited to America. We can see the same anger coming from the public around the globe.

Government is failing to serve the people effectively. The middle class is in a squeeze. A major political revolt of the middle class could erupt, forcing major changes in the political system in America. Due to the economic and financial mess that Washington is in during this long wave winter, we may well see a viable third-party emerge on the American political scene in the years ahead. Politicians of existing parties may even switch to a new party.

President Franklin Roosevelt inherited a government that had low debts and, therefore, a degree of flexibility. During this long

wave winter, government does not have the options that were
available to Roosevelt. The Federal Government is now closing
in on $12 trillion in debt. Before it is over this time around, the
public may well demand that government get out of the way and
let the market and the resilience and hard work of the American
people get the country back on track. So far this has not been
the case, but it may be coming. The Tea Party phenomenon of
early 2009 may be an indication of things to come.

All the problems government has been promising to address
and correct since Hoover have grown worse. Poverty has increased,
crime has surged, education has suffered, banking is in crisis,
and the economy has underperformed. The costs to taxpayers
for these great services from federal government increase every
year. The social forces at work are demanding drastic change
and this mood will grow.

For the record, it is my conviction that President Obama
does not have the socialist leanings that many accuse him of
having, nor do I believe he desires to push America toward
socialism. However, he does appear to favor state capitalism
and intervention. President Obama is no ideologue. He is a
pragmatist and pragmatists play the cards they are dealt. However,
I believe he will ultimately act in the best interest of the country
and the world. It is my firm conviction that, before this global
crisis is over, President Obama will be viewed as an advocate of
free markets and will lead the return to limited and responsible
government. It will not be from choice, but a matter of necessity.
His options will be limited; he will recognize that there is no other
way out.

You may think my forecast and thinking in this regard is
naïve and misplaced, but the global crisis is expected to get
worse before this long wave winter is over. The only way out will
be through radical tax cuts, reducing the size of federal and
state government, and unleashing the remarkable and awesome
power of human action in a new advanced form of unfettered
global free market capitalism. The necessity of radical policy
change that unleashes the pent up potential in the global
economy will become increasingly clear, and I believe odds will

rise that President Obama will act accordingly in the interest of the country. His choices will be limited.

For the record, President Obama did not offer me enough hope to earn my vote. However, I did make the trek to Washington for his inauguration at the behest of my son and a few of his classmates who wanted to experience the history of the occasion. Hope was indeed palpable in the crowd in the middle of the National Mall. However, the true hope for America's future rests in human liberty, individual freedom and the opportunity provided by the greatest free market economic system ever devised by man, not in intrusive and interventionist government and state capitalism. I pray for President Obama regularly. If you are the praying sort, I urge you to do so as well. Scripture teaches us to do so, regardless of your political convictions. Pray that the hope he offers grows more in tune with America's destiny, the destiny to point the way and lead a new world order of less government and more individual liberty, responsibility and opportunity.

My hope is that before this long wave winter is over, President Obama will surprise both the left and the right—all those expecting him to continue to embrace state capitalism, interventionism and socialist solutions. In the same manner that it took Nixon to establish relations with communist China, something a Democrat could not have done, my contention is that President Obama will defend and lead an aggressive return to free market capitalism, market-based solutions, and smaller government relative to GDP. The forces set in motion by this long wave winter will force President Obama and the Democratic Party to make this change for any chance at reelection in 2012. There is a sea change taking place under the surface of American politics. The tide will turn against big government in a profound and fundamental way in the years directly ahead.

I realize that most readers may be a bit incredulous at this point, whether conservative or liberal, but the alternative during this long wave crisis is not something the people of the United States will accept. And at this point in this long wave winter, Obama is the one elected to lead the way. I genuinely believe that those who view Obama as the lead actor arriving on the global

stage just in time to shift of the world toward global socialism–
an opportunity that could arise during the crisis of a long wave
winter season–are going to be sadly disappointed.

Radical change is also coming to government on the state
and local level as well. Municipal governments are bleeding
communities dry with large unnecessary budgets as well as
excessive benefits and fat pensions for government employees that
are stifling the private sector. At some point, the public will not
be willing to take any more. There will increasingly be local and
national tax protests. After a few major municipal bankruptcies
that strip all the egregious benefits being distributed and paid
for by the private sector, municipal governments will take major
steps to address their budget issues. The cutbacks, born of
necessity, will be aggressive and comprehensive.

In looking at the political consequences of the long wave,
we cannot avoid the subject of nationalism. As economies are
in trouble and nations are looking inward, there is a surge in
nationalism around the globe, just as in the 1920s and 1930s.
This is not necessarily a bad thing in and of itself, but there is a
danger of it becoming economic isolationism and being carried
too far. Isolationism could threaten the life of the global economy
and could possibly cause the decline to be far more lengthy and
devastating than it has to be.

This new wave of nationalism has been powerful in the
United States as in the rest of the world. It has been a positive
force in that it has given America a new pride in quality and a
job well done. At the same time, this nationalism could lead us
down the dead-end road of protectionism. There will no doubt
be enormous pressure for the world's new nationalism to bring
increased economic isolation as the economy moves deeper into
the winter season. National leaders will need to convince the
people with authority that this is not the road to take, but it will
be a very hard sell.

We cannot look at politics without considering a major danger
threatening the global economy and our future prosperity. There
is certainly the danger that during this long wave winter we will
not go in the direction of freedom but into the arms of even

more government and bureaucratic tyranny. Indeed, you could argue that this is where we have headed at this stage of the global crisis.

There has been a great deal of talk in recent years about a new world order. It is often mentioned in conjunction with a more powerful United Nations. In the midst of the crisis of this long wave decline, the situation may force major mistakes by national leaders in a state of panic.

Instead of turning away from the failure of big government and back to the market system envisioned by America's founding fathers, U.S. and world leaders may think that uniting under a new form of redistributive world empire is the solution. A redistributive world empire would be a loosely coupled global system of individual nation states increasingly dominated by the rise of state capitalism and interventionism. This rising redistributive world empire would be increasingly managed and administered at the level of supranational organizations such as the United Nations and others that would usurp national sovereignty from individual states. These organizations are helpful, but their power needs to be limited.

More government is the problem, not the solution, when it comes to countering the forces of a long wave decline. A redistributive world empire would simply be one more level of bureaucracy that has to be paid for with higher taxes and decreased efficiency. A redistributive world empire may survive for a handful of long waves, but in the end it would choke off the economy, destroy markets, and suppress individual freedoms. We could enter a decline bigger than Rome's, which led to the Dark Ages.

Sovereign nations of the world must attempt to try and settle their differences and share ideas that are beneficial for all. But to give up even more sovereignty and freedom for one more shot at government as the solution to our problems in the form of a redistributive world empire would be the greatest mistake America and other sovereign states could ever make.

Individual nations must remain sovereign within the global system, just as the individual must remain sovereign within the national economy. The result of a new redistributive world empire would be a global bureaucratic nightmare that is doomed to failure in the long run.

In reaction to global crisis, the United Nations could be offered more funding and more power to exercise over the nations of the globe. A sort of global New Deal would be the cry, as it was in our last long wave decline. A new global money system will likely be part of the Global New Deal. Indeed, the Global New Deal is clearly what national leaders have been offering in this long wave winter.

We will discuss this more at length later as we review the paths out of this global decline. Most of those who will offer global solutions mean well. They are hard-working, basically good people who want to help the situation. They are just wrongheaded when it comes to the political and economic facts and the cure needed. They will likely not succeed in pulling off a redistributive world empire political coup for reasons laid out in this book. The nationalism brought on by the social, economic, and political forces at work in a long wave decline will be too great to overcome and will counteract such attempts.

All nations will be in dire need of leaders who can stimulate great domestic faith during this long wave winter. National leadership will also have to deal in an insightful and meaningful way with the forces at work in the global political and economic environment that will seek to use political power for socialist or excessively nationalist and populist agendas. This will be true of every nation in the international arena-where such visionaries will be in short supply. In America, and even the world, President Obama has been given the lead role in this global crisis of a long wave winter. The world will be watching him closely.

PART III
THE INTELLIGENT INVESTOR

Chapter 13:

LONG WAVE INVESTING

"I am more and more impressed with the possibilities of history's repeating itself on many different counts. You don't get very far in Wall Street with the simple, convenient conclusion that a given level of prices is not too high."

Benjamin Graham

"Adversity has made many a man great who, had he remained prosperous, would only have been rich."

Maurice Switzer

"When prosperity comes, do not use all of it."

Confucius

In the same manner that application of the long wave theory is the most important tool for economic prognostication, as observed by Schumpeter, it is our view that the long wave and smaller cycles are also important tools for long term financial market analysis and short-term market forecasting. Understanding how the long wave, the long wave seasons, and how smaller cycles make up a long wave is essential to successful investing. However, other principles of investment are important to consider in concert with long wave analysis for securing principle and delivering above average returns. If beating the market is not your objective, and safety of principle is not an issue for you, then you should just buy the market with a simple buy-and-hold philosophy. Of course, buy-and-hold is the approach that has now burned millions of investors and destroyed many dreams during this difficult long wave winter season.

If you have not done so, you should read Benjamin Graham's book, *The Intelligent Investor*. It should be a permanent feature in your investment library, worn from frequent referral when you lose your way as an investor. Warren Buffet has called Graham's book, "By far the best book on investing ever written." Graham's book is indispensible to any one that desires to be an investor. His book is the first and last word on value investing, which is based on financial analysis with the express purpose of paying a bargain price today for the cash flows an investment is expected to generate in the future.

Using the long wave and other cycle analysis as part of an investment strategy should be secondary and complimentary to the basic approach of value investing. Understanding the long wave from an investment perspective is about understanding the forces that drive the global economy to increase or decrease the generation of cash flow for companies, and directing your investment decisions accordingly. When you meld the long wave perspective and smaller cycle research to discounted cash flow investing, you greatly increase your odds for success.

Reviewing a chart of the S&P 500 with a 20 year rate of return reveals the long wave impact on the opportunity to purchase future cash flows and, therefore, investment returns in general. An accurate long wave perspective and chart, such as the one included, helps determine when your value investing should be aggressive and when you should be extremely cautious relative to the long wave. Benjamin Graham suggested that systems for determining when to get in and when to get out should be deployed in value investing. Value investors are always in the situation of needing to add to or reduce their investment positions, and determining when to take profits when value investments become overvalued or raising cash is required.

Graham explains how to identify discounted value that has higher odds than average of delivering acceptable cash flow in the future. However, in *The Intelligent Investor* Graham is the advocate of what he terms a "formula timing device" or "formula timing plan" for determining when you buy and sell your value-based investments. Using comprehensive long wave analysis and the study of long wave dynamics is one version of such a formula timing plan. The approach also recognizes that the smaller market cycles added together make up the larger cycles. It is also important to note that the smaller cycles have mathematical and Fibonacci relationships with the larger cycles in price and time and fit into the larger cycles.

There appear to be 16 regular market cycles of an ideal 42-months in every long wave cycle. Each of these 42-month cycles consists of nine smaller approximate 20-week cycles. I termed the 20 week cycle the Wall Cycle in the 1995 edition of this book, in honor of PQ Wall who discovered its relationship to the long wave. Identifying the demarcation between cycles with overbought and oversold indicators produces my proprietary formula timing plan. This method can be used to buy shares exhibiting discounted value, or market indexes for more passive investors. The following are some excerpts from Graham regarding formula timing plans:

> In recent years certain compromise methods have been devised by which the investor can take some advantage of the stock market's cycles without running the risk of an unduly long wait or of "missing the market" altogether. These are known as "formula timing plans." The essence of all such plans is that the investor automatically does some selling of common stocks when the market advances substantially. ... Market movements are important to him in a practical sense, because they alternately create low price levels at which he would be wise to buy and high price levels at which he certainly should refrain from buying and probably would be wise to sell... The sovereign virtue of all formula plans lies in the compulsion they bring upon the investor to sell when the crowd is buying and buy when the crowd lacks confidence. If the reader adopts a formula plan today and it happens to turn out badly—because the market chances to soar upwards to unexpected heights and does not return—it will still prove to have been worthwhile. For the principle and the psychology will remain sound and applicable to the markets of the future, however far

removed their middle range may be from the line of the past.

Theory 144 Analytics is the formula timing plan of Long Wave Dynamics, LLC and that is followed and updated in *The Long Wave Dynamics Letter*. The objective is to discover entry and exit points for value investments. The long wave seasons, as well as the regular market cycles and the 20-week cycles reflect the natural disequilibrium that occurs in markets as part of the markets' ongoing pursuit of price equilibrium. My view is that equilibrium is an illusion, a theoretical notion of the midpoint between the inevitable two extremes of price. To return to our discussion of the application of the hard sciences to markets, the two extremes of markets, overvalued and undervalued, represent the degrees of freedom in the price field. The goal of a value investor that uses a formula timing plan is to buy value reasonably close to price lows and sell at price highs in the action of predictable market cycles. However, the investor should note that the price field is really just the manifestation of the field of human action in markets.

Investors should seek to buy undervalued assets for their above average expected ability to generate cash in the future. The ebb and flow of the long wave, regular market cycle and 20-week Wall cycles on market prices, should primarily be used by investors as a timing tool for the purpose of executing the purchase or sale of investments based on the underlying principles of value investing. Knowledge of these cycles, in conjunction with other technical tools–including Fibonacci ratios in price and time, as well as fast and slow stochastics–can be used as timing tools for your purchase and sell of value-based investments.

The problem with the past ten-plus years of market activity is that very little of it was true investing, as defined by Graham. Most of it was speculation, not investing. The reason to purchase any investment is to acquire the future cash flow the investment can generate at an acceptable price. If this is not the reason you purchase an asset, then you are not investing, you are participating in speculation, entertainment or something else.

The global crisis we now face represents the unwinding of decades of excessive speculation in stocks, real estate, bonds and commodities. Prices paid were too high to represent acceptable value as investments based on expected cash flows. Oversized returns that fed the speculation must decline. This will return prices to acceptable values based on the prospects of real future cash flows. Speculation feeds over production in goods and services in the long wave, which serves to make the prices overcorrect to the downside.

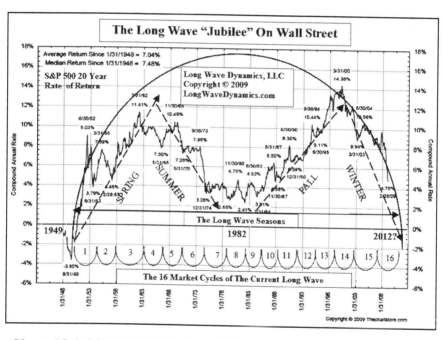

Chart 13.1 S&P 500 Inflation Adjusted 20 Year Rate of Return

The first matter to be covered when considering the long wave's effect on investments concerns timing. An economic cycle of 50 and 70 years duration is highly questionable as a precise investment-timing instrument. You cannot use the long wave to say with precision what will happen next year, or next month, in any market. However, the long wave's long-term trend impact on financial markets is critical information. The long wave's impact can make or break an investor's long-term returns—and even determine a company's survival. Investors should incorporate the most important elements of long wave theory into their general decision-making process. These are the overall inflationary and deflationary forces at work during the seasons of the advance and the decline.

Critical turning points that indicate the change of season in the long wave are what the investor should seek to best understand. The seasonal tendencies in the long wave are crucial to long-term returns. The end of the long wave fall and the advent of the winter season is the period during which history has shown a majority of investors have typically suffered significant losses. It would, therefore, behoove investors to position their portfolios defensively during such an important period-even if a deflationary long wave downdraft is a once-in-a-lifetime event. However, we are now deep into the long wave winter season and values are now beginning to emerge for the next long wave advance, but great caution should be exercised. The transition from spring to summer is also a difficult time for finding great value prices for future cash flows.

The overall allocation of a portfolio during each season of the long wave is obviously important. If critical turning points can be identified in the long wave cycle within a few years, the long wave is worth its theoretical weight in gold.

History has shown that the most successful stock investors take a long-term approach. Investors such as Benjamin Graham, Warren Buffett and John Templeton have proven to be incredibly successful with their approach of finding value in stocks and holding them for the long haul. They find companies that have excellent track records and good management and that offer products or services that are in growing demand. They find these stocks when they are undervalued relative to their potential.

In my view, the Graham's, Buffett's and Templeton's value approach to buying discounted cash flow will continue to be the best approach in investing, except during the summer and winter seasons of the long wave. Long wave theory suggests that two times every 50 to 70 years it would be wise to step aside from the worthy approach of buying value for the long haul, except in a few very select companies, and concentrate on the preservation of one's capital. The problem of course is identifying such major transitional periods.

The compound 20-year rate of return chart of the S&P is a great place to seek to identify long wave value opportunity (see Chart 13.1), and the bottom of a long wave winter. This chart is expected to go under the 0% return level before this long wave winter season is over, which would represent the buying opportunity of a lifetime. Graham's value based investment principles for purchasing discounted future cash flows should be applied aggressively if such an opportunity presents itself. The extreme overvaluation in 2000 is also demonstrated by this chart.

In a long wave winter the S&P 500 20-year total return (including dividends) could fall to 1% or lower. Deploy an aggressive strategy to buy discounted cash flow at such a time. The 20-year S&P total return is expected to approach 1% before this long wave winter season is over. An inflation adjusted version of the 20-year rate of total return chart may decline to 2% return or lower. The focus should be on the most oversold companies offering great values on future cash flows. Please note that the market may not reach these extreme oversold conditions in this long wave winter if it turns out to be a mild one. There will be many great opportunities to buy value based shares before such extreme lows are reached.

Knowledge of the long wave can be frustrating for investors, money managers, and brokers as the fall season draws to a close and in the early years of a long wave winter. Most investors would prefer to take the value approach and just hold solid companies with great prospects for the long haul. But the dangers of the short haul for most stocks outweigh the prospects of the long haul in the winter season of the long wave.

It should be noted that some stocks will do well even in a long wave winter. These will be companies that have low or no debts, have strong balance sheets, and are in high-growth sectors of the economy. A few stocks will actually do great during hard times, if their business model helps cut costs for other companies and they are in rapid growth areas. The problem is that such growth sectors are limited. But stocks aren't the only investment that must be considered. We must take a broad look at all investments and the long wave, including stocks, bonds, real estate, commodities and, later on, gold.

First we must refine our definition of the long wave in terms of investments. The long wave is a global cyclical inflationary expansion and deflationary contraction of economic activity at its very heart. The inflation and deflation of the cycle fluctuates between inflationary periods of economic expansion and deflationary periods of economic retrenchment. The long wave's effects on financial markets and investments are based on these basic trends. Extreme swings of investor psychology and the public mood help create and define these different periods of inflation and deflation. Economic expansion and contraction and the financial investment activity and speculation that surround the four seasons of the long wave are the backbone of the theory.

The periods of inflationary expansion and deflationary contraction must be broken down to the seasons to be useful for the investor. Analyst PQ Wall did some groundbreaking thinking on the key periods of price movement within the long wave by applying Spengler's notion of seasons to the long wave and investment markets. The first phase is early inflation, which is the spring season of the long wave. Late runaway inflation is the second phase, which can be equated with summer. Early deflation is the third phase, also known as the fall season of the cycle. The fourth and final phase in the long wave is a period of runaway deflation, the winter season for the global economy in the long wave.

In the same way that human efficiency is often highest in the spring and fall of the year, so, in the economic long wave, corporate efficiency is greatest in the spring and fall. Stock prices obviously perform best when corporate efficiency is the greatest. Let's briefly evaluate these four seasonal periods to see how they could affect the investor. In this chapter, we will cover the basics. The following chapters will go into more detail on how particular investment instruments are affected by the long wave cycle.

Early inflation takes place in the first half of the advance of the long wave, which is the spring season. In the most recent long wave cycle, this would represent the period from the late 1940s to the mid-1960s. Prices of raw materials, commodities, real estate, and stocks rise during this period. The level of general price increases during this period tends to be slow and steady–except for stocks, which trend up fairly strongly and make for great investments by outpacing inflation. Global stock markets did fairly well from the early 1950s until the mid-1960s. This was basically a period of slowly rising real prices and steady economic expansion. You won't get rich buying real estate early in this period, but patience will pay in the long run. Stocks would have bottomed in the previous long wave winter before the spring period had begun and would have entered their long wave climb. Interest rates also trend slowly upward during this period, so bond prices tend to turn down in a long wave spring and underperform other investments.

The summer period of late runaway inflation comes when the long wave economic expansion has heated up significantly. The generation that experienced the pain of the last decline is being replaced with a new generation of managers and investors. They have their hands on the controls of the engines of economic growth and finance. The latest long wave summer lasted from the mid-1960s to the late 1970s. Prices of commodities, real estate, and raw materials rise sharply during the overheated summer season. Look at what the price of oil, coal, gold, coffee, and lumber did during the last long wave summer. Investment in farmland, timber, oil wells, advanced agriculture production, construction, and energy production would make good investments early in this period.

Stocks tend to go through bear markets during the summer period. In real terms, the bear markets are severe during spring, but don't look as bad because of inflation. Stocks will sharply underperform real assets in the inflationary long wave summer. Inflation accelerates during this period, rising most rapidly in the last years, as was the case in the late 1970s. Everyone jumps into business because they believe the advance and prices are going to constantly increase, bringing ever-rising profits. Final spikes in raw materials and commodities come as the long wave summer period of late runaway inflation draws to a close; in the late 1970s, wheat, gold, and oil had inflationary blow offs. Interest rates rise sharply during the summer phase and reach their final highs at the end of the summer in late runaway inflation. This means bond prices decline sharply during a long wave summer, especially at its inflationary ending.

The primary recession of the long wave is what brings this runaway inflation phase to an end. The shift from late inflation in the long wave summer to early deflation in the long wave fall is taking place. The primary long wave recessions in the early 1920s and early 1980s are classic examples of this final price peak that ends the long wave summer period of fast-paced economic expansion and runaway inflation. The price of commodities, raw materials, and farmland reach their peak at this time. Raw material and commodity producers such as farming and energy can enter industry specific depressions when the runaway inflation ends.

The third phase is the fall period of the long wave, which is really the beginning of the long wave decline for the underlying economy. You would never know it because it is a period of positive feelings and is rife with financial speculation. All the money floating around in the global economic system after the summer inflationary expansion phase has to go somewhere; it pours into global stock markets and paper assets. Prices of raw materials and commodities are falling during this period, while wholesale and retail prices still rise-even if not as fast as they did in the runaway inflation phase. Speculation also hits residential and commercial real estate along with the stock markets of the globe during the early disinflation and deflation phase of the long wave fall season.

Interest rates fall during the early deflation of the fall season. There is typically a brief rise in interest rates and prices late in the fall season when the speculative manias take full effect and actually create significant demand for expansion. The activity at the end of the fall season, which appears to be an improving global economy, is the ultimate Indian summer boom. At the end of the early deflation fall phase, commercial and residential real estate reach their speculative peaks and the global economy is set up for the runaway deflation winter phase of the long wave decline. We witnessed this real-estate price peak in Japan in the late 1980s, just as we had seen it in the late 1920s in the United States. Since interest rates typically decline during the fall season, bond prices rise during most of the fall.

The next phase is the one remembered in the history books. The most fascinating thing about the runaway economic deflation of the winter phase of the long wave decline is that virtually no one sees it coming. The generation driving the system has come to believe first that inflation–and then that low inflation–is a permanent fixture in the system. Even as prices sink lower in deflation, the press and public are looking for inflation just around the corner–as falling prices accelerate. Virtually all U.S. prices were crashing in the early 1930s. Consider Japanese real estate in the early 1990s or in the United States in the early 1930s. During the early years of this long wave winter in the U.S. and many other countries low interest rates and deficient regulation fed a global real estate boom that has now gone major league bust.

Looking back over history, we see distinct phases of runaway long wave winter deflation following third-phase fall seasons in every long wave decline. Governments always try to step in and prop up prices because deflation destroys the basis of the financial system. In the 1990s the Japanese government was doing just that, but prices sank lower and lower. This is just what Hoover and Roosevelt tried in the 1930s. The U.S. government and Federal Reserve are once again trying to stop the deflation. But not even government is bigger than the long wave and global markets.

Almost all prices decline as the runaway deflation winter phase of the long wave accelerates. At some point, in the panic, chaos, and crisis of the runaway deflation, gold becomes a great investment because of the banking problems that always develop. The problem is that gold may get caught in the deflationary downdraft for a while before it shines as an investment due to its monetary value. Real assets such as real estate and commodities also fall in price during the long wave winter. Interest rates continue their downward trend, although they may spike up in a short-lived scramble for funds as the crisis accelerates in the beginning of winter. Interest rates don't reach their bottom until the end of the runaway deflation winter phase, just prior to the beginning of the next early inflation spring phase of the long wave; therefore, bond prices rally in winter. In general residential and commercial real estate, stocks, commodities, raw materials, and farmland have a tendency to decline in price as the long wave winter season works havoc and chaos on a global economy that is going through major restructuring in preparation for the next spring season.

There will always be brief inflationary rallies during long wave economic deflationary declines that in time give way to more economic deflation. Stocks and oil will have strong rallies in overall declines. The deflationary phase may last a decade or longer. Since the fall season was extended with liquidity fed booms the deflation in this winter season may last to the end of the current long wave.

It should be obvious that you don't want to own most stocks and real estate during the runaway deflation phase of the cycle, although there are exceptions to every rule. A few industries and numerous companies will do extremely well even during a long wave winter. High-quality corporate bonds and stable government securities will do well as interest rates decline in a long wave winter.

The problem with timing is that the bottom in each area of the economy will come at different times in the decline. The lowest levels in prices in stocks and real estate may come years apart. By the time it is clear that the economy has entered the next advance of the long wave, the latest spring cycle phase of early inflation, the best buys will have already been snatched up in most markets by savvy investors. The best buys in stocks will come before the next spring season begins. Investors aware of the long wave will have to be on their toes and ready to act contrary to popular opinion. When the public thinks the world has come to an end and is throwing in the towel, it means that we have most likely reached bottom and that a new advance of prosperity and expansion has already begun in the global economy. However, there will be false starts.

Even though the different inflationary and deflationary phases of the long wave give overall direction for different investments, you never want to cast your views in stone. In the different seasons of the cycle, there will always be particular cases that move against the general trend. Some commercial real estate did great in the late 1980s and early 1990s when the general trend was down. Some Japanese stocks have gone up during their vicious bear market, and a few U.S. stocks may be buy-and-hold investments. There will be a few buy-and-hold stocks in every bear market. Always be open to rare opportunities in every area of investment: stocks, bonds, real estate, commodities and gold.

In terms of real-estate, certain areas of every country will not be hit as hard as others and some cities within those general areas will fare better than most. Specific areas in a specific city will often do better than the entire city or region.

A word about market timing is important at this point. It has already been stated that the long wave can't be used for exact timing. Kondratieff himself said there must be a several-year margin of error when observing the turning points in the cycle. He was looking back at the history of actual events. Looking forward is even more difficult. Investors face the daunting task of looking into the future for what will happen to the economy, financial markets, and their investments. This is where the four Kitchin cycles that come within each season of the Kondratieff long wave are helpful and the 20-week Wall cycles within the Kitchin. See the Theory 144 Analytics chapter and The Theory 144 matrix chart to better understand how the smaller cycles fit in and create the market cycle framework for the long wave.

Investors should look at the powerful forces of the Kondratieff long wave for general guidance in asset allocation. When the signs of the major long wave seasonal turning points are clear in the marketplace, one should invest accordingly.

There is another critical consideration for investors in relation to the long wave. During the fall and winter of the cycle, there is a drastic increase in failures of financial institutions. Many banks, insurance companies, and brokerage companies face major trouble in the winter season–especially during the runaway deflation of winter. Banks collapsed in 1933, and Roosevelt declared a banking holiday. Many brokerage firms failed in the early 1930s. Many financial institutions have and will fail during the latest long wave decline. It is very likely that government bailouts will eventually be curtailed, shut down completely, or simply fail by being too-little-too-late. Budget constraints will be far more important this time than in the 1930s. The money just will not be there.

Millions of' investors will likely suffer because financial institutions that they do business with will go belly up. This has clearly already occurred. Anyone who has money on deposit with a financial institution should check the safety of that institution. This principle should apply at all times, but especially when faced with a winter season decline of the long wave cycle.

Eventually, we might have a true market-based financial system where financial institutions survive on their market and business merit and not with government props and bailouts that encourage bad management. It will be important to be able to decipher the safety of the institutions you do business with. Independent rating agencies should replace taxpayer funded government insurance for financial institutions. Depositors could find out the risk they are taking before they put money in. Risky banks would pay higher returns, while safe banks would pay lower returns. If a bank failed, it wouldn't cost taxpayers a dime. The system would be self-cleansing, not glued together with extorted funds from taxpayers to pay for bailouts, which make the banking system corrupt, weak, and inefficient.

Identifying the new opportunities of the spring season of the new long wave advance is just as critical as being cautious and conservative during the winter season. There will be an abundance of opportunities available, but it will take astute investors to identify the new trends and investments that will capitalize on the new economy that will emerge.

Investors always face tough decisions, but especially during critical periods in the long wave. The years we are presently in are just such a critical time.

To summarize the investment implications of the seasons of the long wave, the following review of the general tendency of markets should be helpful. In spring you have stocks up, commodities up, and bonds down. The summer season sees commodities up and stocks and bonds down. A long wave fall season sees stocks and bonds up and commodities down. During a long wave winter, bonds are up while stocks and commodities are down.

This chapter was meant as an overview of investments relative to long wave theory. The chapters that follow look at the effect of the Kondratieff long wave on specific types of investments. But first, a discussion and review of the inflation versus deflation arguments and schools of thought are necessary to clarify a few long wave fundamentals that have a major impact on various investment instruments.

CHAPTER 14:

INFLATION VS. DEFLATION

"If Americans ever allow banks to control the issue of their currency, first by inflation and then by deflation, the banks will deprive the people of all property until their children will wake up homeless"

Thomas Jefferson

"The real price of everything is the toil and trouble of acquiring it."

Adam Smith

Throughout this book we have reviewed both the inflationary expansion and deflationary contraction of the Kondratieff long wave. It is critical that the driving forces of the long wave inflationary advances and deflationary declines are understood and interpreted correctly, since these are the essential trends of the long wave. Every investment class is invariably influenced by where the global economy is in inflationary advances and deflationary declines of the long wave.

Typically, the long wave economic inflation in the advance and the economic deflation in the decline are mirrored by prices. By "economic" inflation or deflation, I mean what is going on in the real economy adjusted for price changes–how many houses, refrigerators, and manicures are being produced and demanded, regardless of their price. Basically, economic inflation and deflation refer to what the economy is doing–not the prices in the medium of exchange charged and paid to do it. It is important to note that there is a big difference between real economic inflation and deflation and "price" inflation and deflation.

By "price" inflation and deflation, we refer to the amount of a particular currency it takes to purchase desired goods and services such as houses, refrigerators, and manicures with dollars, yen, marks, pounds, and so on. Unfortunately, you can have rising prices and still have an economically deflating economy. The true meaning and implications of long wave inflation and deflation runs far deeper than just prices.

The heart of the Kondratieff long wave is the direction of global economic activity in terms of real output, real income, real gross domestic product, real global product, and, in the end, the real standard of living–all adjusted for rising or falling prices in the economy. These components, which are the central forces of the economy, are expanding year-after-year in the long wave advance and are more likely to contract year-over-year during a long wave decline, particularly in the winter season.

Perhaps far more important than even these economic factors is the critical long wave component of human psychology. The long wave advance is a period of expanding or inflating material human expectations and demands: The mood of humanity is positive. A long wave winter is a period of contracting or deflating human psychological expectations and demands of the material world: The mood of humanity is negative.

The underlying inflationary and deflationary economic forces and the trends of individual and social psychology are critical to long wave cycle theory. They are far more critical than price inflation during the advance and price deflation during the decline. Strip away the direction of prices in any particular currency and there would still be a clear boom and bust in the real economy of the long wave cycle. Prices usually reflect what is going on underneath the surface of the economy, but they don't have to.

In long wave advances and declines, prices have also gone through inflationary and in turn deflationary trends along with the real economy. However, in a more fundamental sense, this does not have to be the case for long wave theory to be valid. Without price observations, long wave theory goes a long way to explain what is happening in the global economy at any given time. Prices are just the more obvious icing on the long wave economic cake. This brings us to an important point of observation of long wave theory and its influence, particularly when it comes to investments and the impact of inflation and deflation.

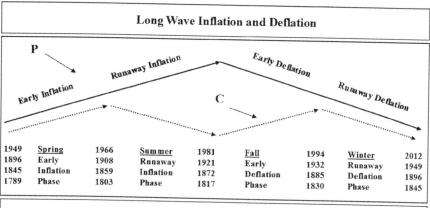

Chart 14.1 Long Wave Inflation and Deflation

The economic inflation advance of the long wave, the spring and summer seasons, typically see rising prices–price inflation, as in the cost of houses, refrigerators, and manicures. The greatest price inflation follows spring and comes in the summer, such as we saw in the late 1960s and the decade of the 1970s. The disinflation and some actual deflation, falling prices, come in the fall and economic deflation winter season of the long wave cycle. This was evident in the 1920s and the 1930s. It was also clearly the tendency in the 1980s and 1990s and has accelerated more recently as we head for the bottom of this long wave winter season. However, it is important to clarify that these price trends are surface reflections of the more fundamental economic inflation and deflation of the long wave cycle. Once again, that is to say that the key to the long wave is not inflation and deflation in prices, but in the developments within the real economy.

There has been a lot of discussion in recent years as to the nature of the economic crisis the global economy is facing. Basically, two schools of thought have emerged.

The largest camp has always been made up of those who see a hyperinflationary crisis in the cards. This group thinks the United States and other major economies are headed for a banana-republic-style economy of hyperinflation. They certainly have solid arguments favoring their view. Government debts and disturbing inflationary central bank policies are their best arguments. Chairman Bernanke of the Federal Reserve wrote of using a helicopter to dump money on the global economy in order to stop deflation. I must concede that the central bankers around the globe have shown a tendency to bailout economic problems by printing money, which has obvious inflationary implications. This has been the clear attempt as this long wave winter season has accelerated.

The smaller school of thought–wherein most of us quote Kondratieff and principles of long wave theory–has argued that falling prices and deflation are the most likely direction for the global economy during the most difficult years of this long wave winter decline. The forces created from debt defaults which produce what is termed a "debt deflation" is the linchpin of this argument. Excessive debt in the system combined with collapsing demand for goods and services, and very importantly, collapsing capacity utilization, are powerful deflationary forces. Based on the chart presented of the annual rate of change in the CPI, the long wave camp is presently carrying the day, but we recognize that Bernanke's helicopter still has plenty of fuel, in the form of all the taxpayer funded and insured liquidity he can pack in his helicopter. I must confess that part of me wants him to win this bet, since the implications of global long wave winter deflation are a very scary affair.

We are now at an interesting point in this grand experiment of a global fiat money based central banking system, as we are sailing full steam into the headwinds of a long wave winter. Central banks are seeking to create inflation during the greatest global debt bust in all of human history. This is where it gets really interesting. It is questionable whether governments truly can print their way out of a global deflationary debt bust due to the forces that are weighing on global prices during this long wave decline. This especially goes for economies with dominant global currencies that are less controllable by their respective central banks, namely the U.S. dollar. There are a lot of financial black holes to fill in a long wave decline, especially this one. There are over $50 trillion dollars of debt in the global economy, including the obligations of entitlement programs. If you add in all the theoretical derivative debt, you could get over $100 trillion, and some estimates go much higher. There has not been a prior test as to whether you can create inflation during the collapse of such a global empire of debt.

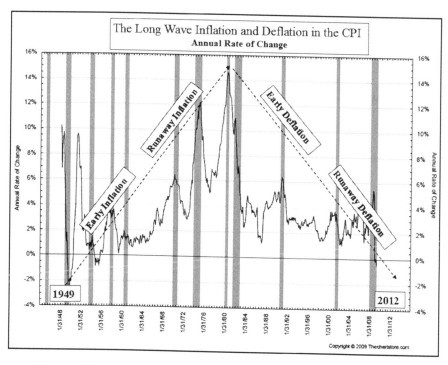

Chart 14.2 Long Wave Inflation and Deflation in the CPI

So what's the problem with priming the money pump and generating inflation? During the long wave winter season, such as the one we are now enjoying, the real demand for money is collapsing. We are in a fundamentally deflationary economic long wave descent, which makes creating price inflation a real effort for the Federal Reserve.

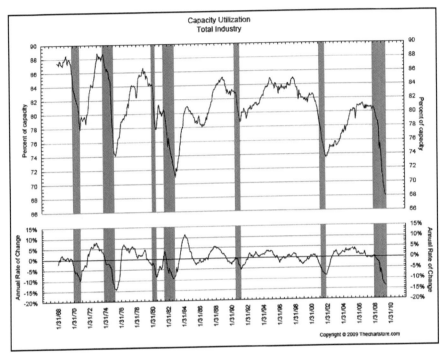

Chart 14.3 Capacity Utilization

This is where grasping the fundamentals of a long wave winter season are so crucial. It is not just a matter of creating money so banks, companies and individuals will borrow to produce and purchase goods. The global economy is overproducing every possible good and service you could possibly desire, but at a time when companies, individuals, and governments are borrowed to the hilt and debt loads are maxed out. Psychologically, a growing number of people are repulsed by the mindless consumerism that has coaxed them into the debtor's prison with no way out. They neither want more goods and services nor debt to purchase them. They don't want the new debt the central bankers want to create, even at 0% interest. Just look at the Japanese experiment of the past 20 years. The U.S. consumer has also lost the will and the way to buy more. They are literally and figuratively spent. The long wave winter season combines overcapacity in production with the reality of no more spending capacity, coupled with the psychological revulsion of spending.

U.S. capacity utilization just dropped under 70% for the first time since the Great Depression. What CEOs in their right minds are going to borrow money to build another plant and what bankers in their right minds are going to lend to them, when global capacity utilization is in free fall. It is not just every segment of the U.S., but every segment of the global economy that is overproducing, so it is difficult to force enough money into the system to ignite prices. At the slightest hint of demand manufacturers are cranking up production and cutting prices to make payroll and pay their debt. They have no choice. Competition is incredible. Clearly, it takes significant effort to create price inflation in a long wave decline.

It is a testament to the underlying power of a long wave decline that the incredible amounts of monetized debt–the trillions in new money created by the Federal Reserve in recent years by buying government debt and pumping dollars into the system–has not created a big jump in inflation. The hawks at the Fed are still waiting for this to happen; they have never met the late January chill of a Kondratieff winter. The new dollars aren't creating inflation because we are in a long wave winter that is oversupplying everything from toothpaste to luxury autos. This oversupply is keeping a lid on prices. Producers and retailers have trouble raising prices in a glut–even if there are more new dollars sloshing around in the system. There is another reason we see no real inflation while the Fed is making billions in new money: On top of the glut of goods, consumers are maxed out in debt and can't afford to buy the excess goods. The consumer is retrenching in a big way and becoming price conscious. This principle of consumers being maxed out financially and psychologically is a key to the inner workings of the long wave inflation to deflation clock that ticks full circle.

In the 1990s the new dollars that central banks were creating to stop the shifting long wave seasons from fall to winter were chasing financial assets and pouring into stocks and bonds. They were perpetuating the long wave financial bubble in global stock and bond markets. All the Fed has to do is look at falling producer prices and the stagnant consumer price index and then look at stocks trading at 30-to-40-plus times earnings to know where the new dollars were going. Next the real estate bubble was pumped up from the Federal Reserve's easy money attempts to prevent the natural deflation of the emerging long wave winter. The new dollars the Fed was creating were producing financial inflation instead and real estate inflation, wages and goods and services price inflation. Eventually stock market and real estate bubbles collapsed due to the collapse of the credit bubble. This came in spite of the Federal Reserve pumping money in an attempt to prevent long wave deflation, even if they did not realize the deflationary forces are being driven by the long wave. They only achieved their goals temporarily, but the excessive credit is now only feeding the deflation and making it worse than it otherwise would be.

Don't interpret my observations as Fed bashing; they are not. The Fed has to manage money supply and economic growth targets, while the government spends itself blind drunk on the taxpayers credit tab. The Fed could do its job effectively if government would control spending and run a balanced budget. Government spending is to blame for this mess, not the Federal Reserve System and fiat money.

The Fed knows it cannot seek to generate inflation forever without destroying the creditworthiness of the U.S. government, its own credibility, and in time, the entire global financial system. The Fed knows that new money-financed bubbles do not exhale in an orderly fashion. They bust. Most importantly the Fed's knows that recent aggressive money creation and quantitative easing to stop deflation will ultimately hurt United States debt ratings if they go too far. At some point too much U.S. debt will ultimately decrease the willingness of investors to hold dollar-based debt. There is only one way that the United States government can defend its credit rating and that is by ending runaway spending and reducing the United States deficit as a percentage of GDP.

The U.S. government and the Fed cannot both stop deflation and maintain their AAA rating in this long wave winter season. They will have to choose. My belief is they will choose the AAA rating over stopping the long wave deflation. They will slowdown the rate of growth in spending, which will insure the natural forces of long wave winter deflation.

Then there are the trade war implications in a long wave winter of "beggar thy neighbor," dollar-pumping, currency-devaluation policies. We have already reviewed the pressure for trade war and the sensitivity of all global trading partners to any acts that are perceived as trade protectionism. The fight against deflation that becomes an official act of currency devaluation by any country is an official unfair trade practice. It is the firing of real shots in global trade warfare. This is a critically important point in terms of where the global economy is in the long wave winter. And it has everything to do with the ultimate outcome of inflation vs. deflation.

Fighting deflation and pursing inflationary fiscal and monetary policy is the same thing as pursuing a weak dollar. If you are a trading partner with the U.S. you view any government and central bank policy that is seeking to support and create demand for U.S. business by decreasing the value of the U.S. dollar as an act of unfair protectionism. An anti deflation and weak dollar policy is being viewed or will be viewed as shots fired in a trade war by our trading partners and will increasingly be viewed as unfair heavy artillery.

If you are China trying to sell tires in the U.S., or India selling pharmaceuticals in the U.S., then a weak dollar caused by the Federal Reserve trying to stop deflation is a trade subsidy and protectionism for the U.S. tire and pharmaceutical industries. If capacity utilization were running over 90%, there would not be a problem, but it is not, it is below 70% and falling. Remember both the U.S., China and India are all seeing capacity utilization fall in their tire factories and pharmaceutical factories. The factories in the U.S., China and India have an imperative to pay their wages and pay their bank debt. It is an issue of survival.

Herein lies the deflationary debt-collapse Catch 22 regarding inflationary fiscal and monetary policy that seeks to stop the deflation. U.S. inflationary policy is clearly an attempt to export its deflation to the rest of the world by boosting U.S. demand and making U.S. goods and services cheaper in the global marketplace than foreign goods and services. Every high school physics student knows that every action produces an equal and opposite reaction. It's also true in global trade. Every country in the world will respond in some manner to avoid importing U.S. deflation. They will in turn seek to drive down the value of their own currencies or put in place tariffs or subsidies to make their exports more attractive on global markets. If they take the route of closing their borders, then U.S. manufacturers will lose markets and capacity utilization will fall faster, driving even more deflation. With global capacity utilization collapsing in a long wave winter, every dollar of deflation the U.S. exports by flooding world markets with dollars or protecting its own markets in other ways, will produce a dollar of deflation in China or another country–in the price of tires, wheat, cars, chewing gum, etc.

One of the clearest writers and lucid thinkers on the risk of deflation thus far during this global crisis is New York Times columnist and Nobel Laureate economist Paul Krugman. It would be well advised to follow his views regarding deflation as this long wave winter unfolds. The deflation discussion has been moving into the mainstream, and Krugman would be an expert to follow on the matter of inflation vs. deflation in the final years of this long wave winter, and the risk of inflation as a new long wave advance begins in the years ahead. You are encouraged to read Krugman's 1999 article, "Can Deflation be Prevented?" This piece is more relevant today than when he wrote it and addresses the subjects of 1) Excess capacity, 2) The liquidity trap, 3) Saving, investment, and the paradox of deflation, and 4) Policy implications.

In this chapter we have addressed the connection between excess capacity and deflation, and aspects of the liquidity trap and deflation, which Krugman articulated as what occurs when "further increases in the real money supply have no further effect on real spending." Krugman's (1999) ideas and discussion of the paradox of deflation related to saving and investment is unique and essential.

> Japanese-type deflation is an economy's way of "trying" to get the expected inflation it needs. This conclusion sounds very peculiar, but on reflection it is the same as the logic we commonly use in thinking about asset prices. Suppose that a country reduces its interest rate: this makes its bonds unattractive to investors unless they expect the currency to rise; what must happen then, as Dornbusch taught us, is that the currency must overshoot, depreciating below its long-run value in order to be expected to rise. The logic of deflation in a liquidity trap is the same; it is because spending in the current period is unattractive unless prices are expected to rise that the current price level is pushed down.

Krugman's 1999 article "Deflationary Spirals" and 2003 piece "Fear of a Quagmire?" are also recommended reading. He is expected to keep readers abreast of his thinking on the matter of deflation as this global crisis unfolds.

Certainly the foremost undisputed expert on the subject of deflation during this global crisis is Robert Prechter of Elliot Wave International fame. His book *Conquer the Crash; You Can Survive and Prosper in a Deflationary Depression* is must reading for anyone interested in the deflationary vs. inflationary argument that will be settled in the next few years. New Classics Library released an updated edition of this book in 2009.

Those who believe we are in for hyperinflation are making a simple call. They believe the Fed will support the declining economy and try to save the imploding global debt structure over the value of the dollar. You have to believe that such polices will not produce retaliation in the form of trade subsidies that will produce even more global deflation in goods and services. They believe the Fed, as the lender of last resort, will monetize at full throttle, creating new money by buying as much debt for as long as it takes to stimulate the economy, even at the risk of hyperinflation. I've not changed my view in 25 years. This won't happen, even though they appear to be trying it now. The Fed will not simultaneously destroy the U.S. AAA debt rating and fan the fires of global trade wars, at least for an extended time. The Federal Reserve will realize the need to cut its losses, huddle with and force the U.S. government to rein in spending, end the attempt at reflation, and support the dollar, necessarily taking the deflationary route, which, all things considered, is a better solution, than the disaster of the hyperinflationary route that will wreak havoc on all concerned.

The only way to hyper inflate and avoid a currency crisis in the sort of trouble that's brewing would be an international hyperinflation effort, with all central banks in perfect agreement and working in unison in the midst of a global panic. Nationalism and introspection are on the rise in a long wave winter. PQ Wall (1994) used the term "fortress America" to describe the emerging mentality in the United States. This is a trend we are going to see accelerate in all nations around the globe. In the real world of economics and finance, nations tend to give up global cooperation in a long wave winter in order to address domestic realities and necessities. All nations turn inward to correct the many problems created by a long wave decline, especially as the chill of winter goes to the bone.

The complex synchronized plan and agreements it would take to create hyperinflation in leading nations will never come about. Gridlock happens. By the time they all agreed on the plan, we will be registering the coldest day of this Kondratieff winter season. I personally believe that the resolution of the global crisis we face will be price deflationary. Prices will fall along with the real economy. In many respects, it already is deflationary: falling real-estate values in Japan, England, the United States and other countries; falling farmland prices and commodity prices; and falling consumer prices. However, if a government or its central bank is dead-set on creating inflation during a Kondratieff wave decline, and is willing to destroy the value of its currency to do so, it is conceivable that it could be done, but historical examples are few and far between. Central banks are in fact trying their best to inflate during this latest long wave decline, or at least stop the growing deflationary forces. We now all have a front row seat in the global debate between inflation and deflation in a long wave winter. A winner will be decided. Presently, it looks like deflation is winning.

As the global economy seeks to survive this long wave winter, central banks and national governments walk a narrow path between price inflation and price deflation. Imagine a narrow path running along the center of the face of a huge cliff. For most of the fall season, the path is fairly wide. But the further the economy moves into the real long wave economic contraction and fundamental deflation in terms of real income and real growth, the harder it is to balance the emerging economic forces pulling between price deflation and price inflation. The path narrows until there are no alternatives left, prices have to move sharply in one direction or the other. But remember, the real economy will take its predestined, contracting, deflationary direction no matter what prices do.

In *Black Swan* (2007) Nassim Nicholas Taleb recognized the increasingly narrow path that the central banks and national governments are walking between inflation and deflation. In a May 2009 article, Bloomberg quoted him as saying:

> "The global economy is facing 'big deflation,' though the risks of inflation are also increasing as governments print more money, Taleb told the conference organized by Bank of America-Merrill Lynch. Gold and Copper may 'rally massively' as a result, he added."

You cannot sustain stable or no price changes, while, on one hand, incredibly powerful deflationary forces, such as bankruptcy, overproduction, and declining asset values are pulling the system into contraction, and, on the other hand, central banks are monetizing debt and printing money like there is no tomorrow, trying to inflate enough to patch the system together, so it will keep expanding. One or the other will win out and change prices. No central banks are talented enough to do a balancing act on a path that doesn't exist. And there is no turning back to where the economy began. Time pushes the global economy ever forward. One direction or the other must be taken: hyperinflation or deflation.

The bankers and politicians want to print enough money to pay for the mistakes of overshooting the economic target during the long wave advance. However, they don't truly want inflation. This is why they usually fail to inflate prices. They don't realize the magnitude of the deflationary forces and don't go far enough with the inflation.

History has shown us that bankers and politicians have never been able to move quickly enough on monetary and fiscal policy stimulus to counter the deflationary forces of a long wave decline. They are also restrained by global market forces more than ever before, forces that limit their options. We have always seen price deflation as well as economic deflation during long wave winter declines of the past. It is legitimate to ask whether they can create inflation during this decline since they have never done so before. I'm betting on history, which suggests they won't be able to inflate their way out of the latest long wave winter either.

The German economy during the fall and winter seasons of the 1920s and 1930s is one of the few examples of hyperinflation when the global long wave was in its decline phase. The central bank and government of Germany were able to create inflation by monetizing debt and printing currency. One positive aspect of this, at least from the government's perspective, was that their World War I debts were inflated away, which may have had something to do with the policy. However, it must be noted that the German mark was not the world's reserve currency in the 1930s. If it had been, they may not have been able to inflate.

A question obviously worth asking is whether the United States will be the Germany of this long wave winter season. The government could attempt to avoid the inevitable consequences of the real economy in a natural long wave winter deflation. I'm keeping an eye on Federal Reserve policy and government fiscal policy. They probably won't move fast enough, and the building global deflation will kill their efforts. However, I intend to pay close attention to the price data to see if the U.S. central bankers and politicians are able to take the route of hyperinflationary Germany.

Most can make the inflationary argument. The greatest argument against deflation and in favor of inflation is that the monetary power of central bankers and fiscal power of politicians are more powerful than ever before. They have clearly stated that they are willing to use their power to avoid deflation. Quantitative easing (i.e., the Federal Reserve buying U.S. debt), is a powerful tool. With the Monetary Act of 1980, the Federal Reserve can monetize all debt–even the local sewer-bond debt of towns in Zimbabwe. The political and monetary tools for inflation are more powerful during this decline than at any time in history. This basically means the Fed can create–at the drop of a hat or the stroke of a computer key–an incredible amount of dollars, which they hope will chase goods, services, and assets. However, consumers and businesses must be willing to spend the money the Fed is willing to create.

If global central banks take the inflationary route, it only means there are more dollars, yen, or pounds in the system. It doesn't create a growing economy in real terms. Price data only measures the economy in debased terms, not real terms. Remember, the real economic and psychological contraction is still going to go on during the long wave decline. To a real extent the old cliché is accurate: The governments and central banks that chose inflation would only be pushing on strings. They may create a pile of higher prices, but no real economic growth. They would not stop the long wave winter season from running its course, only shift perceptions of what is happening.

It is possible we see a situation where price inflation hits a few countries in the global economy such as the United States and Japan, which may develop even more aggressive inflationary policies. The Federal Reserve may cave into government pressure, throw all caution to the wind, and give into government spending demands with unlimited quantitative easing. Germany, Switzerland, and other nations with more conservative fiscal and monetary policy this time could see deflation. In fact, Switzerland just recorded a solid deflationary consumer price number in 2009. I doubt this division will occur and I think we will all see price deflation before this long wave is over. Even so, I'm not willing to say price inflation cannot occur in a long wave winter if the bankers and politicians go over the deep end and totally embrace inflationary mechanisms in a state of money-printing panic. Russia may be the best candidate for a hyperinflationary depression like Germany the last time around, and the political fallout could be similar. Russia is already in bad economic shape and has proven it is willing to destroy its currency for political purposes. Russian efforts at reform could backfire. The people may endorse totalitarian rule in an effort to fix the crisis.

This book has presented a case for price deflation in a long wave decline. The following chapters on different investments also take this approach. Obviously, if I'm mistaken and we do see hyperinflation in a long wave decline, it will change some of my investment philosophy. However, I believe it will be easy enough to see inflation coming and to make the necessary changes. There will be clear signs that inflation and hyperinflation are on the way in any particular country. The consumer price index will see occasional rises during the long wave decline and real economic deflation but they should never spike to double-digit levels during the duration of the decline. If double-digit inflation, or even levels over five percent annualized, hold on the consumer price index or producer price index for more than a few months, a red flag should go up immediately: Banana-republic-style hyperinflation could be coming to the first world. All thanks should be sent to the U.S. Congress; the Federal Reserve is just reacting to the outrageous debts created by the politicians that are spending your money.

Another possibility is that we could see global deflation for a few years in the decline and then a drastic change. Bankers and politicians could then use the crisis to consolidate their monetary and financial power and resolve to inflate the system. We could see a global effort on the part of central bankers to inflate the system. We could come out of the decline and into the next long wave advance with much more inflationary pressure than previous cycles. This would produce deflation-inflation whiplash. Once again, the politicians would be fighting last year's battles while the markets move on into the new economy.

In conclusion, we are rapidly approaching the end of the path in this long wave winter. Since most are still expecting inflation, deflation remains the most likely outcome. The U.S. government debt credit rating will be defended by a slowdown in spending. When government taps the brakes to defend its credit rating and in response to a growing global trade crisis from long wave overproduction, deflation will slam the economy in the final years of this long wave winter.

It is important to note that if my primary count for the smaller market cycles is accurate, we are not far from the beginning of the next inflationary long wave advance. Although I'm skeptical about the Federal Reserve and other central banks creating inflation in the next few years, there is a very good chance that the liquidity injected into the global economy in the final years of this long wave decline will create major pent up inflation for the next long wave advance and spring season. As major new global markets recover with rapid growth, such as China, Brazil, Russia, India and others, the inflation forces will be powerful. There should be no doubt about it, the next long wave advance is going to be spring loaded for inflation. This will have a major impact on your investments and should be considered in your investment strategy.

Chapter 15:

STOCKS AND THE RULE OF EIGHT

"Cast thy bread upon the waters: for thou shalt find it after many days. Give a portion to seven, and also to eight; for thou knowest not what evil shall be upon the earth."

King Solomon

"I don't believe any of us have the pretension of believing that by being very good analysts, or by going through very elaborate computations, we can be pretty sure of the correctness of our results."

Benjamin Graham

"What mental grasp, what sense have they? They believe the tales of the poets and follow the crowd as their teachers, ignoring the adage that the many are bad, the good are few."

Heraclitus

"He who wishes to be rich in a day will be hanged in a year."

Leonardo da Vinci

One of our main objectives in studying the long wave and the long wave family of cycles is to develop a formula timing plan. The purpose in having a formula timing plan is for determining when to buy stocks based on the basic Benjamin Graham principles of value based future cash flow investing. The plan is also used to determine when to take profits, and when to reallocate stock investments. This chapter reviews the basics of the long wave impact on stocks and presents charts, which demonstrate our cycle based formula timing plan for stocks.

Also essential to our approach is that when invested in stocks we also follow what we call "The Rule of Eight." This is the rather simple but important proposition that the minimum number of stocks in which you should invest is eight for the purpose of diversification. You may invest in more than eight, which makes sense for many investors, but no less than eight. You should have no more than two investments in any one industry if you are only invested in eight enterprises, and your minimum of eight investments should ideally be diversified globally. For large investors and institutional investors additional diversification is obviously required.

Global stock markets have long been barometers of the world's economic and business activities, as well as measurements of swings in human emotions and expectations. As an investor begins to fully realize the great impact the long wave can have on the global economy and financial markets, questions as to its effects on stock prices are typically the first to be asked. The stock markets of the world hold the future to the lives of millions of people whose retirement and therefore future sustenance are dependent on the performance of individual stocks, mutual funds, pension funds, and personal investments in global equity markets.

Before reviewing stocks in light of long wave theory, it is important to note that to sell all stocks, based on belief in the beginning of a long wave winter, or to buy any stock during a long wave spring for fall season, based exclusively on long wave theory, would be foolish. There will always be a few great opportunities for stock investors, even during a long wave winter. Some of the industries that will lead the next long wave advance have already been formed and are emerging. The key is to find the diamonds in the long wave rough. The objective isn't to sell all stocks in a long wave winter, but to buy and hold only the right stocks.

In general, global stock-price trends in the long wave are fairly simple. Each long wave experiences two great bull markets: in the spring and fall seasons. Each long wave experiences two periods marked by a number of bear markets: the summer and winter seasons. Stocks rise during the long wave spring along with a slow rise in inflation and improved corporate efficiency.

They experience a few corrections along the way. In the summer season, stocks have major problems due to inflation and rising interest rates that destroy corporate efficiency. Stocks boom in the long wave fall as disinflation and corporate costs–wages and raw materials–stagnate and decline, thus boosting corporate efficiency. In the winter, it is severe deflation that harms corporate efficiency and creates bear markets in global stock markets. Note that these are general trends. The exceptions will still offer reward to investors.

Remember that the long wave represents what is going on in the real economy. The constant-dollar Dow, which adjusts stock prices for inflation, actually experiences a crushing bear market in a long wave summer. In real dollars, the long wave summer bear market, during the season of high inflation, may well be worse than the long wave winter bear market, during the season of deflation. The summer bear market in real stock prices is hidden by inflation. In winter, the deflation makes the bear market feel worse than it actually is in terms of the real prices in the economy, since the dollars that represent stock prices are typically increasing in purchasing power.

Stock prices rise more slowly in nominal and real terms in the spring but explode upwards in nominal and real terms in the fall season, spiking to new highs in the last few years of fall. The price of a majority of stocks will decline during the bear markets of the long wave winter season. Fortunately, bear markets occur far more quickly than bull markets. The sharp bear markets in a long wave winter will present incredible buying opportunities for long-term investors. By the time investor psychology has reached bottom, many great stocks will already have begun their next long wave advance ahead of a new bull market.

To understand how the long wave winter will unfold, it is important to closely observe the long wave seasons and smaller cycles. The 42-month Kitchin cycle is more important than the long wave or long wave seasons for stock investing. The 42-month period is simply the ideal; the actual cycles, although they may run exactly 42-months on occasion, will typically run short or long by Fibonacci ratios to the ideal (i.e., ~38.2%, ~50.0%, or even ~61.8% short or long). These will also correlate, but not exactly, to the regular business or trade cycles that are often impacted by fiscal and monetary policy around elections. Stock will lead the real economy by six months or more, both up and down. What is important is where these cycles come within the long wave cycle. Remember, there are ideally four Kitchin cycles in each of the four seasons of the long wave. That means there are 16 Kitchin cycles in one long wave. Identifying and paying attention to where a market is in the Kitchin cycles will greatly assist investors in timing buying and selling opportunities.

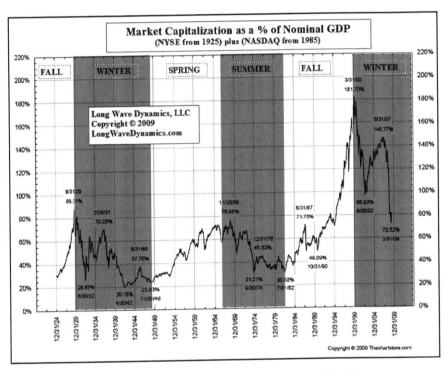

Chart 15.1 The Long Wave in Stock Market Capitalization as % of Nominal GDP

Just as important, and potentially more important to long term returns, are the 20-week Wall cycles. There are nine such Wall cycles in every Kitchin cycle. (See the Theory 144 Analytics chapter for a chart of the Theory 144 matrix to see the various relationships between all the cycles.) To use long wave dynamics to develop a formula timing plan for stock investing, you must use the smaller cycles, which could be viewed as the ribs of the long wave.

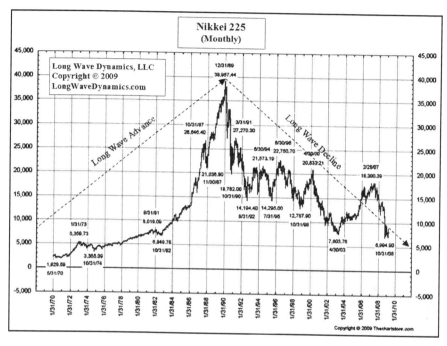

15.2 S&P 500 Since 1982 and the Kitchin Cycles

Many were under the illusion that a major bear market in stocks could never happen again because of new rules, regulations, and government safety nets. They pointed to increased margin requirements, close SEC regulation, welfare, and government financial insurance. Long wave theory, however, with the weight of 200 years of history on its side, demonstrates that a bear market in stocks, the major generational long wave bear market, is inevitable.

The turn of global stock markets mark their slow realization and acceptance that the global economy really is entering a protracted economic decline that could last for more than a decade. However, financial markets are smarter than the individuals who drive them, and it takes investors a while to catch on to the new facts of life. A few of those who only become aware of the long wave economic winter as global stock markets accelerate their descents, and those who can't handle the new realities, are sometimes seen jumping from bridges and windows.

How does this long wave in equities really occur? In the chapter on psychology, we briefly explored the generation gap and demonstrated that as old pessimistic blood is drained from the leadership in the economy, a new generation and breed of risk takers take over. The great pendulum of pain and pleasure takes its rhythmic course, and the pain is long forgotten. The belief that the economy can only expand takes precedence in a long wave advance. The liquidity created during the long wave advance has to have some place to go. It moves into stocks during the fall season.

When the bullish psychology takes over, everyone believes markets will hit a pothole on occasion, but no one really believes we could ever skid off the road. This creates a natural upward bias in stock markets based on what one could call the pendulum power of the generation gap. The upward momentum of the markets becomes somewhat of a sporting event, and everyone truly wants to see the score get higher and higher. The only problem is that in a real sense the forces and people driving the market are all on the same team, creating the illusion that everyone can be a winner.

It was humorous to listen to the great variety of reasons put forward for the bull markets of the latest speculative fall season. One day it was interest rates, the next day it was earnings, then came falling oil prices. Sure, there are the intermediate cyclical conditions and the technical factors that all play an important role in the market, but the most important and overriding element comes from the sweeping effect of the Kondratieff long wave as nothing–including the Dow Jones Average in New York, Nikkei in Tokyo, Hang Seng in Hong Kong, FT 100 in London, CAC 40 in Paris, DAX index in Frankfurt, and all other global markets–can escape its relentless path.

The forces driving global bull stock markets in the 1980/90s were the same forces that were at work in the 1920s. Remember, the United States was the leader of the long wave last time around, while Japan assumed financial speculation leadership this time around. On August 21, 1921, the Dow Jones Industrial Average was sitting at 63.90. In just over eight years, on September 3, 1929, the Dow hit 361. This height was not seen again for 25 years, late in 1954. In the interim, the Dow bottomed at 40.56 on July 8, 1932. The parallels with the Japanese market in the 1990s were ominous, but few outside of Japan played attention. In the 1950s, the Japanese market was less than 500; in the 1980s, it started out under 7,000. It rose to over 39,000 in December 1989 and has since plunged in a protracted long wave winter.

The Nikkei followed the exact pattern sketched by the U.S. market during the fall season of the 1920s when it plunged in the long wave winter of the Great Depression. The worst in Japan could be over, but the Japanese market could easily see a decline of 80 to 90 percent or better before this bear has finished its mauling. There will always be bear-market rallies of as much as 50 percent retracement of declines or better between each stage of the bear-market decline.

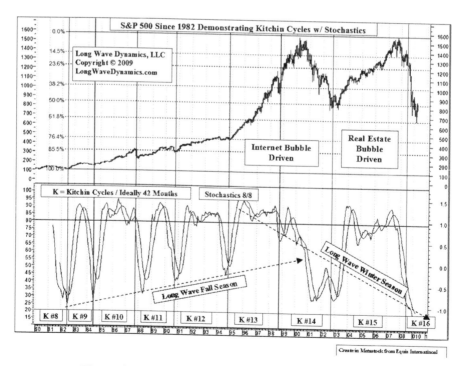

Chart 15.3 The Long Wave in the Nikkei 225

Many would like to attribute the entire crash in the markets in the 1930s to speculation and the lenient rules and regulations that led to the boom and, therefore, the bust. These were factors, but are in themselves reflections of the psychology of the long wave. The many long wave forces at work are responsible for the collapse, and not only investors buying on margin. An article (Feinberg 1987, 226-227) that quoted Robert Prechter, discussing a crash to come during the latest long wave fall season and anticipating the long wave winter season, had exceptional insight into the foolishness of faith in today's margin requirements. I chose to leave the older reference in this new edition as it demonstrates that many saw the global crisis of this long wave winter building far in advance:

> Those hoping that any future collapse will be cushioned by post-1929 safeguards are misguided, Prechter says. Like fellow doomsayers James Grant and Jim Rogers, an investor, Prechter believes that today's 50 percent margin requirement, as opposed to 10 percent in 1929, offers only illusory protection. 'These days,' he says, 'with options and futures and second mortgages, you can get much more than 10-to-1 leverage. And at the top, people will be tremendously leveraged.'

Although many who invested in the market in the 1920s were wiped out, there were numerous astute investors who became quite wealthy during the period. There are a number of cases of people in high corporate positions whose companies and banks were boosting the market but who were personally selling out or going into short positions. They made vast fortunes while the rest of the world was in panic. The same thing clearly occurred again this time around in the latest long wave winter season.

As upper middle-class society becomes more and more affluent during an upswing and expansion, more people are able to invest in the markets with their increasing discretionary income. In the United States in 1952, only approximately 6.5 million Americans owned stock, which was close to 1 person in

20. By the early 1990s, this number had grown to better than 60 million by some estimates, or more than one in four. By the late 1990s top, these numbers were greatly exceeded, with over 50 percent of all families owning stocks, and cabbies were once again pitching stocks to their fares.

The sad fact is that the axiom of greed takes over late in the long wave fall season and a large majority of the newcomers are novices. They always want to stay until the end of the party. After volatile corrections in the market that always seem to rebound, investors decide they have become smart and will buy and hold for the long haul. As the market collapses further, they change their minds and begin to sell. Many ride the long wave down until most of those who bought at the top sell at the bottom.

Let's take a closer look at the forces other than psychology that drive booming stock markets higher in the long wave fall season, and examine the forces that drive stock prices lower in the Kondratieff winter decline. There is an added increase to the profits and earnings picture by the existence of the long wave fall season. The early deflation of the fall season creates a corporate efficiency boom. A great deal of the improving profit picture is due to sagging and falling prices. This sounds unusual at first, but when we take a closer look, the reasons become evident. The falling prices in the fall season first come in raw materials and commodities. For most industries, this means their cost of production is lower. Of course, falling prices are not good for the commodity and raw material producers. The depression experienced by agriculture and commodity producers in the fall is an example of what is to come in the rest of the economy in the long wave winter.

The falling prices seen in commodities in the 1920s and the 1980/90s were due to overexpansion and overcapacity, which created oversupply. Raw material producers had extrapolated the growth rates of the long wave advance into the future, but the long wave hit the fall season phase of economic decline. We all know that when the rest of the industrial world gets savings from commodities and raw materials industries, it is quite some time before those savings are passed on to the consumer, and they never pass those savings along entirely.

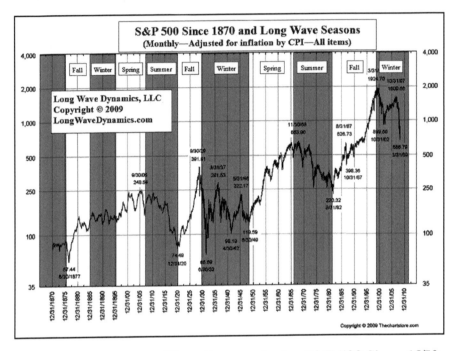

Chart 15.4 The Long Wave Seasons in the S&P 500 Since 1870

The retail gasoline industry is a perfect and clear example. When we see a fall in oil prices we do not see gas prices drop the same percentage at the pump. This happens in all areas of the economy during the long wave fall season. Costs are dropping, yet retail prices are holding their ground or even advancing. This naturally produces an increase in profits and earnings for non-raw-material producers. As the quarterly reports are released, higher earnings drive up the price of stocks. However, when the fall season has ended and winter decline begins, it is the consumer-goods manufacturers, wholesalers, and retailers who are overproducing or over expanding and have excess supply and space.

During the long wave fall season a cooling of inflation and dropping prices is perceived as an improving and stabilizing effect when taking an overall view of the economy. This positive perception helps bring buying strength into the stock market. There is evidence to suggest that stocks can maintain a higher price-to-earnings ratio during a period of disinflation. Lower costs in the form of lower commodity and raw materials prices make most industries more efficient during the fall season.

Because of the overexpansion, there is no need for mature companies to sink as much investment into new capital outlays. One only has to look at textiles, computers, autos, agriculture, and other industries to see that the entire world was overproducing in the latest fall season and into the winter. There is certainly capital investment, expansion, and development going on in the fall season, but the bulk of this is mostly by new and young companies. Many of these new companies go heavily into debt and do not survive the decline.

Mergers, takeovers, and stock buybacks sweep the markets in fall seasons of the long wave. The true reasons are simple, while telling of the reckoning that is to come. If a company had excess capital and profits during the long wave advance, it automatically went into new outlays and expansion of production facilities. This was because the economy was still in its rapid growing stage, and every dollar was needed for investment to keep up with growing demand. When companies no longer need to spend as much cash for expansion, you see large corporate cash positions.

The 1980/90s fall season in the U.S. was a case in point. As corporate cash positions begin growing during this time of slowed expansion and higher profits, there is the natural tendency to start shopping around to see what can be bought. The sad situation is that debt is added to the cash in these buyouts. This causes companies to take on more and more debt when the smart move would be to pay down existing debt. Companies should tighten the belt in preparation for more difficult times to come.

Just as in the 1920s, the 1980/90s saw a global explosion in acquisitions, mergers, and buyouts. The size and types of takeovers were unprecedented at their peak. The buyout mania that swept the globe and then ended abruptly proved to strengthen arguments of the long wave's existence. The same

thing occurred in the 1920s and will no doubt take place during
the next speculative fall season in the future.

The fact is that during this latest fall season the general
economy was overextended. The big money was not going into
new layouts and production capacity, but into the financial
markets in the form of takeovers and acquisitions.

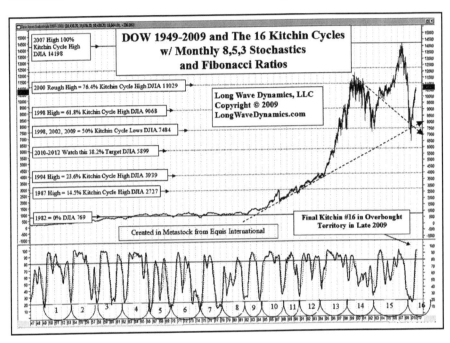

Chart 15.5 DOW 1949-2009 and the Kitchin Cycles

When is less more? When the number of outstanding shares
on the market is shrinking, while the number of dollars chasing
those shares is rapidly increasing. All of these takeovers, as well as
the stock repurchases by many companies who were seeing their
own stocks as attractive investments, were rapidly diminishing
the number of shares on the market. Estimates show that the
number of outstanding shares on the New York Exchange fell
sharply throughout the 1980s. When supply is shrinking and
demand is on the rise, the market has only one place to go:
up. The massive global bull markets of a fall season pull small
investors into global stock markets at the top to a degree not
seen since the last long wave stock peak.

The trend toward stock buyouts changes late in the fall season, as fall turns to winter. The trend of a shrinking number of shares on the market reversed in 1990. This is because the number of shares hitting the market rises as a public hungry for gains buys up the new stock offerings and new issues at a record pace. Record numbers of new stocks were listed on global markets in the early 1990s and then late into the 1990s with the Internet bubble, along with new offerings of mature companies. The number of total shares on the market soared. Shares were snapped up by the public's new love affair with stocks. Japan, however, had already made the long wave turn in 1989, and so the Japanese public was backing away from stocks while the U.S. markets partied into the winter season.

There will always be some winning industries and stocks that investors should own on the basis of valuable discounted cash flow. Some of the new companies and old ones that made new and secondary offerings are in businesses that will do well, even great, in a long wave winter. The sectors that will outperform and actually gain will be the best-run, low-cost entertainment companies, and certain high-technology companies. Certain healthcare companies with top-flight management, which will be helping other companies cut costs in hard times, will do well. Other existing industries will also do well, as well as industries that will emerge as time passes.

The Kondratieff long wave cycle is a fundamental approach to the global economy and international financial markets and does not lend itself to precise technical analysis and short-term stock market timing. You cannot look at long wave theory and say that in this year the stock market will be up or down. The Kitchin cycle and Wall cycle are much better tools for this. Long wave analysis can only present general time frames. It can be utilized to say that we are in the fall season phase and headed for a stock market decline that will lead the world economy into an era of recession and depression, or it could indicate we are in a long wave winter that will see stock market lows that will provide great buying opportunities. Evidence indicates that the global stock-market decline of the latest long wave began its shift from the speculative fall season to the beginning of the winter season in Japan in 1989, but globally the onset of the winter season in equities began in earnest at the peak in 2000, with some markets setting new highs in 2007 due to fiscal policy and central bank provided liquidity.

In a mild, long wave winter, global equity-market declines could range from 30 to 50 percent. We have already exceeded these numbers in most major global markets. A mild long wave would actually have many advantages, such as disinflation or low inflation and low costs of capital. If it is a severe long wave winter, global stock markets should find their bottoms after 50-to-90-percent declines. Since Japan had the greatest stock boom, it will most likely suffer the greatest percentage bust before this long wave winter is over.

Once again, the great long wave pendulum is ushering in the next era of purifying economic pain. Market bottoms, just like market tops in different nations, could be years apart. All global stock markets will experience a few strong countertrend rallies before reaching their ultimate lows of this long wave winter decline.

Many of the best stocks in markets around the world will present buying opportunities before the broader global economy has reached its long wave bottom. Remember, stock prices reflect future not present economic activity. In the U.S., as of this edition in 2009, markets appear to be in Kitchin No. 16, the final Kitchin cycle of this global long wave. A new low in the U.S. and many other equity markets will likely come before final Kitchin No. 16 and the long wave ends.

During the final years of this long wave winter, it is my view that it is time to employ the investment philosophies of men like Benjamin Graham, John Templeton and Warren Buffet once again. There will be incredible quality and value in global stocks, as the pendulum of human emotion will have swung back in fear. Exceptional yields and great buys on stocks will be prevalent. Unfortunately, most investors will turn them down in pursuit of safety.

After a few years of violent swings that present opportunities for short-term gains in both directions, the markets will embark on a comparatively boring upswing. Out of the long wave winter, global stock markets will embark on a rise that will last years. A key will be knowing which industries and nations are leading the next long wave advance. Except for in a few high growth industries, stock price gains will be slow and steady, not comparable to the rapid profits during the speculation that energized markets in the 1920s and the 1980/90s.

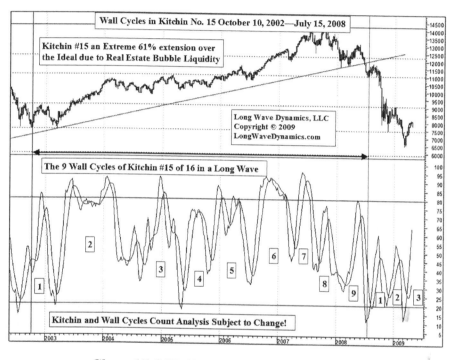

Chart 15.6 Wall Cycles in Kitchin No. 15

The U.S. market could be one of the first markets to find a major bottom in prices and begin to move up, along with a number of Asian and Latin American markets. It will be important to stay in touch with long wave fundamentals and the Kitchin cycles to know which global markets are finding their final lows in stock prices. These lows in specific stocks that offer great value will likely be in advance of strong long wave winter rallies before the next long wave spring season and advance.

The new global economy that lies ahead will witness the exploration of space and magnificent technological advances not presently imagined. It will be exciting and profitable for investors to become owners in the next advance by buying stocks in the companies that lead the new revolutions in communications, transportation and many other industries, and the thousands of other companies that benefit from a reviving global economy into the next spring season. However, the greatest opportunities will exist in the midst of this long wave winter. It will be hard to go against the trend and public mood of gloom and despair and be optimistic, buying the best companies when others will be selling.

There will be intermediate bear markets during the next long wave advance and lengthy periods of market stagnation. The next long wave summer will see bear markets once again. The next peak in stocks of the next long wave fall will come. We will probably see new investment products not dreamed of in the latest cycle top in the next long wave peak.

In spite of my long wave and cash flow based investment convictions, there are always a few great stocks that are buy-and-holds for investors. If you own excellent companies that are in a position to benefit from the cost control efforts of a long wave winter or that are in new high-growth sectors that will outstrip all the long wave negatives, they may make excellent long-term holdings.

Value investing by buying shares for their discounted cash flows at Wall cycle lows and selling at Wall cycle highs during a long wave winter season, will be a strategy that should produce great long term results. To implement our formula timing plan using market cycles we first seek to recognize where we are in the long wave and the long wave seasons. This will determine how aggressive to be in stock market investing and how much risk to take. Clearly, an investor wants to be more risk averse in a long wave winter season. Using the ideal lengths of the smaller long wave family of cycles, particularly the Kitchin cycles and Wall cycles, we calculate the ideal target date for a cycle from a past cycle low. These cycles can be identified on a market index chart.

We also calculate the optional Fibonacci ratio target dates relative to the ideal target dates. We then review market stochastics to determine if our target dates for cycle lows for buying and highs for selling are being validated by the market. This is done by using an appropriate market index to generate a chart with an appropriate date range, stochastic interval and stochastic oscillator parameters. When a cycle moves strongly under 20 on the stochastics and matches one of our target low dates it becomes a potential time to buy value based stocks. When the cycle moves over 80 in a time frame we are targeting for a market high, it becomes a potential time to take profits in our value based stocks.

To summarize, our basic formula timing plan based on market cycles is what we call Theory 144 Analytics, based on the long wave family of cycles. We use Fibonacci ratios in price and time and stochastics to help identify the highs and lows of the cycles. The miniature long wave, which is the ideal 20-week Wall cycle, as well as the ideal 42-month Kitchin cycle, are the cycles best suited for tracking in order to buy in and take profits, no matter where the economy is in a long wave cycle. Greater caution in summer and winter of the long wave, and more aggressiveness during the spring and fall of the long wave should be the strategy of an intelligent investor looking for value in their stock investments.

Chapter 16:

BONDS AND INTEREST RATES

"In spite of the general perception that monetary policy should be conducted so as to avert deflation, a central bank cannot lower interest rates below the zero lower bound."

Toshihiko Fukui

"Every trend must go too far and evoke its own reversal."

PQ Wall

"The best way to suppose what may come is to remember what is passed."

George Savile

Of all the investments available, investors typically consider fixed-income securities; government bonds, notes and bills, and investment-grade corporate bonds to be the safest. The overall return on fixed-income securities tends to be lower than stocks over time since the income investor assumes less theoretical risk than does the stock-market investor. It is thought by many that fixed-income investments are immune from the effects of the business cycle, but this is far from the truth.

To begin our look at fixed-income investments and the long wave cycle, we should first state the obvious. Generally speaking, when interest rates go up, the price of fixed-income instruments goes down, and when interest rates go down the price of fixed income instruments goes up. In this chapter we will review the impact the long wave has on bonds and interest rates.

Kondratieff (1951) stressed the relationship between interest rates and bond prices and the flow of the long wave cycle. He saw emerging from his analysis a very distinct long wave pattern for bond yields and prices. Kondratieff concentrated his study on government bonds, which are more stable than most corporate issues. However, he believed corporate bonds followed the same long wave pattern of yield and prices as government bonds.

At this point in our research and study of the long wave, it should be fairly easy to understand that the powerful economic currents that drive the long wave cycle would also push global bond markets in a predictable direction. The predictable path of credit markets is not conjured up for the sake of the long wave evidence, but stands on its own as an independent witness to the long wave ebb and flow of the global economy. Even so, the relationship of bond yields and prices to the long wave is a bit more difficult to understand than other factors that we have observed, but it is nonetheless extremely important for investors.

For long-term investment purposes, it is crucial to know the general pattern interest rates and bond prices follow in the long wave. In stating that, we must first confess that the fiscal policies of government, as well as the monetary policy of the Federal Reserve and other central banks, have an impact on bond markets. However, their effect is not as great as most economists would have us believe. The government and the Federal Reserve receive far more credit than they deserve as they scramble about to give the illusion that their actions are more important than the facts warrant. When we look closely, we see that the government and the Federal Reserve can only react to the dominant forces at work as the economy takes its predictable long wave path. They cannot change the inevitable, even when they spend trillions of dollars on the effort.

Short-term effects are all the credit we can legitimately give the money supply manipulations of monetary policy. It would perhaps be safe to say that the long wave doesn't react to policy, but that policy reacts to the long wave. The long wave cycle is a market force far greater than any government and is beyond the scope of government to affect in the long term. These are important considerations in relation to the bond markets. Bonds owe their short-term activity to government policy and Fed action. Long-term bonds are guided by the inflationary and in turn deflationary long wave cycle. This observation has proven to be critical information to the long-term bond investor.

Kondratieff's research indicated a clear pattern for bond prices and yields emerging from his data. It became very clear that bond yields and interest rates reached their lowest levels during the low points or troughs of the long wave, around 1848, 1896, and 1949. Yields began an upward movement in 1789 and peaked around the years just prior to the first downturn of the long wave. The downward pressure continued on yields and interest rates in the first long wave decline until we moved into the next upswing of the long wave in the mid- to late-1840s. This next rise in rates began in the 1840s and continued until the early 1870s, as the economy prepared for the next fall and winter seasons of the long wave.

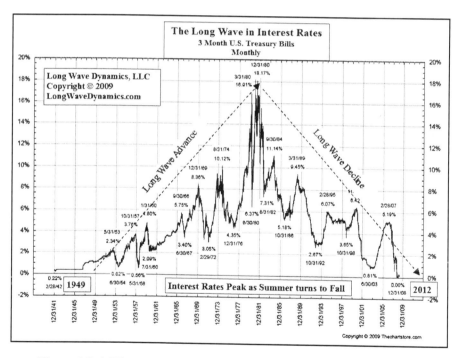

Chart 16.1 The Long Wave in 3 Month Treasury Bill Rates

The evidence clearly shows interest rates declining from their peaks in 1870 to the next trough of the long wave around 1896. During the first few decades of the 20th century yields and interest rates were slowly rising to their peak in 1922. After 1922 they turned sharply down, but then picked up slightly in 1928 and 1929, and then began to fall sharply as the long wave decline set in during the Depression, and they fell until the bottom of the long wave in the late 1940s.

The comparisons of the current long wave with the last long wave cycle are all too clear, as we saw interest rates rise once again from the 1940s to their peak in 1981. Interest rates peak as the long wave summer moves into the long wave fall season. We saw them fall off sharply during the early 1980s, just as they did in the 1920s. They rose slightly in the late 1980s and then began to plunge. The Federal Reserve was forced to begin slashing rates to stimulate the economy as the global long wave began its fundamental shift and the economy was no longer demanding money. Interest rates are nothing but the price of money. The Fed is ultimately controlled by the market and, therefore, the long wave cycle.

The Federal Reserve cut the discount rate drastically in the early 1990s. Japan was also forced to cut rates drastically as it led the global economy into the latest long wave decline. Past declines have effectively brought interest rates down to almost nothing. Demand for capital vanishes as the economy slides toward long wave winter season and deflation. This lack of demand for money causes interest rates to collapse.

However, there is a brief period as the economy shifts from the fall to the winter season when lower quality interest rates spike up. We saw this severe credit crunch in 1931 and 1932. Although we are into the winter season now, we may still see a greater default driven rate spike for poor quality corporate and government debt. Poor quality rates on BAA, BBB and lower-rated bonds and risky mortgage and business loans ultimately rise the most in this spike and prices of fixed-income securities tumble. The rates on AAA-corporate and solid government interest rates ultimately rise the least in this transitional spike phase.

This spike primarily occurs as individuals, companies, and governments in poor financial shape scramble for funds for their survival. It is the last few months of the spike when participants in debt markets begin to appreciate the magnitude of the economic problems and speculative and debt excesses that must be wrung out of the system.

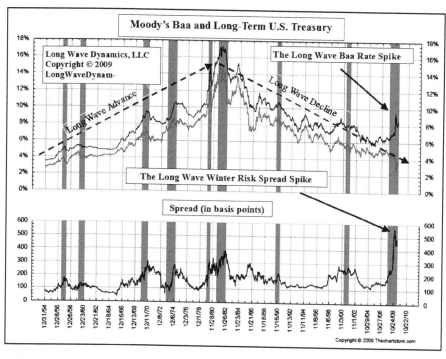

Chart 16.2 The Long Wave Spike in Low Quality Interest Rates

After this short-lived spike in interest rates, as fall turns to winter turns, rates resume their fall and bond prices rally. Only the bonds issued by companies and governments that are going to survive the long wave winter resume the rally. The long-term long wave decline rally in bond prices that began with the fall season after being interrupted by the spike, lasts until the bottom of the long wave winter.

It is during the spike of the credit-crunch period when the survivors, individuals, companies and governments, are separated from those that will fail the test of a long wave winter. This was the case for the 1931-1932 spike. Many will panic, thinking it is a new upward trend in interest rates, and will make the wrong moves. During the current long wave winter we are seeing the debt of the companies that will not survive fall in prices and their interest rates spike.

Over the past 200 years of history we have clearly seen price increases in bonds, and, therefore, falling interest rates from around the peak in long wave expansion as the summer long wave season turns to fall, until the end of the winter season. Bond prices peak and interest rates bottom just as the long wave winter is turning into spring and the demand for money begins to rise. The greatest bond rally in history was from the early 1920s until the 1940s. We have witnessed the same phenomenon since the early 1980s and it should last until the end of this long wave winter. There have been and will continue to be intermediate fluctuations of yields and prices. Long wave theory concentrates on the overall trend in both yield and price, where the existence of a long wave pattern is all too obvious.

The role debt plays in understanding the long wave is very important and is closely related to bond prices and interest rates in the bond markets. Outstanding debt is lowest as we begin a long wave expansion in the economy and highest in the peak of the financial markets at the end of the fall season and the beginning of winter. This time debt levels continued to rise into winter, before the crash. Access to debt dries up in the winter phase. A new generation becomes converted to financial conservatism. It is not important that all debt be flushed from the economy during the decline, but that the debt which is unproductive and nonperforming be eliminated. This includes the outrageous debt built up for Third World nations, leveraged buyouts, needless expansion, and real estate speculation, as well as all types of corporate, government, and individual debt.

This debt is flushed out–in part, by simply being paid off and, in part, because of the bankruptcies and failures taking place during the Kondratieff winter. Individual, corporate, and state debts are at unsustainable levels in this long wave winter. There are many companies that kept their heads as the economy roared during the long wave advance and speculation boomed in the fall season. Some companies do not expand beyond their means. These companies should survive in the winter contraction, even if their stocks take a hit. They will have to cut back and streamline operations, but will not be in danger of defaulting on their debt obligations, but these are only AAA-rated companies and there are not many.

The decreasing amount of debt due to defaults and pay offs also puts downward pressure on interest rates in a decline for the most simple demand reasons. The price side of the equation is that a decrease in availability of quality bonds as debt is retired puts upward pressure on the prices of remaining quality bonds in the winter season.

The sad fact is that most companies did not use prudent judgment in the past and will thus suffer for it in the long wave winter. Debt is a useful instrument for business at the right time. However, too much of a good thing can be fatal.

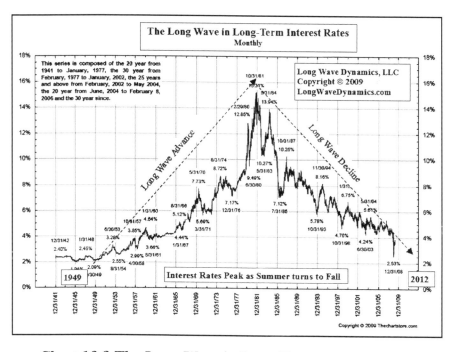

Chart 16.3 The Long Wave in Long Term Interest Rates

The latest long wave contraction and winter season will force companies, which are inefficiently structured, into default and bankruptcy. As we move deeper into the decline, an increasing number of companies will be forced into submission. The banks which made the foolish mistake of lending to companies, real estate projects, and individuals, beyond the creditors means to repay will be forced out of business. Default will purge inefficiency out of the global economy. Only the financially fit of the business world will survive, unless the government bails out poorly run banks and allows them to survive. They need to be sold to the strong banks.

The bonds that survive the long wave winter, those issued by stable governments and prudent companies at fairly high interest rates, will turn in their best price performance in years. This has been the case in this long wave winter once again. However, investors must realize that any company with competent enough management to maintain a strong position in such a volatile and reckless economy will be smart enough to call in these high-yielding bonds and issue new debt at the new low rates. Such a potential development should be taken into consideration when mapping a strategy for the years ahead.

So why do interest rates and bond prices follow these long wave trends? The inflation of the economic advance and the deflation of the long wave economic decline are critical to understanding why interest rates rise during the advance and fall during the decline. When companies and individuals believe prices will always rise, they don't mind borrowing and having debt on the underlying assets that are collateral for the loans. They believe inflation will bail them out of their debts if they have to sell. The inflation of the advance, therefore, increases the demand for borrowed funds. The opposite takes place during the decline, as no one wants debt on assets that are falling in value because eventually they will owe more than the assets are worth. The deflation of the decline decreases the demand for borrowed funds.

The reasons that debt is productive in a long wave advance and destructive in a long wave decline for individuals and companies are fairly easy to understand. A simple example would be helpful. If you borrow 90 percent of the value of a house–say, $90,000 on a $100,000 house–and the house doubles in value, you will only have 45 percent debt instead of 90 percent– or, $90,000 on a $200,000 house–and some of the debt will have been paid down. This concept applies to farmland, factories, machinery, and commercial real estate. Enough inflation bails out debtors and, therefore, creates more demand for money and, therefore, higher interest rates.

Eventually the cycle runs its course and runs in reverse. The global economic system is overbuilt with homes, factories, and wheat fields. Prices begin to fall. No one wants to borrow money if prices are falling. The person who borrows 90 percent on a home– say, $180,000 on a $200,000 home–and watches the price drop to $100,000, then has 180 percent debt on the home's new market value.

The above illustration was in the 1994 edition of this book. The Phoenix Business Journal reported April 28, 2009 that Phoenix was the first major U.S. market to report that home prices have declined by 50% with the headline "Phoenix leads nation in home price declines in February." Where my example and projection was off was that we had zero money down at the top of the bubble, so now the debt is 200% of value in many cases, and rising. If the borrower has to sell, he or she is now most likely a bankruptcy statistic. Instead of inflation bailing the borrower out, deflation is destroying the borrower and most likely his or her foolish lender. This is happening around the world during the latest long wave decline as it has in all declines of the past. And it is not just the homes, but the factories, oil rigs, and wheat fields that are falling in value. You can especially see the effects of deflation in Japan, Australia, England, and the United States; Japan is by far the best example since it experienced the greatest speculation. Apply the principle to stocks bought on margin and the picture becomes even clearer.

Once you comprehend the inflation and deflation of the long wave, you understand why no one wants to borrow money in a long wave decline. No Japanese wanted to borrow money to build commercial buildings in Tokyo in the 1990s since prices were collapsing. This is now occurring in other major markets. Europe and the U.S. are experiencing or facing the same deflation. They will likely do so once again some 50-70 years hence. If no one wants to borrow money, then the price of money, i.e., interest rates, naturally fall. The Federal Reserve can lower interest rates all it wants. It is the fool who borrows money when prices are falling. The economic lessons of the decline decrease the number of economic fools walking around looking for a loan. In the late 1930s, short-term interest rates were under one percent and virtually no one wanted to borrow. This is occurring once again. The process becomes a vicious cycle in both the advance and decline that must play itself out.

Investors realize that there is something different going on when the Fed can drastically cut interest rates and no one shows up at the banks applying for loans. The whole process and the reasons behind it are really quite simple if you think about it. Long wave theory and this book are only pointing out the obvious human tendencies for swings from one extreme to the other.

The effect of supply-and-demand for money becomes obvious as the economy enters the spring of the long wave. When the new expansion or next upswing in the global economy begins, there is once again a demand for money. This naturally puts upward pressure on interest rates and yields-the price of money. Interest rates will begin and continue to rise until the next peak of the long wave and changing of seasons from summer to fall-once we find the bottom of the latest decline and winter season. Just as with any commodity, when the demand for money increases so does the price we pay for that money in the way of interest rates. We saw this phenomenon as real interest rates started to rise after 1789, 1846, 1896, and in the late 1940s. We will no doubt see it again when the next long wave advance and spring season get underway in the years ahead.

Another major consideration when planning bond investment strategy based on the long wave is the psychological change taking place as we enter a major world economic decline. Bonds have a safety factor since they take priority over stock, if the time ever comes for liquidation of the issuing firm. Bonds receive a safety premium over stock. As the decline sets in, the psychology of the marketplace is changing from one of extreme optimism to one of extreme pessimism.

The demand for safety in a decline produces a strong upward pressure on the price of bonds and a downward pressure on interest rates and, therefore, yields. At the same time, we see a great decrease in the demand for stocks in the winter season. There is growing strength in the minds of investors toward risk aversion as the new era of pain is ushered in.

The debt of the U.S. government has been considered one of the safest investments in the world for years. In a long wave winter, government securities will have increasing prices brought on by the safety factor. I say this with caution. Rising prices should also be the case for the bond issues of stable foreign governments whose people will participate with citizens of the United States in the rush for security–this I also say with caution. Governments must maintain the faith and confidence of investors in their government issued debt. The bull market in government bonds in a long wave winter has clearly been confirmed during the current long wave winter season.

The one avenue of government investment that should definitely prove to be safe and liquid is Treasury bills. Treasury bills are the government's short-term borrowing instruments. The government must keep this market liquid otherwise Washington would have to shut down. Without a liquid T-Bill, market politicians won't get their paychecks. Count on government T-Bills remaining a liquid and safe investment. Most direct treasury U.S. government obligations should survive, but I would keep an eye on the deficit in the event Washington opts for a hyperinflationary solution. I would avoid all U.S. government-agency debt obligations (i.e., non-direct Treasury government debt), during this winter season. If Uncle Sam does have to stop payment or reshuffle its debt portfolio in a crisis, agency debt will be the first to get the ax.

A word of caution on the municipal bond market is appropriate as we review bonds and interest rates related to the long wave. Following a Moody's warning on the U.S. municipal bond market James Quinn made the following observation in an April 2009 article in the UK *Telegraph*:

> The unprecedented warning–the first time Moody's has made such a warning about the US local government system as a whole–was made in the light of the continued recession and the problems that it is causing for city and state governments. Moody's said that it was assigning a negative outlook to the entire $2.6 trillion (£1.8 trillion) US municipal bond sector–operated by local town, city and state governments–because of the combined collapse in the financial and housing markets. Analyst Eric Hoffman said what could prove to be the worst recession since the Great Depression of the 1930s will pressure "many if not most local governments" over the next 12 to 18 months. Local governments have been hit by reduced tax intakes as more residents lose their jobs, and as more companies in their areas either close or have produced losses. ... Mr Hoffman said that those localities most at risk of a downgrade will be those heavily reliant on car manufacturing, property and financial services, as well as those who have been heavily reliant on property taxes or those that have a high proportion of fixed costs.

Rushing to municipal bonds for perceived safety and tax advantages may prove very hazardous for investors for the remainder of this long wave winter season. As real estate prices continue to decline, revenues for municipal governments are increasingly constrained. As municipal governments are forced to cut back on spending, hiring and generous retirement packages, they will feed the deflationary cycle. The negative implications of this global crisis on the municipal bond market naturally come late in the cycle.

An interesting bit of Great Depression history is that Asheville, North Carolina had the highest debt-per-capita ratio of any municipality in the United States in the roaring 1920s. Asheville North Carolina was a boom town during that era, due to the cool breezes before the invention of air conditioning and the beautiful views. It is interesting to note that Asheville did not default on its debts. The city paid all their 1920s obligations, but it took them until 1977. That is why some of the great architecture from the 1920s still remains in Asheville; the city was paying off old debts for fifty years and could not afford fancy new buildings. The moral of this story is to be leery of municipal bonds over the next few years. If the civic leaders of the municipality do not have a strong moral and financial ethic, your bonds may not survive the global crisis. Even if the civic leaders do have a strong moral and financial ethic, you may need a long-term time horizon. Asheville's sewer bonds should do well in coming years; I know the power behind the throne and suspect they will pay their bills.

There is a bit of ironic history here in that this long wave author was founder of a research company still located in the beautiful Grove Arcade Building in Asheville. The Grove Arcade is a remarkable piece of architecture that was being constructed when the Great Depression hit. The planned 18 stories in the building ended at five. As the last long wave building boom was coming to an end in 1927, W.E. Grove said of his building, "It is generally conceded that the Arcade Building would do justice to a city many times the size of Asheville. It is by far the finest structure in the South and there are few, if any, finer in the entire country." The Empire State building was of course the world's greatest building of that long wave era. The Burj Dubai is a remarkable and beautiful building and the global crown jewel of the most recent long wave boom gone bust (see BurjDubai.com). Although the Dubai municipal market has not been studied, caution would be recommended in relation to the municipal bonds in such a market, as is the case with any municipal bond market during this long wave winter season.

It should be pointed out that the rally in bonds that comes with a long wave winter decline is greatest in high-quality instruments. Much of this rally has already been seen this time around. Low-grade and junk bonds will vaporize with the companies that issued them. A prudent move would be to steer clear of any poorly rated bonds during a decline and winter season. The streetwise investor will be able to pick through the rubble and find some incredible winners in the junk bonds of companies that end up surviving. But this game will not be for inexperienced investors or the weak at heart.

I cannot emphasize enough that, when facing a long wave winter decline and looking at corporate bonds, the only ones you should consider are the highly rated issues from stable, blue-chip companies. Other, lesser-quality companies could be considered if they are closely analyzed and have secure market positions with low debt-to-equity ratios. Keep in mind, when investing in bonds, that most are callable by the issuer after five years, so you could be caught by having your bond called.

For speculative investors, there are excellent profits to be made in bond futures and interest-rate futures at critical long wave turning points. Such investment instruments are, again, not for the inexperienced investor.

In reviewing bonds and interest rates, we see that they do indeed follow, both in price and yield, the flow of the long wave. It should be noted that mortgage rates and bank-CD rates will tend to track the government and solid corporate interest-rate patterns discussed in this chapter.

The investor should be aware of the long wave effect on his or her corporate and government bond holdings. Investors should be clear on the position they want to find themselves in during the remaining years of this long wave winter and as the next long wave advance gets underway. The risk-averse bond investor as well as the risk taker has a great deal to gain by observing the Kondratieff long wave in relation to bonds and interest rates. Quality bonds tend to rally during long wave declines as interest rates fall and the demand for borrowing dries up.

Another global long wave winter is underway at the writing of this edition. However, when the economy begins to move into the next advance and spring season, the bond investor would be wise to take note. The demand for money, and, therefore, interest rates, will begin their next long wave ascent, and the price of bonds will decline for years. The fact that governments and central banks around the world are trying to inflate their economies, means that when the next long wave spring season begins, inflation will roar, and bonds will crash in price. It will potentially be a bigger and longer term crash in prices than global stock markets have experienced in the winter season. To summarize, when it comes to interest rates and bond investments, the intelligent long wave investor is generally a bond buyer for the fall and winter season, but will find other investments more to their liking during a long wave spring and summer season.

Chapter 17:

REAL ESTATE

"Humanity does not profit by experience .... We should say: Profit by history; because the life span is too short to permit more than one ride."

James M. Funk

"No real estate is permanently valuable but the grave."

Mark Twain

"I would give a thousand furlongs of sea for an acre of barren ground."

Shakespeare

The real estate bubble in the U.S. and globally had a major impact on the amount of debt in the system in the current long wave. It was a major driver of U.S. consumer spending and therefore the overproduction of many global industries. Real estate trends are critical to the long wave. However, it would be wrong to view the collapse of the U.S. residential real estate market bubble as the singular or even the most important force at work in the unfolding global financial crisis. The collapse of the U.S. housing market is critically important, but still only one piece of the long wave mosaic.

Real estate first collapsed in Japan in the early 1990s, which was a key piece of the emerging global long wave deflationary decline. The U.S. real estate bubble was merely the final debt binge of this long wave. The colossal global debt structure had been building for years and the U.S. housing bubble served to push it over the edge. There are many other real estate markets around the world that experienced rapid price growth that are now collapsing during this long wave winter.

The reality that the value of a home, apartment, office building, or acre of farmland can go down in price just as easily as it goes up casts a revealing light on the idea of an economic long wave passing through the global economy every half century or so. You might even say it makes the long wave theory "hit home."

A major concern for average homeowners and investors alike is the effect the long wave has on the value and price of residential real estate-mainly their own home. This has proven to be especially true over the past few years, as real-estate values have dropped in many major economies around the globe. At this writing the crash in real estate prices is largely viewed as synonymous with the global financial crisis.

After prior editions of this book regarding the long wave impact on real-estate, I had conversations with individuals from California to New England who said in effect, "Sure, real-estate prices might fall in other places, but not here. Prices are booming." The same thing was said about Japan-Tokyo in particular. Well, we now know that the commercial and residential real-estate bubble of the last long wave advance has burst. California, Florida and Arizona and Las Vegas have been some of the worst hit thus far. The United States, England, Japan, France, Spain, Canada, Australia, and even Switzerland, along with numerous other countries, have seen real estate falling in price.

The world became addicted to rising real-estate prices and was blindsided by the debt deflation impact of the long wave cycle. Although prices were falling in areas before then, it is likely that the history books will look at 1989 as a peak in global commercial and residential real-estate prices in Japan that will hold for decades, but in other countries, such as the U.S., the real-estate bubble peaked and burst in 2005, driven by the most aggressive central bank monetary and interest rate policy in history.

The erosion of global prices that we have seen during every long wave decline has also been seen clearly in the value of real estate. This is of utmost concern to the homeowner who has taken on enormous debt over the last few decades of the upswing in the long wave. Many homeowners are faced with large monthly payments on an asset that is decreasing in value. Over the past few years, we have seen collapsing home values for the first time since the Great Depression.

For many years, if a family came on hard times and came up short on payments, they could sell their house for a gain without much effort. It was unfortunate, but not financially devastating. Things have changed. In increasing numbers, families are finding that their homes will not sell on the open market the amount of debt they owe on the home. Under such circumstances, many are finding it is wise to simply allow the bank to foreclose and take the home. We are also seeing situations where it is the seller who writes the check at closing instead of the buyer. Such situations were unheard of during a long wave advance. Owners simply walking away and sellers writing the check at closing are occurring with increasing regularity as the latest long wave winter decline proceeds along its predictable path.

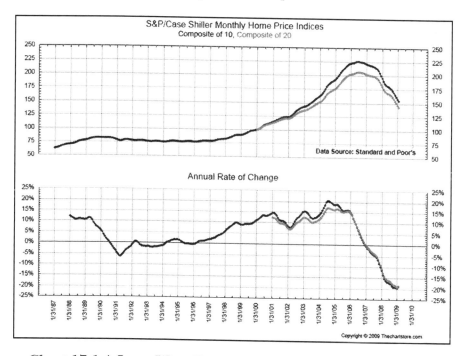

Chart 17.1 A Long Wave Bust in Residential U.S. Real Estate

Early in the latest long wave fall season, the worst-hit areas for real estate were in the central United States. The problems in the heartland spread quickly to both coasts as the fall season progressed. Prices on both coasts began their plunge in 1989. Real estate prices in Los Angeles, Boston, and other cities plunged by 30 to 40 percent in many cases. Aggressive monetary policy and the Internet and real estate bubbles gave housing in the U.S. a second chance, which came to an end in 2005

The changes occurring today mark the need for tremendous strategy changes on the part of families and businesses involved in real properties. This is of course a majority of the families and most businesses. Average prices could fall from 40 to 90 percent before the declines are over, although just as in the stock market there will still be opportunities and periods of rebound in real estate. The next substantial rebound in U.S. real estate will likely be in the spring season of the next long wave advance.

Many who use real estate as a tax shelter and a hedge against inflation are finding in this long wave decline that the game is being played on an ever-tilting playing surface. This calls for positions to be closely analyzed and restructured, but at this point it is likely too late for such action. Vacancy rates in commercial real estate are reaching unheard-of levels. In many cities, development has come to a screeching halt in this long wave winter season.

Most real-estate owners and investors believe this is a short-term phenomenon. They don't want to accept that major shifts are going on in the structure of the global economy, brought on by the long wave cycle. The long wave is right on schedule, and deflationary developments in real estate haven't surprised anyone who understands the fundamentals of what the forgotten Russian, Nikolai Kondratieff, observed about capitalist free market economies. Many who were once skeptical of the long wave are beginning to change their tune as they observe the real estate evidence, which is overpoweringly in favor of the long wave hypothesis.

To gain direction for what position the home owner and investor should be taking concerning real estate in regards to the long wave, we must first take a close look at what has created the situation in which we now find ourselves. When the economy initially moves into the spring season expansion of the long wave cycle, inflation is just beginning to show its face; prices, including real estate, which have been in decline for as long as several decades, are beginning to move in an upward direction. The economy is digging itself out of the long wave decline and into the next advance. Demand is rising across the board. As the new upswing begins, interest rates begin to pick up from the lows they reached in the trough of the decline of the long wave. These factors all have the effect of moving real-estate prices in a steady upward direction throughout the entire long wave upswing of the economy.

Inflationary pressures are increasing as the economy moves further into the expansion phase, making real estate extremely attractive as a hedge against inflation. A rising money supply increases the amount of money chasing real estate and, therefore, chasing prices higher. The further we move into the expansion, the easier it is to forget that prices will eventually come down. Eventually, the generation that created the last speculative bubble in real estate retires. A new generation of infinitely optimistic investors and developers drive capital into global real estate markets during the advance of the long wave and into the fall season.

We know that inflation subsides as the long wave summer comes to an end. There comes a point during the fall and winter season of the long wave where there is no longer the rush into real estate, as during the extremely inflationary period through which the global economy had just passed. The late 1970s and 1980s saw classic global long summer to fall season real-estate bubbles, but the real estate bubble that will be used to measure all bubbles in the U.S., from the late 1990s to 2005, outdid all prior U.S. real estate bubbles, as central banks around the world cut rates to try and prevent the natural long wave winter deflation. However, even the U.S. bubble was not as impressive as the Japanese real estate bubble that ended in 1989.

Farmland is typically the first real estate to take a hit in the long wave fall season. We only have to look as far as the average family farm in America to see the long wave having its effect on real estate in the 1980s. The average price of farmland dropped approximately 50 percent between 1981 and 1992. That is serious deflation. The effect this has on the agricultural industry was all too obvious as we witnessed failure after failure in all parts of the country.

This real-estate situation was created by oversupply and overexpansion built into the system during the advance. The head of steam in the system just overshot the true needs of the economy. The growth and price trends were simply projected into the future by investors and developers-a classic long wave expansion overkill.

No trend runs to the sky. There is always an equal and opposite reaction in economics just as in physics. Too many buildings were built, creating a real-estate glut. Further, the long wave advance created too much liquidity, chasing those prices higher; therefore, prices had to come down in a bust, as illiquidity spreads as a long wave decline deepens.

What happened to farmland in the fall season is an excellent example of what is in store for the rest of the real-estate market in the later years of the decline. Residential and commercial real estate was overbuilt. Japan was the most inflated this time around and is, therefore, experiencing the greatest real-estate crash and its consequences, but the U.S. is not far behind.

For the next few years there will likely be fire sales not seen since the 1930s in real estate. These bargains will represent excellent buy-and-hold investments for the next long wave advance. Deals will be everywhere, in farmland as well as in commercial and residential properties. Real estate becomes a buyer's market that reaches its best deals in the long wave winter season before the next advance of the cycle begins.

Investors who don't care to invest directly in real estate and manage it themselves would be wise to find a solid real-estate investment team that will acquire and manage for them the exceptional commercial, residential, and raw land properties that will be available in the worst years of the decline. Excellent returns and long-term investments will be available before the current long wave winter season is over.

There are exceptions to every rule for investing based on the long wave. Some real-estate investments purchased during the previous advance and fall season will do well during the long wave winter season. But these properties and opportunities are extremely rare. The real opportunities for real-estate investment based on long wave theory come in the winter season, when prices have collapsed and the excesses are being wrung out of the system.

I don't advise everyone to go out and sell all their real estate before a long wave decline. It is too late during this latest long wave anyway. Some investors will choose to hold real estate right through the decline and will do just fine. However, they will have to be liquid and have little debt. But there is no investment that has the permanent safety value of real estate. This includes raw land, farmland, homes, office buildings, and apartments. Investment in real property protects the investor from what I consider to be the long wave unpredictables.

There are any number of complications that can arise during a severe economic downturn that will affect other investment instruments, but not real estate. Stocks, besides decreasing rapidly in value due to overall economic conditions or individual corporate failures, are subject to complexities in transactions and in the brokerage end of transfer of ownership. Even if you were flawless in your market picks and your overall timing, your broker could still make a mistake that could cost you dearly. Many will find that their brokerage firms themselves are in financial trouble and will be forced into bankruptcy because of their own leverage and foolish transactions. This has already occurred with Lehman Brothers. So even without making a wrong move yourself, you may find your investment washed away by another's mistakes, or you may find your assets frozen for years while litigation drags on and you are left helpless. Bonds could face the same problems as stocks. You may also find your banking deposits frozen during the restructuring of the banking system. No one knows for sure what will happen to the money and banking system in a long wave decline. An absolute worst-case situation would be the default of the U.S. government on its obligations. It could happen. On the other hand, if the government chooses to hyperinflate its way out of their debt and create an inflationary depression, real estate will be a great hedge.

These sorts of market and transaction problems will not affect an investment in real estate. As long as the title was thoroughly searched by an experienced, dependable lawyer, you will not run into the predicament of suffering for someone else's mistake. Real estate is something you can jump up and down on, grow or saw a tree down on, see with your own eyes, and walk on with your own two feet. A debt-free family farm saved many families from starvation in the Great Depression as members of the family returned home. The key is to be sure that rent or cash is available to pay the taxes in a worst-case situation.

Years back I read of the president of a bank who resigned and bought a farm in the country because he didn't want to be in the city for the long wave winter that was coming. He obviously didn't buy his farm for price appreciation.

Taxes on real estate that is losing its value are an important consideration for anyone looking at the pros and cons of owning real estate in a long wave winter. In Chicago in the 1930s, rents would not pay the taxes in most cases. Debt should be avoided on real-estate positions that are held during a long wave winter decline. Lack of debt gives the owner options and flexibility so that hard times don't dictate action. It may be advisable to use debt to buy real estate at the bottom of the decline before the next inflationary advance phase of the long wave. However, debt should always be used with moderation so that the debt works for the investor, not the other way around. Remember that in a Jubilee system debts would be highest early in the cycle and then constantly falling. Once you understand the long wave, you realize the parallels with the long wave and why that makes sense.

When ultimate safety is a consideration, real-estate reigns supreme. This brings us to the conclusion that the investor should be concerned with far more than selling at a gain. The investor must realize that even though real estate will probably not rise in price and will most likely even fall, it possesses a quality no other investment has: permanence. The short of it is that there are reasons other than profit for owning real estate. Even so, some profitable, well-structured, real-estate deals will be put together prior to and during the worst of times.

Another word of caution on the matter of real estate comes under the topic of debt and concerns your personal residence. The first and foremost investment of anyone during this time would be to have your principle residence debt-free, with no liens or claims outstanding from any source. This is a tall order for most families and individuals. You may choose to rent and then find a bargain in the worst years for real estate. Since we are now deep into the price collapse, it is now time to begin evaluating the buying opportunities; however, the final lows will likely not come until the end of this long wave winter season.

The most serious drawback to the tax laws in the 1980s was that due to the elimination of the consumer interest-deduction, a lot of homeowners shifted their consumer debt to their home equity lines of credit. During this decline, many a homeless family is going to wish they had never heard of the home equity loan. Again, one of the smartest moves any family could make before a long wave decline is to get their home as debt-free as possible.

It should be noted that certain cities in the United States, and around the globe for that matter, did not become nearly as inflated as others during the long wave advance and real estate bubbles that lasted into this winter season. Property values could hold up quite well in the long wave decline in areas that didn't experience drastic price increases in the advance. Areas that will be hit the hardest are the resort locations of the wealthy and other properties that do well in times of general prosperity. Areas that experienced the greatest price booms usually experience the greatest bust. Well-established and historical neighborhoods should suffer the least. The price of real estate in different countries, regions, and cities around the globe will bottom and begin the next long wave advance at different times.

Property-tax bills could prove to be a major issue for real estate investors in coming years. Since all prices will be adjusted downward, we should see a substantial drop in taxes on real property as we move into the decline, due to the falling value of real estate. Of course, local governments may just raise tax rates to compensate for falling prices. Doesn't that sound like the logic of a politician? You should be quick to have your home or other property reassessed at the new lower values for property-tax purposes.

In summary, let me emphasize that there is no investment with the physical security of real estate. However, real estate will continue to decline in price into the long wave downturn and winter season. The bottom of a deflationary long wave decline is a great time for investors to buy real-estate bargains and hold on for the next inflationary advance of the spring and summer season of the long wave cycle. During the long wave winter deflationary bust, real estate should be avoided. Above all, it is real estate that provides a roof over your family during the good times as well as the bad.

Chapter 18:

COMMODITIES

"I'm going to see the handwriting on the wall, and I'm not going to be here to read the last sentence."

American Farmer

Commodity and raw material prices are typically the first to peak and decline in the long wave. The peak can sometimes come during a long wave summer season as the commodity and raw material producers are the first to begin overproducing with too much debt. There will be rallies during the fall and winter season of the long wave, but these typically give way to lower lows as overproduction swamps the markets.

In every recorded long wave decline, there has first been a sharp deflationary and debt-liquidating decline in commodities and agriculture in particular during the fall season. The rest of the economy suffers the worst years of decline and debt liquidation in the winter season. A more detailed review of the agricultural industry will provide insights into why virtually all commodities experience the full turn of the long wave. The fundamentals driving all commodities in the global economy are driven by the long wave. The reader can take this review of agriculture and apply most of the fundamental principles to other commodities.

Falling land prices, sliding commodity prices, and enormous amounts of debt are a few of the problems farmers have faced in the 1980s and 1990s, the same problems they faced periodically every 50 to 60 years in the past.

This history of long waves in agriculture and their connection to other forces at work on a society is a rather extensive and disturbing history. Some of the evidence predates Kondratieff's own work. In his book on economic cycles, Jake Bernstein (1991, 58-59) observed:

> Lord William Beveridge in 1922 isolated and studied extensively an approximate 54-year cycle in European wheat prices. Using historically reconstructed data, Beveridge tracked the cycles in wheat as far back as the 1200s ... In addition, there is evidence that 50·60 year cycles are present in other phenomena as well. Records of the Mayan civilization suggest that its economy fluctuated in approximately 50-year cycles. The Aztec Indian calendar was, in fact, based on an approximate 50-year cycle ... In reporting his validation of the 50-60 year Beveridge wheat cycle, Dewey observed that the wheat cycle appeared to be closely correlated to the 54-year cycle in Arizona tree-ring widths.

Our primary concern in this book is with more recent and documentable history. American and European agriculture was suffering fearfully around the time of the defeat of Napoleon in 1815 during the first long wave fall season. Prices were plunging, and the agricultural industry was in deep trouble. This was the case again in the late 1860s and 1870s, as the global economy entered the second long wave downturn phase. In the fall season of the third decline of the long wave, the 1920s, falling prices and overproduction was once again plaguing the industry.

Is the repeat of the farming crisis in the 1980s just a coincidence? Is it a fluke with no real significance? Or is a periodic decline in agriculture another manifestation of the global forces at work that begin the long wave decline. It seems a bit far-fetched that these agricultural depressions–all in the fall season time-frame of recorded long waves–are isolated incidents, unrelated in their causes and timing. Long wave theory suggests that they are not.

As Kondratieff emphasized so effectively, as the fall season begins, commodity prices peak and begin to drop due to overexpansion, which brings even more overproduction and extreme competition. This erosion of prices does not happen automatically, across the board, but begins slowly, first in farmland and agricultural prices, commodities, and raw materials. This occurs early in the fall season. Then the process works its way along until it finally reaches wholesale and consumer goods in the winter season of the long wave.

Farmers are caught in a squeeze. They are paying high prices, which are still rising for machinery and production products, while the price they are getting for their produced goods is falling. Caught in the middle during a period of rising costs and falling prices on world markets for their products, farmers are the first to feel the pain of the long wave decline. The long wave forces that hurt farmers and other commodity and raw material producers are actually making many industries more efficient and productive by lowering their raw material costs.

The value of U.S. farmland fell 49 percent from 1981 to 1992. A cut in value of almost one-half is no small drop. Anyone who questions the deflationary principles of the long wave need look no further than the price of agricultural land during long wave fall seasons. Many farmers were going into debt in the late 1970s and early 1980s, buying more land for expansion and increased production. It is not too difficult to realize where the problems have come from in the industry. Crop prices fell almost as much as land in most cases.

Financing of farmland and the desire to borrow was based on bankers' and farmers' expectation that production and demand would rise at the rates of previous years. The reason farmers fail when prices actually decline in a deflationary fall season should be obvious. The same phenomenon occurs in almost all other industries as the long wave decline progresses. Residential home owners and commercial real-estate owners, such as Donald Trump, who have seen the price they paid for real estate drop by 20 to 50 percent, are now coming to understand the plight of the farmer in the 1980s. The computer industry is the latest consumer industry to realize the impact of long wave deflation due to excesses in the system. What happened to agriculture in the 1980s is the first act of the Kondratieff decline phase play being acted out on the stage of the global economy.

One would tend to ask at this point why it is that prices first begin to fall on farmland and in agricultural, raw material, and commodity products. The answer most likely lies in technology developed during the decline and implemented during the upswing. This new technology helps to pull agriculture out of its slump and make it more productive. Through innovation, the farm becomes more efficient and competitive on world markets. The improved technology and productivity pushes agriculture into a period of overproduction first as the long wave advance comes to an end.

We are all aware that food is the most basic of human needs. This need will be met before the world delves into other projects as the new upswing is getting under way. There is a change in priorities during a decline. Things that seemed to be important as the economy moved into the peak of the long wave, such as sports cars and mink coats, are given a back seat to agriculture in the new advance. However, just as the world economy peaks again, agriculture, as it enters its phase of overproduction, takes a back seat to the luxuries of life. The luxury goods market did great in the long wave fall season as the cost of agricultural products fell.

Food is a priority that will be met before humanity endeavors to meet other less basic needs. Herein lies one of the reasons for agriculture being the first to begin the upswing of the long wave cycle and why it is the first area to implement the new technology developed during the decline. It could also be said that because agricultural and many other commodity products are the most basic and practical of all products, they give a better reflection of true value, so they dictate to the rest of the market what prices should be doing and are thus a leader as the economy goes into a deflationary period. This is to say that agricultural prices clearly make the statement that enough is enough and that it is time for world prices to come back to earth.

The agricultural decline is in no way independent of the rest of the long wave cycle. As we reach the top of the cycle, we see agriculture put in a triple squeeze. Agriculture is first caught in the situation of rising operating costs and falling land and commodity prices. These price shifts come during a period of high interest rates, before interest rates decline in the fall and winter. To top it off, agriculture is asked to do business in a world of growing international protectionism. This is especially difficult since agriculture is the United States' largest export. The pressure is just too much and the farming community is thrown into depression a decade or more earlier than the rest of the global economy.

A visit to any Midwest farming town in the 1980s would have convinced you that no one in these areas was under the illusion that an expanding, growing economy existed, unlike people in the rest of the world. The farming community is a reflection of what the rest of the world invariably experiences in a long wave decline.

An article in *The Wall Street Journal* (1986, 1) gave exceptional insight into the situation on the farm during a long wave fall season when early price deflation had already begun. The insight provided into the long wave overproduction and excess capacity forces at work is relevant to other commodities and industries, including computers, mining and autos. The long wave winter is about removing excess capacity funded with expensive debt from the global economy.

> The farm economy, still burdened by tremendous overcapacity, is merely pausing before another long bleed, many economists say ...
>
> Capital will be slowly wrung out of the sector, as lenders eventually push billions of dollars of land onto the market at lower and lower prices. As the farm depression drags on, a swelling number of farmers and farm suppliers will lose the war of attrition and some analysts see the exodus of the next four years exceeding that of the last four ...
>
> Certainly, for some farmers and suppliers, the worst is over. Land prices, having plunged more than 50 percent in some areas, won't fall as far or as fast in the future ....
>
> Excess capacity will plague U.S. agriculture for the next decade, a study by the Food and Agriculture Policy

Research Institute suggests. It predicts that enough land will come out of production as the result of federal policy or economic pressures to restore equilibrium by the mid-1990s. But idled land is still there and if farmers again planted all available acres, they would still produce about 30 percent too much wheat and 35 percent too much cotton, the study calculates ...

Farmers were going broke in the 1980s at rates not seen since the Great Depression, due to the many debt and price pressures we have been discussing. The farms that survived the difficult times of this long wave fall season took on many new characteristics. These changes were the result of financial necessities brought on by the pressures created by long wave forces. Agriculture is likely to continue to suffer in this long wave winter as commodity prices continue to be hit by the deflation of a long wave winter. Before it is over the farm will likely be forced to do without many of the price subsidies, government purchases, and other supports. Government will simply not be able to afford all the agriculture support programs of the past.

Price supports and government props do nothing more than increase the inefficiencies in agriculture. There will be great pressure for more government in agriculture as things get worse, but these pressures should be resisted as the free market is the best regulator in any industry. The worsening of the decline will be an excellent opportunity to remove Washington from the farm by purging inefficiencies through failure. Unfortunately, we may see Washington become even more involved in the farm economy in the years ahead, as it did in the Great Depression, and, therefore, do more damage to the system.

It was interesting to hear the public and those in other industries in the 1980s say, "The farmer got himself in this situation; let him get himself out." These people are now caught in the same situation of falling prices in their industries and too much debt service to cover their expenses. They are now seeing the value of their collateral eroded so that their pleas for working capital at the local bank are falling on deaf ears. As we now know, many industries are rushing to Washington in their private jets to receive their taxpayer funded bailouts. The farmer is now at least given more sympathy, since the rest of the economy is also suffering.

New inventions and genetic engineering breakthroughs, coupled with more efficient computerized machinery, will bring agriculture out of the long wave decline before the rest of the economy. We have already seen this to some degree. As we enter the next advance of the long wave, agriculture will once again be seen as a priority, not as an expendable part of the economy. Planet earth could well be populated with over 7 billion people by the year 2012; the only industry that can feed them is agriculture.

Seely G. Lodwick (1983, 517-521), former undersecretary of Agriculture for International Affairs and Commodity Programs, has some insightful ideas on the direction of U.S. agriculture in the years to come that are still relevant in this latest edition:

> The other certainty, along with taxes, is that the world's people will want to eat better than they have in the past. Those who are hungry and malnourished want to have adequate diets and the world must find ways to meet that need. Those people with only adequate diets want to have food that is more nutritious, more varied, richer in protein. Not only do they want more protein in their diets, they need it. As developing countries increase their consumption of poultry, dairy and livestock products, their people become stronger, healthier and longer lived–more capable of contributing to the advancement and development of their countries and ours too. We can no longer afford to squander the energy and talent that are lost in people who cannot fully perform because they are not well fed. The problems of the world are too numerous and too large and we need the capabilities of all the world's people. This invites innovation on the part of American farmers and traders to find ways of serving those needs. We have the opportunity to expand exports

of processed foods and other high-value products that increase dollar returns to this country and also create non-farm jobs in processing and food manufacturing. We also have the challenge to find new methods of trading–barter and countertrade, for example–and the linking of trade with development projects that make imports possible for the poorer countries. All this adds up to a growth opportunity for those Americans who produce food. Food producers will be the key to progress towards a future world of peace and plenty.

The old proverb, "the only thing that is permanent is change," comes to mind as we observe agriculture moving through the long-wave cycle. Farmers must look to the next spring season and advance of the long wave and realize that once again agriculture will come into its own. Agriculture is now a more efficient, productive industry that will face the needs of a rising world population.

It appears as if in the first two long wave cycles the fall season was more severe in many respects than in the most recent cycles in terms of bankruptcy and business failure. This was because agriculture made up a far greater portion of total economic activity during these periods. In the last cycle decline of the 1920s and 1930s, agriculture made up less of the total economic activity than previous cycles, but the winter season of the 1930s was far worse than the fall season of the 1920s. Agriculture was certainly a far larger portion of the economy in the 1920s and 1930s than in the more recent fall season of the 1980/90s. The most recent fall season of the long wave decline was mild because agriculture and raw materials represented the smallest portion of the total economy in history. The bottom line of this line of thinking is that a larger portion of the total economy appears set up to take a hit in the latest winter season than occurred in long waves of the past.

During the hard times many are wishing for the good old days on the farm, but there is really no more exciting time to be alive than when the world is going through major changes.

As we pull out of the latest long wave winter and enter the next long wave spring advance, it will be a very rewarding time to be involved in agriculture. Many will be saying, "We never had it so good."

The coming long wave spring season will prove to be a boom for agriculture and other commodity producers. In the depths of a global long wave winter, spring seems a long way away. For the intelligent long wave investor, in the spring and summer seasons of the long wave, commodity prices boom. During the fall and winter season, watch out for disinflationary and deflationary periods.

PART IV
THE FUTURE

Chapter 19:

THEORY 144 ANALYTICS

"Pattern is the sunlight of the mind."

PQ Wall

"What experience and history teach is this that people and governments never have learned anything from history, or acted on principles deduced from it."

George W.F. Hegel

This chapter is included in the final section of this book on the future since Theory 144 Analytics is our unique cycle based formula timing plan that attempts to determine the future direction of financial markets. Our objective is to increase the odds for success in a value based approach to investing. It should be evident at this stage that we agree with Harvard economist, Joseph Schumpeter (1939), that the Kondratieff long wave is the most important tool at our disposal for economic prognostication. However, we view the long wave as simply the largest cycle in the long wave family of cycles. The long wave is most useful for investing when the smaller cycles are considered in their long wave context. While reading this chapter it is important to note that our view of cycles is that they measure the fields of human action.

The reason the long wave is essential to investing should be clear. The long wave's length is approximately 50 to 70 years. It, therefore, allows most of us to experience only one complete cycle in a lifetime. However, longer life expectancies are allowing an increasing number of people to experience either the bounty of two booms or the dubious pleasure of two busts, but few live the 100-plus years necessary to experience two complete long wave cycles. Certainly, no one is actively engaged in the economy and financial markets for two full cycles.

This single full-cycle experience says a great deal about the Kondratieff long wave. The long wave and its seasonal stages have proven to have the greatest bearing of any economic or financial cycle on the life and investments of a given individual.

A key to personal development and worldview is the age at which an individual experiences a long wave winter. If experienced at a relatively young age, it will mold an individual's perceptions and views for the remainder of her or his life. If experienced late in life, it can be traumatic and drastically alter an individual's remaining years–especially if major financial loss is suffered in retirement.

Other seasons of the long wave have a significant impact on an individual, but the long wave decline and winter clearly draw attention to themselves. The worst years of long wave declines inevitably become mile markers on the road map of history that are remembered and spoken of with respect and appreciation for the damage they do to investors for several generations. A generation born in the summer, spring, fall, or winter of a long wave has its own unique way of looking at the world and reacting to it, which molds and influences the economy and all of society in future years. For example, the generation born in a long wave spring and summer advance is inevitably spoiled by the wealth created by their parents' generation and sure to drive the system over the edge, without the experience of the past decline to provide financial and economic perspective and sobriety.

Clearly the long wave is the key to any cycle research related to social development and long-term investing. In my view, the Kondratieff long wave is the most important cycle–bar none; but what of the other cycles? Over years of cycle research, it has become increasingly clear that the entire long wave family of cycles is essential to any relevant cycle analysis. Even Kondratieff (1951) wrote of a few of these cycles, as already briefly mentioned.

Other cycles can have a major impact on the way a Kondratieff long wave cycle is perceived in society and can influence its impact on investments. The following discussion of other cycles is meant to briefly address other cycles and their relevance for the future direction of financial markets and the global economy.

A good starting point for a review of cycles is Schumpeter's (1939) classic work, simply and appropriately entitled *Business Cycles*. The three cycles that were the focal point of his research were the Kitchin, Juglar, and Kondratieff cycles. Schumpeter does an excellent job of discussing all three.

The Kitchin cycle is named for its earliest advocate, economist Joseph Kitchin (Schumpeter 1939), and is often called simply the regular business cycle; we sometimes refer to it as the regular market cycle, since it can occur without a clear recession. Observers see the Kitchin cycle as ranging from as short as three years to as long as five.

My own position is that the regular market Kitchin cycle is an ideal 42-months in length, but will fluctuate by Fibonacci ratios in time, i.e. length, to the ideal. Remember that a cycle merely represents a field of human action in space and time (see the Economic Field Theory chapter). The print of a cycle bottom on a major index chart is simply the demarcation between two fields of human action, a phase boundary if you will. Fibonacci ratios represent the possible external degrees of freedom that will determine the cycle or field's actual length, similar to the external degrees of freedom in the quantum field as expressed by quantum mechanics. Since there are no natural laws yet discovered that govern these external degrees of freedom, beyond their tendency to exhibit themselves in approximate Fibonacci ratios to their ideal, the subject, therefore, becomes a philosophical or theological one; but that's another book.

It should be noted that presidential terms fit nicely with the approximate parameters of this business cycle. The Kitchin business cycle is greatly influenced by U.S. presidential elections and has a great deal to do with what is called the economic theory of elections. Presidents try to boost the economy for election years and don't mind taking a recession early in their first or second term because it will be forgotten by the time the next election rolls around. They like a growing U.S. economy in the last year of their second term, if they get a second term, to be remembered fondly and to boost the chance of their party keeping control of the White House. This clearly did not work out in 2008, which has set the U.S. election cycle up for an interesting 2012 election cycle. The regular Kitchin business cycle in the U.S. economy has had a big impact on the long wave and global economy.

The Long Wave Family of Cycles								
Theory 144 Analytics								
Fields "Cycles" of Human Action								
Cycle Name	"Ideal" Length	Div. By	Div. By	Cycle Count	Direction	Start Date	Target End Date	Next Best Count
Long Wave	56 Yrs.	4	144	Ending	DOWN	1949	2012	Beginning
LW Season	14 Yrs.	4		Winter	DOWN	2000	2012	Spring
Kitchin	42 Mths.	3		16 of 16	LWD	LWD	2012	1 of 16
Kitchin Third	14 Mths.	3		LWD	LWD	LWD	LWD	LWD
Wall	141.94 Days	4	144	LWD	LWD	LWD	LWD	LWD
Quarter Wall	35.48 Days	4		LWD	LWD	LWD	LWD	LWD
1/16 Wall	8.87 Days	3		LWD	LWD	LWD	LWD	LWD
1/48 Wall	2.95 Days	3		LWD	LWD	LWD	LWD	LWD
1/144 Wall	0.98 Days	4	144	LWD	LWD	LWD	LWD	LWD

Table 19.1 Theory 144 Analytics - Cycles "Fields" of Human Action in Markets; see LongWaveDynamics.com (LWD).

It is my conviction that after the Kondratieff long wave, the Kitchin or ideal 42-month cycle, and the 20 week Wall cycle are the most important cycles for financial market analysis. Schumpeter believed there were 18 Kitchin cycles in every long wave. This interpretation of his threw me off for years. Between the first and second editions of this book, I learned of another cycle scenario, which I have now come to accept as the actual cycle count of Kitchin cycles in the Kondratieff long wave.

The work of market analyst and philosopher PQ Wall (1993) must be credited with what I believe is an extremely important discovery in the relationship between the Kitchin cycle and the Kondratieff long wave cycle—and, in fact, one of the most important discoveries in technical market analysis and market cycle research (www.PQWall.com). As an integral part of his prime family of cycles, Wall observed that there tend to be four

Kitchin cycles in each of the four seasons of the Kondratieff long wave. Therefore, there are a total of only 16 Kitchin cycles in each long wave. This may not seem like an important distinction at first, but it is revolutionary for a market technician searching for value in cycle research, and is important for the extended implications for technical market analysis.

PQ Wall's (1993) work is built on concepts of an inherent threeness and fourness within all cycles. He has found that divisibility by the number 144, which he arrived at by 3 squared x 4 squared or (9 x 16). In PQ's work and our work this is important to the structure of cycles. Each Kitchin business cycle can be divided into three subcycles or Kitchin thirds. Wall goes further and divides each Kitchin third into three cycles; so that there are nine cycles in each Kitchin cycle. The approximate 20-week cycle, nine in every Kitchin cycle, we have termed the Wall cycle, after the man who explained its real importance to market analysis. The Wall cycle is 1/144th of a Kondratieff cycle. This approach to cycles means the Wall cycle is effectively a miniature long wave. The ideal 20-week Wall cycle often exhibits long wave characteristics. PQ passed away just prior to the release of this new edition in 2009. He will be missed.

My contribution to PQ's unified theory of market cycles combines the 144 divisibility of the long wave with Fibonacci ratio analysis in price and time. The ideal 20-week Wall cycle shows a tendency to fluctuate by Fibonacci ratios in time to the ideal (i.e., 38.2%, 50%, 61.8%, etc., long or short). This Fibonacci methodology can also be applied to the Kitchin cycle as well.

Using the cycle and Fibonacci tools for interpreting and projecting these cycles is what at LongWaveDynamics.com we call Theory 144 Analytics. This methodology of technical market analysis helps to pinpoint probable market bottoms and tops in all cycles. This is central to long wave dynamics and the analysis presented in *The Long Wave Dynamics Letter;* every issue will present the Theory 144 Analytics matrix and analysis of the current directional trend and count of every cycle in the long wave family of cycles.

In 1929, the U.S. stock market appears to have peaked in the third Kitchin cycle of the fall season and tumbled to its low in 1932 at the bottom of the fourth and final fall Kitchin cycle. This time around, Japanese stocks peaked in the third Kitchin cycle of the fall season, just as they did in the United States in 1929, and collapsed into the fourth Kitchin cycle of the fall season.

The Juglar cycle, named for the work of economist Clement Juglar (Schumpeter 1939), is the intermediate business cycle and is considered by most cycle analysts to range between 7-and-11 years from peak-to-peak or trough-to-trough. A Juglar cycle is likely more in harmony with commodity prices than stock and bond prices. This cycle is not incorporated into the Theory 144 Analytics matrix, except that it likely represents two to four Kitchins in a trend together, which could sometimes be a single long wave season or half a season.

This ends our brief review of what we term as Theory 144 Analytics. It would be nice to stop here in my review of cycles and only cover the long wave family of cycles. However, there is evidence of a number of cycles that are degrees larger than the long wave, which could be larger iterations of the Theory 144 Analytics matrix.

Extensive work on climate cycles and their impact on business cycles were done by the late Raymond H. Wheeler (Zahorchak 1983) at the University of Kansas. Using over 200 researchers and over 3,000 reference sources over a 20-year period that began in the 1930s, Professor Wheeler assembled a massive data base for his study of climate and cycles. Over 20,000 items of climate evidence went into his work. In a nutshell, Wheeler found that, historically, wet weather accompanied booms, and dry weather accompanied busts. The fact that agriculture was historically the largest segment of economic activity is likely one reason for this finding. With less of the economy dependent upon agriculture, weather patterns shouldn't be as important. The bottom line for Wheeler in terms of cycles is that he discovered climate and, therefore, business cycles ranging from 7 years to 1,000 years. What he saw as most important were the 100-year, 500-year and

1,000-year cycles. Of these three, the 1000-year cycle was critical to his research and findings.

Wheeler's work supported long wave theory and the Kondratieff cycle. Wheeler (Zahorchak 1983) actually tracked what he considered to be a Kondratieff long wave cycle going back to 600 B.C. As pointed out by Michael Zahorchak (1983), who has edited many of Wheeler's papers, Wheeler saw his 100-year climate cycle as being made up of two complete Kondratieff cycles.

Instead of looking to the 1930s for the most accurate clues for this long wave decline, Wheeler's work would suggest we look at the decline of the late 1800s, and after that the decline of the late 1700s, for guidance as to how the latest long wave decline will play out. Wheeler (Zahorchak 1983) basically says you must go back two cycles to find a cycle most similar to the current long wave cycle. This effort presents mixed blessings for stock-price analysis since the bear market that bottomed in 1784 was 15 years long, came at the end of an exceptionally weak long wave, and wiped out stock values by as much as 50 to 70 percent, while the bear market in stocks from the late 1880s to 1896 wasn't nearly as long and wiped out only 46 percent of values.

The economy could be out of rhythm with weather patterns in this cycle. To look more closely at Wheeler's work, pick up the book of his papers edited by Zahorchak (1983), *Climate: The Key to Understanding Business Cycles*. Wheeler's work also covered a 1,000-year climate cycle that he seems to have uncovered. He further divided this cycle into two 500-year cycles. According to Wheeler (Zahorchak 1983), the Roman Empire began its rise around 575 B.C. His exact dates are certainly debatable. Rome peaked around the birth of Christ and declined into total collapse by A.D. 460. The Middle Ages rose from A.D. 460 and ended around A.D. 1475.

According to Wheeler (Zahorchak 1983), what we have come to know as Western civilization began its rise around A.D. 1500, and should reach its peak in the present time frame. This is certainly debatable. Wheeler noted that at the end of a 1,000-year cycle, an old world passes away and a new one is always born. This would suggest Western civilization passes away for good around the year A.D. 2500. Fortunately, this would imply we should have a few solid centuries left, unless you have unearthed this book in an archeological dig. Please note that I do not agree with Wheeler's analysis. For a number of reasons I believe there is the potential for our current civilization to continually improve with each long wave, if we embrace the promise of what I call The Great Republic and increased individual freedom and liberty.

If Wheeler (Zahorchak 1983) is correct, a new culture will begin its rise around 2500. Given the evidence of these cycles, the time frame we are now in is a critical turning point. However, there is not a great deal you or I can do about it if a 1,000-year cycle really exists, except hold on for the ride.

Another cycle I feel compelled to mention is one that has been introduced to most students of cycles by Robert Prechter, of Elliott Wave International (ElliottWave.com): the grand supercycle. Mr. Prechter's (1989) analysis of the grand supercycle removes hope for a shallow Kondratieff Wave decline this time around. In Prechter's analysis, a supercycle is the equivalent of a Kondratieff long wave cycle, while a grand supercycle is the next degree larger. If his analysis is correct, the advance in stocks from the bottom of the bear market in 1932, at 41 on the Dow Jones Industrial Average (DJIA), into the latest highs is the fifth and final wave of the grand supercycle advance since the market bottom in 1784.

It should be noted that we haven't seen a grand supercycle decline since the South Seas speculative bubble burst in the 1720s. This created a financial panic and economic crisis that lasted for decades and threatened to return England to the Dark Ages. The theory calls for a potential return to the 1932 low of 41 on the DJIA. Prechter's interpretation calls for a low between 41 and 382 on the DJIA. We can only hope that Prechter is wrong, but he makes a compelling argument.

Prechter's (1993) argument for the latest advance being the fifth wave of a grand supercycle is important for another reason. Elliott wave theory argues that third waves are exceptionally strong. This would explain why the long wave decline in the late 1800s was fairly weak and stocks declined only 46 percent since the decline came within a third-wave, grand supercycle advance. If Prechter is right, this would dash hopes for a weak long wave winter decline this time, based on Wheeler's (Zahorchak 1983) argument for comparing a long wave's prospects to the long wave that was two waves prior. The extremes in valuations and debt levels of the latest long wave fall season give Prechter's arguments disturbing validity. Once again, let's hope for the Wheeler outcome of a weak decline and that we have not just experienced the fifth wave of a grand supercycle and are now descending into the abyss of a grand supercycle decline. I am personally far more optimistic than this, for the reasons elaborated on in this book.

If the idea of a grand supercycle is not disturbing enough, Prechter (1993) also has written of what he calls the millennium cycle–obviously a 1,000-year cycle. He notes that the advance since 1784 could be a fifth and final wave in a millennium cycle that began around A.D. 1000, but he hopes it is only a fourth wave. If we are in the peak of a fifth wave of a millennium cycle and facing a millennium bear market then ... well, let's not discuss the possibilities. Let's simply hope, once again, that he's wrong.

Then there is the ultimate cycle, relative to world history, that needs to be mentioned briefly. Oswald Spengler, in his two vast volumes, entitled *The Decline of the West*, writes of four civilization cycles. PQ Wall's interpretation of Spengler's work ups the cycle-ante a notch with his proposition of what would be an 8,000-year cycle made up of four 2,000-year civilizations. Since the last edition of this book, I purchased on old set of Spengler's two-volume set and reviewed his work more carefully. The idea of full 8,000-year cycle is not fully described, but Spengler does write in detail about four civilization cycles lasting as long as 2,000 years each and their seasons were as long as 500 years. The particularly interesting thing about the notion of an 8,000-year cycle with four civilization seasons is that when you divide 8,000 by 144–for the next iteration on the Theory 144 Analytics matrix–you come up with an average Kondratieff cycle of 55.5 years–very close to our estimation of an ideal long wave of 56 years. I've never been a big believer in coincidence. However, although such a Spengler cycle of four civilizations that is a long wave times 144 can make for light dinner discussion, it will not be proven with any data we can collect and is mere conjecture.

Based on Spengler's work, western civilization is in the process of moving from its fall season into the beginning of its winter season. Most of Wheeler, Prechter, and Wall's work fits into and reinforces the Spengler framework. Spengler concludes that European-American dominance will pass to the beginning rise of a new culture around the year 2500. This is obviously several cycle degrees larger than would be beneficial for us to spend a great deal of time fretting about. The present long wave winter season provides sufficient cause for concern.

The interesting thing about cycles that should be noted is that by their very nature they have beginnings and endings. Cycles are in essence and at their very heart defined by time. Cycles are in many respects the fingerprints of time, which measure complex interconnected fields of human action.

Whatever your own beliefs and convictions on the origins of and future of cycles, we appear to currently be in the midst of a critical juncture in cycles marked and defined by time. This is most clearly recognized by the long wave winter season and global crisis that has all of our attention with front page news. My research now indicates that the end of this long wave winter phase and the beginning of a new long wave cycle will take place globally in the next few years, as the Theory 144 Analytics matrix of cycles in human action shifts to a new long wave spring season; whether this long wave cycle coincides with larger cycles of major change to come for civilization will be left to future historians to figure out.

All this cycle discussion could make one think that it is human fate to be stuck in cycles and the rise and fall of civilizations forever. Please note that I'm not a fatalist in this regard. In fact I have grown more optimistic over the years. My conviction is that as humans we have an opportunity–perhaps not to beat cycles, but to use them to our advantage.

It is my contention that the rise of The Great Republic will not eliminate, but subdue cycles to background noise in a new millennium of progress and prosperity in human action and affairs, where good does, in fact, win the day. Here I use millennium not as a fixed period of 1,000 years, but as a genuine hope for the rise of the greatest civilization of all time, built on individual human liberty, freedom and responsibility. The Great Republic is our best hope for allowing humanity the opportunity to fulfill our individual purpose driven lives as directed by the gentle nudge of the invisible hand.

Chapter 20:

DIGITAL GOLD CURRENCY (DGC)

"The greatest gift is the power to estimate correctly the value of things."

Francois, due de La Rochefoucauld

"Divers weights, and divers measures, both of them are alike abomination to the Lord."

King Solomon

"Money is only a tool. It will take you wherever you wish, but it will not replace you as the driver."

Ayn Rand

The basic premise of this book is highly optimistic. The "coming" global financial crash has arrived. Radical changes are underway that are even now setting the world up for the next long wave spring season. The changes that come during a long wave winter, and the necessary retooling of capitalism, ensure that international free market capitalism will not only survive but thrive in the future. The long wave winter creates new innovations, methods and institutions for ensuring the prosperity of the system during the next long wave spring season and advance. Clearly there is a genuine optimism underlying long wave analysis, even excitement about how a long wave winter will spawn great innovation and changes that will ensure the future of international free market capitalism.

Nowhere do the long wave winter changes this time around have more potential for ensuring the survival of free market capitalism than where technology and the Internet are combining to create an alternative free-market-based international currency system, a system anchored in the natural monetary characteristics and foundations of gold. The prior editions of this book predicted that a high-tech and flexible gold-based currency system was coming. At the writing of this edition, just such a system has been created and is now, during this long wave winter of economic contraction, one of the fasting growing businesses in the world.

Although it is still in its infancy, such an international currency system will in time naturally provide a check on government spending and force fiscal policy constraint by providing market feedback to government decision makers. The natural forces being unleashed by such a market-based system will force governments to reign in out-of-control spending, or suffer the punishment and retribution of the market. By reigning in bad fiscal policy, this new currency paradigm will allow for more effective management of national and regional fiat currencies by respective central banks.

Many readers are likely skeptical at this point. The recent financial disaster of commercial banking during this long wave winter that led to aggressive government fiscal stimulus response does not engender confidence or optimism in the international financial system. Many will point to central banks seeking to counter the spreading global deflation by printing money and quantitative easing as a sign that we are all doomed to inflation and sure financial disaster in the years ahead. The facts indicate something entirely different is happening. No less than a currency revolution is underway that will transform international finance and the international political economy as we know it.

The deflationary global financial and economic crisis of this long wave winter season has seen gold rise in price. Gold has flexed its intrinsic monetary muscle and demonstrated that it has a role to play in the global currency system. Gold has rallied with this long wave winter crisis. The rising monetary role of gold is not just a hedge in a time of fear and crisis, but it appears that it is destined to play an ever-increasing role in the new economy that will emerge with the next long wave advance. It will play a key role in the rise of The Great Republic.

One of the most important financial and monetary developments in this long wave crisis has received little notice or coverage by the financial or other media, although a few important publications have taken note. Gold itself has received a great deal of coverage, but the impact of technological changes on the potential monetary role of gold has received little notice.

Soon after the advent of the Internet, the advent of high-tech, private gold banks arrived, offering a new type of gold account. These new banks and accounts effectively created a new form of international digital gold currency (DGC). The account holder's gold is stored in a secure vault in New York, London, Switzerland, Singapore, Dubai, etc. The account holder can convert major currencies into their gold deposit balance or convert out of gold deposits into major currencies from their DGC account. These DGC accounts are now exploding in popularity, with some of these private gold banks growing deposits well over 100% a year. The implications of DGC are far reaching, no less than a fundamental change in the world of banking, finance and international currency.

The potential for private gold banks and DGC filling a major market void in international finance was floated in a trial balloon in a 2007 article in *Foreign Affairs*, the publication of the Council on Foreign Relations. It should be noted that the Council on Foreign Relations and *Foreign Affairs* play a vital and important role in vetting U.S. policy options.

The potential for DGC emerging globally to become a new, highly efficient, technology-based alternative to fiat money has only become possible with the advent of the Internet. The vast changes to financial and economic life that will come from the Internet are still in their infancy. New stages of Internet development and implementation will be a key driver of the next advance of the long wave, as evidenced by DGC.

Benn Steil, author of the article "The End of National Currency," which appeared in the May/June 2007 issue of *Foreign Affairs*, published by the Council of Foreign Relations, recognized the dramatic rise of private gold bank DGC when he wrote:

> So what about gold? A revived gold standard is out of
> the question. In the nineteenth century, governments

spent less than ten percent of national income in a given year. Today, they routinely spend half or more, and so they would never subordinate spending to the stringent requirements of sustaining a commodity-based monetary system. But private gold banks already exist, allowing account holders to make international payments in the form of shares in actual gold bars. Although clearly a niche business at present, gold banking has grown dramatically in recent years, in tandem with the dollar's decline. A new gold-based international monetary system surely sounds far-fetched. But so, in 1900, did a monetary system without gold. Modern technology makes a revival of gold money, through private gold banks, possible even without government support.

What is noteworthy about DGC, which many users may not have even realized, is that as they move from fiat money into their gold account and then back out into fiat money to pay a financial obligation or make a purchase, they are effectively using a form of currency that was sanctioned for use in the U.S. Constitution by America's founding fathers. The difference is that, since you cannot make purchases and payments directly in gold in most cases, you, therefore, have a two-tier transaction that converts the gold into the given fiat currency of the seller. If both the buyer and the seller have DGC accounts, then a transaction can be executed without the required intermediary two-tier fiat currency portion of the transaction.

Advocates of returning to a gold standard need to take notice. The market, using Internet, database–and, no doubt, object-oriented programming technology, high-security vaults and remarkable entrepreneurial talent–has stepped up to the challenge and created a remarkably flexible and useful international digital gold currency.

However, there is good reason to not support a return to the gold standard for the dollar or other fiat currencies, since such a system would ultimately be manipulated by the government and the gold backing would invariably be jeopardized in the future.

DGC is a non-government free market response to the need for a gold currency, allowing individuals and businesses to avoid the pitfalls of poorly managed fiat currencies that are constantly in crisis due to out of control government spending.

DGC will rise in popularity if there is truly a market demand for gold money. DGC is offered by private gold banks and cannot be manipulated by governments. But it has the upside of allowing the saver, investor or business to trade back into a fiat currency at the click of a button when the issuing government and managing central bank of the fiat currency get their act together. This is of major importance in bringing fiscal discipline to national governments. If governments are fiscally responsible, their respective central banks will be able to effectively manage monetary policy without destroying their currency.

What I am basically stating is that what some would view as the U.S. Constitution sanctioned money based in gold is already available and in use. The free market has risen to the occasion and created a sophisticated, technologically secure system that is precisely such an international currency, the currency Adam Smith recognized as the currency and backbone of the great mercantile republic. Although you cannot use it as tender for government and all other payment transactions in the U.S. just yet, you can convert it to dollars and do so in real time. Such a two tier process actually has its advantages.

Additional advances in DGC will invariably come. Third parties will create more efficient real-time, market-based, seamless methods and services to facilitate exchange–into and out of DGC from any fiat currency–for any global transaction. Major financial intermediaries are effectively doing the same thing now. If you visit Tokyo and use your Visa card to purchase dinner, your card company will convert the cost in yen into dollars, Euros, Swiss francs, etc. There is already an international currency three-letter code for gold established by the International Organization for Standardization (ISO) 4271, just like for all other currencies. The gold code is XAU. In the future, Visa, MasterCard, Google, PayPal, and potentially others would all be candidates to create third-party currency conversion services tied into existing credit and debit card services that allow for converting into and out of DGC accounts from any fiat currency.

The rise of DGC and the new monetary role for gold helps explain my unconventional perspective on the historic event of Nixon closing the gold window and its important implications for financial markets. My view is that history will judge this as an astute move by Nixon to preserve U.S. gold reserves, since the gold window was only available to foreign entities at the time. Tons of gold were leaving U.S. vaults for foreign accumulation on a daily basis just prior to Nixon closing the gold window. The gold window only being available to foreigners was a result of the Bretton Woods system established in 1944. Early on Nixon believed in reducing the size of government. However, Nixon could not stop the U.S. Congress from the deficit spending and growth of government that was the real cause of the destruction of the value of the dollar, the driver of the demand by foreign entities to trade their dollars for gold.

President Nixon stopped the greatest gold heist in world history, when he closed the gold window to end the outflow of gold and preserved U.S. gold reserves. Had he not done so the U.S. would likely have few if any gold reserves today. It is my view that the importance of Nixon's decision may become apparent as this long wave winter crisis and our global financial and monetary future unfolds.

It should be noted that I do not expect the emerging system of DGC to replace central banking or fiat money; however, it will provide a real time market feedback on the job government and central banks are doing with managing their fiscal policy, deficits and their fiat monetary systems. This will be an essential role played by DGC.

DGC will actually force national governments toward fiscal responsibility by creating healthy competition for fiat money. A change to more fiscally responsible governments as a response to this global crisis will allow their respective central banks the potential to actually manage their fiat currencies effectively. When they do so, there will be a flow of capital from DGC back into the best-managed fiat currencies.

DGC is the alternative technology-driven global monetary system that is outside the domain of government manipulation. DGC will become more popular as U.S. fiscal policy continues to add to the U.S. deficit and, therefore, management of monetary policy by the Federal Reserve will become increasingly impossible. Global financial markets will be further destabilized if the U.S. government doesn't get its financial house in order, including entitlement crises with Social Security and Medicare. If and when the U.S. does get its financial house in order, funds will likely flow from DGC accounts back into fiat dollars.

DGC accounts can be opened now and you have options as to the country in which you store your gold. My advice would be an account with a reliable company, such as the bank established by James Turk called GoldMoney, which allows you to store your gold in Switzerland or London. There are a growing number of gold banks offering such services, but trust will be critical. Once DGC becomes more established and accepted, other secure and flexible storage options will be available in most countries.

My view is that their will be major DGC banks that will emerge in the future. The big change ahead, even before this long wave winter comes to an end, will be that some of the DGC banks may be managed by sovereign governments. Sovereign states will see state run DGC banks as an opportunity to create financial stability and economic growth.

A new national or international currency that is only partially backed in gold and based on SDRs or some other basket of currencies offered in response to the global crisis will be subject to government manipulation. China, India and Russia have recently advocated such a system, as earlier editions of this book suggested they would. DGC is a better option. DGC offers a pure alternative to a fiat monetary system and can exist along with fiat money. DGC should remain independent of such fiat currencies. I believe that this global crisis will force China, India and Russia to create DGC banks run by their respective state treasuries.

A Constitutional amendment should clarify the right of every U.S. citizen to have a DGC account in the institution of their choosing. Governments around the world must allow and will be under great pressure to allow DGC as a constitutional right and option for their citizens. Any political party or elected official who opposes DGC should be voted out of office. Every country in the world should provide this basic human right of financial self-preservation and financial freedom to their citizens.

It is certainly a speculative call on my part, but I'll go out on a limb and suggest that, in time, Fort Knox may manage the vaults that house the deposits of the largest DGC bank in the world, run by the U.S. Treasury, operated alongside the fiat U.S. dollar managed by the Federal Reserve. Such a dual system would hold Congress responsible for their policies. President Nixon may be looked upon more favorably by history, as a result of closing the gold window and keeping U.S. gold on hand for a rainy day, rather than allowing it to be shipped to foreign banks and governments. The U.S. Treasury would likely keep a minimum amount of U.S. government owned gold on deposit, but could sell the rest, and earn storage fees. The Chinese may want to trade some of their U.S. bonds for such gold. Instead of paying interest to the Chinese the U.S. could earn gold storage fees. If a U.S. Treasury run DGC system is executed correctly, the amount of gold stored in Fort Knox will surge. The U.S. is still the safe haven of the world. Fort Knox is protected by the U.S. Army. Many sovereign states may want a portion or all of their sovereign gold wealth held in Fort Knox.

Since DGC is a pure gold currency, an account holder will require transparency and security from the manager of the DGC bank. Any watered-down DGC will not be accepted in the marketplace. Unless a national government, including the U.S., provides a constitutional right of citizens to hold DGC accounts of pure gold and provide a transparent system, they will have no account holders when they offer a DGC system. The U.S. Treasury should set the global standard for a quality run transparent and safe DGC bank.

Russia is a prime candidate to offer a national DGC account system, since they have significant gold resources. It would be a boom to the Russian economy and create great economic growth potential for Russia. They will also need to pass a constitutional amendment that ensures the integrity of DGC accounts for account holders. India could create one of the largest DGC banks in the world, as they have the largest private holdings of gold in the world, and citizens of India would likely be willing to monetize much of their holdings. The Swiss could also effectively offer a national DGC account service with their extensive gold reserves.

Swiss expertise in banking, along with the Bank of International Settlements in Basel, makes Switzerland a natural location for private DGC banks. Switzerland is a natural location for providers of DGC services that could automatically convert DGC accounts from or into any fiat currency around the globe. The Swiss central bank could offer such services and private Swiss banks may also introduce DGC and DGC support operations. Commercial banks may offer both traditional banking services with fiat currency and have separate operations that offer DGC, but depositors will likely be suspect of such banks since they are not pure DGC enterprises.

There are those who do not believe such a change could occur and be implemented on a major global scale. They do not realize the power for change pent up in a long wave winter. Necessity is the mother of invention. When the U.S. government and the Federal Reserve realize they cannot stop a global debt deflation by printing their way out of it, they are going to have limited options. They will be forced to reduce spending, balance budgets and implement more restrictive monetary policy. At some point the latent potential and power of DGC to restore global financial health and actually restore health to fiat currency systems will become more evident and the rush to DGC will begin.

Many readers may not appreciate the change, but over the past 25 years of studying the long wave and its implications, particularly regarding global banking and the international monetary system, I've come to believe that fiat banking is not the origin of the destructive forces that most believe it to be. Fiat money does not automatically produce a bad monetary system. Central banks could manage a fiat money system quite effectively, with minimal or even no inflation, if it were not for the fact that

they are constantly forced to be reactive to bad government fiscal
policy, government overspending, and deficits. The politicians
overspend and the central bank has to manage a monetary
system destabilized by government deficits. When governments
run surpluses, they never put any of it away for a rainy day, they
spend it. When the rainy day comes, they must borrow more.
The central banks have the thankless task of trying to stabilize
a monetary system that is constantly being destabilized by the
politicians; this naturally produces an inflationary system. If we
get government overspending under control, central banks could
manage a zero or low inflation monetary system and business
cycles and long waves would not be nearly as severe, although
they would still exist.

Benn Steil recognized this role of bad fiscal policy in
destabilizing the monetary system when he wrote in the above-
referenced article in *Foreign Affairs*:

> ...the dollar's privileged status as today's global money
> is not heaven-bestowed. The dollar is ultimately just
> another money supported only by faith that others will
> willingly accept it in the future in return for the same sort
> of valuable things it bought in the past. This puts a great
> burden on the institutions of the U.S. government to
> validate that faith. And those institutions, unfortunately,
> are failing to shoulder that burden. Reckless U.S. fiscal
> policy is undermining the dollar's position even as the
> currency's role as a global money is expanding.

Well-managed central banking, and even fiat money, will
greatly increase the potential for economic growth, productivity
and stability if government spending can be controlled. DGC will
constantly keep a check on fiscal and monetary policy, issuing
real-time market feedback on the fiat currency in the form of
DGC activity and pricing in the fiat currency (i.e., the price of
gold in dollars, yuan, rubles, etc.). Any government and central
bank that does a good job of managing fiscal and monetary
policy will be rewarded. The DGC will change in value relative

to the various fiat money systems into which it can be converted. If Congress continues to spend money like drunken sailors on port leave, the Federal Reserve will not be able to manage the monetary system for stable growth. Steil highlights the difficult job of the Federal Reserve in managing monetary policy when he concludes his article:

> As for the United States, it needs to perpetuate the sound money policies of former Federal Reserve Chairman Paul Volcker and Alan Greenspan and return to long-term fiscal discipline. This is the only sure way to keep the United States' foreign tailors (China), with their massive and growing holdings of dollar debt, feeling wealthy and secure. It is the market that made the dollar into global money—and what the market giveth, the market can taketh away. If the tailors balk and the dollar fails, the market may privatize money on its own.

Steil was clearly being overly generous with the Greenspan legacy, but his point is clear and critically important: the U.S. government must rein in spending and the Federal Reserve must quickly shift to a more conservative monetary policy to defend the dollar as the world's reserve currency, once this long wave winter season has been stabilized and the risk of global financial meltdown has been averted. One way they could do this is to promote a dual U.S. monetary track that promotes fiscal and monetary discipline in the form of a Treasury administered, U.S. Constitution authorized, pure gold-backed DGC, where all the gold in Fort Knox is put to use driving economic growth and financial stability. A U.S. Treasury administered DGC would provide a constant barometer of the job the U.S. Government and the Federal Reserve are doing in terms of providing sound policy to support to the U.S. economy and U.S. dollar stability.

Let me be clear, I support central banking and the Federal Reserve, their foreign equivalents, and their role in the management of monetary policy and commercial banking. However, there is a great risk that central banks lose their independence during this global crisis and that monetary policy is politicized. Politicians around the world would love to get their hands on monetary policy in order to monetize the debt they create and inflate their way out of the fiscal disasters they have created. They are even now seeking to blame central banks for the crisis and politicize monetary policy. DGC has the potential to stabilize the financial system and insure central banking independence from the political process, not just in the U.S., but around the world.

To fully understand the rise of DGC during this long wave winter, it is important to review gold as a commodity and the history of gold to understand why its star is once again rising in international finance. A brief review of gold will help explain why gold is loved by savers, investors and the advocates of individual liberty and responsible governments all over the world.

Gold has always played an important role in the long wave. But before we try to project how gold should perform throughout the cycle, we need to take a quick look at its history. It is important to understand why gold is a unique commodity.

"What makes gold the noblest of metals?" asks writer Timothy Green (1981, xvi-xvii).

> Its greatest strength is its indestructibility. Unlike silver, it does not tarnish and it is not corroded by acid–except by a mixture of nitric and hydrochloric acid. Gold coins have been recovered from sunken treasure ships after two centuries beneath the sea, looking bright as new... Its beauty and versatility swiftly recommended it above all other metals. One ounce of gold can be beaten into a sheet covering nearly 100 square feet. It is also so ductile that one ounce can be drawn into 50 miles of thin gold wire. It is such an excellent conductor of electricity that a microscopic circuit of liquid gold "printed" on a ceramic strip saves miles of wiring in a computer.

The World Gold Council estimates that at the end of 2007 about 161,000 tonnes of gold is in above-ground stocks. This total world supply of gold if priced at $1000 per ounce would come to $5.67 trillion dollars. A sobering thought, in light of this fact, is that all the gold in the world couldn't payoff half of the U. S. government's debt. The fact is, gold was in very short world supply before the middle of the 19th century and has only been available in large amounts for some 130 years.

Russia was producing some three-fifths of the world's output of gold in 1847, just prior to the discovery of gold in California. Mines near Mongolia and the Lena River east of Lake Baikal and on the Amur River, discovered in the late 1840s, were producing over 40 tonnes in 1880 and over 50 tonnes in 1914. The "Age of Gold" was ushered in by California in the rush of 1848-1849 . Up until that time, it is estimated that only about 10,000 tonnes of gold had been mined in all of history.

It all began one afternoon in January of 1848 when James Marshall, a carpenter, found small specks of gold at John Sutter's mill at the junction of the American and Sacramento Rivers. The United States was in the process of completing the purchase of California and New Mexico from Mexico for $15 million in early 1848, just as the news of the gold find was spreading. By 1852, tens of thousands of fortune hunters and adventurers had flocked to California and had mined well over $81 million in gold in 1852 alone. California was probably one of the last good investments made by the U.S. government.

Australia was the nation next hit with gold fever when, in 1850, there was a major gold find in New South Wales that yielded 26 tonnes in 1852. Gold was discovered in a number of places in Australia, but the world's largest finds were yet to come in South Africa where production reached 120 tonnes by 1898.

One last big strike before the end of the century came in the Klondike in 1896 as a couple of salmon fisherman saw a glimmer of gold on the bottom of a stream. The Klondike rush yielded over 75 tonnes of gold in the last three years of the 19th century, the biggest century for gold discovery in history.

Gold poured into the money centers of Europe in the mid-19th century, producing dramatic effects on the world's economy and monetary systems. This was during the upswing of the second long wave cycle. The gold discoveries did a great deal to boost the world economy and stimulate global trade. These great discoveries of gold paved the way for the introduction of the gold standard, which became an international basis of money. A majority of currencies were attached to a fixed amount of gold from 1879 to 1913. Most of Europe abandoned the gold standard in 1913 and the United States finally followed suit during the banking crisis of 1931, after suffering a great drain on gold reserves.

On April 5, 1933, under the leadership of President Franklin Roosevelt, it became illegal for U. S. citizens to hold or own any form of monetary gold, either coins or bullion. The government was doing this in 1933 in an effort to relinquish its responsibility to repay in gold. Today the government has no such obligations and should not find such a policy necessary.

In order to understand the present dynamics of gold in global markets, we must go back to the Bretton Woods agreement of 1944. The international banking collapse of 1931 left the world monetary system in shambles. Countries were unable to control and carry on fiscal policy without seeing their currencies depreciate in terms of gold, their capital flee the country, or their credit markets crippled. This led to a meeting in Bretton Woods, New Hampshire, which resulted in the creation of an international monetary agreement that would, because of its inherent contradictions, come crashing down 25 years later.

The basis of the agreement was that the dollar would be redeemable in gold–but only by foreigners. United States citizens and banks were not allowed to exchange dollars for gold. The price of gold would be fixed at $35 per ounce for the foreigners. The foreign currencies would be required to maintain fixed exchange rates with the dollar. They were allowed to rise and fall by only one percent from their fixed rates.

This had the effect of treating the dollar as gold, at least in relation to foreigners. Due to deficit government spending the United States Federal Reserve had the U.S. Treasury print more and more money. Naturally, the dollar became extremely overvalued against foreign currencies. The dollar was overvalued by all measures. Being convertible into gold, the dollar was being traded in for gold almost as fast as it was being printed.

Foreign governments very much preferred gold locked away in their vaults rather than owning overvalued dollars. The dollar was convertible by both foreign commercial banks and the central banks of foreign nations. And converted it was, as the gold reserves peaked at 701 million ounces in 1949 and plummeted to 296 million ounces in 1968. During this period, the United States Air Force was said to be making constant flights with cargo planes loaded with gold from Fort Knox to Europe.

Because of the significant devaluation of the dollar, as the presses rolled on during the Bretton Woods agreement, there began an upward pressure on the market price of gold during the early 1960s. In order to stop this upward pressure, the central banks had begun open-market efforts to hold the dollar up and hold gold down. These open market efforts were mainly composed of the United States selling large quantities of gold in an effort to keep the price of gold down.

At the realization that gold could not be held down indefinitely, a meeting was called in Washington in 1968 during which a two-tier market was established, where central banks would continue to operate in gold at the official level of $35 per ounce, and the free market would be allowed to find its own price.

Central banks were forbidden to participate in the open market. This of course did not stop the erosion of the dollar. All European currencies were coming closer to pushing through their limits set in the 1944 agreements. This was clearly because the gold dollar was losing its shine.

England was the first to violate the agreements and devalue its currency. All of Europe soon followed suit. This caused a massive flight into gold, but the United States still honored its gold dollar at $35 per ounce. In 1971, United States gold reserves against the dollar were getting low and were pushing below their 25-percent backing of reserve notes (dollars).

Rumors began to spread that the United States was going to close the gold window. No longer would gold be exchangeable for the dollar. This would cut the dollar loose from any backing and allow the devaluation of the dollar to go unchecked. This rumor caused a new-style gold rush, and in one week some $4 billion in gold left the country for European vaults.

On Sunday, August 15, 1971, rumor became reality as President Nixon in a televised address announced the closing of the gold window; no more gold would be given in exchange for U.S. dollars. Afterward, the only market that existed for gold was the free market and gold prices took off with a vengeance. When the gold dust had settled, U.S. gold reserves had fallen from over 22,000 tonnes to under 8,300 tonnes, while European gold reserves had exploded to over 17,000 tonnes.

We have seen gold prices soar from a low of $34.75 in 1971 to their high of $850 per ounce in 1980 and over $1,000 in 2008 and 2009. After the agreement collapsed, foreign banks could sell the gold they had heisted from the United States under the Bretton Woods agreement on the open market.

Kondratieff related the buying power of gold and the production level of gold very closely to the long wave. Since production prices reach their peaks as the long wave expansion peaks, it becomes extremely expensive to mine gold. At the same time, the purchasing power of gold is declining. This tends to slow production as we enter the peak of the industrial expansion of the long wave cycle.

The opposite occurs in the decline, with production costs falling and the purchasing power of gold increasing. As the decline deepens, the cost of labor and the price paid for mining equipment gets cheaper, while the purchasing power of gold is on the rise. This naturally leads to greater production efforts and output as the long wave reaches its low point in the trough of the winter season decline. The confusion in the markets and the crash of the banking system will create a rush for the safety of gold, which has occurred in recent years. The free markets we have today in gold will put great upward pressure on the price of gold as gold takes on its natural monetary role during this long wave winter season.

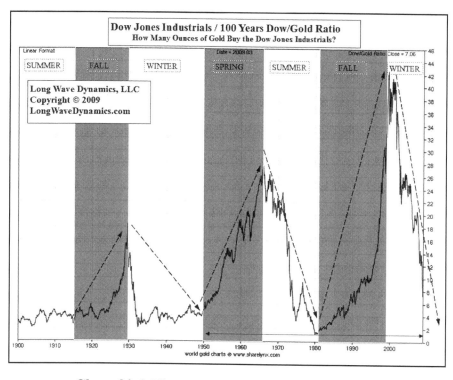

**Chart 20.1 The Long Wave as Seen Clearly in
100 Years of the Dow/Gold Ratio**

The investor would particularly want to hold a position in gold during the summer and the winter of the long wave cycle. In a free market, it should perform well during the advance due to natural economic inflation and monetary inflation. Gold makes an especially good investment during the late runaway summer inflation seen during the last decade of the advance phase of the long wave. This was the case in the 1970s. However, during the fall season and the first few years of the long wave winter, gold should be avoided because of the deflationary forces of the long wave cycle. A few years into the decline, a global financial banking crisis tends to hit that makes gold important for investment insurance and as a disaster hedge, which is exactly what we have seen in this long wave winter season.

Throughout history, those who have held a portion of their portfolio in gold have always come out on top when times get really tough. The buying power of gold has consistently gained, while all else has fallen by the wayside in long wave declines. Fiat money supported by nothing but government overspending can only last for a season and in time will come to nothing. Gold will have a double advantage in the latest decline. It increases in purchasing power in a deflationary economy, and is emerging as the basis to new national and international currency in the form of DGC.

A major factor to consider when looking at gold is the impending changes and potential collapse of the international monetary system as we know it. We have seen an international banking shakeout in every decline of the long wave cycle. This has always led to major changes in the money and banking system that include a changing role for gold. We have already made the case for DGC in this chapter. The rise of global DGC banks would be an alternative free market gold-based banking and money system that would exist in parallel with fiat currencies managed by central banks. DGC can be used to trade in and out of the fiat currencies. In this clearly defined and parallel system DGC will play a major role in the explosive growth of the new long wave economy and keep fiat currencies in check. This system would allow the global economy to perform far better than the economy of the last long wave advance.

However, the world's politicians, central bankers and the IMF may come up with another option in the form of a single international currency unit backed fractionally in gold and run by the IMF and/or World Bank, ultimately under the authority of a more powerful United Nations. This is the system recently pitched by China and Russia. This system would be limited in its economic potential, although the global economy would still move into the next advance with such a currency system, but potential for growth would be greatly restricted. DGC options could exist along with such a centralized fractional gold system, but such a system would likely limit the use of DGC due to government intervention and restrictions in favor of the centralized fractional gold reserve system.

Gold will play a role in either one of these potential currency systems and is, therefore, an important part of an investor's portfolio. Either system could bring us into the next advance of the long wave. One thing is certain: change is coming as the failed system that has lasted since the beginning of the latest long wave crumbles during this long wave winter season.

Gold stocks may be an attractive form of investment in gold for the small, as well as the large, investor. This should be closely considered. It may be smart to divide your gold investments between gold stocks or gold mutual funds and actual physical gold holdings. One-half in stocks and one-half in DGC could be a good mix. The tendency for gold stocks to move up more on a percentage basis than gold itself should be kept in mind. Gold stocks may perform better than the actual gold in an international financial crisis. Once the long wave decline is over and the financial crisis is a thing of the past, a gold position should be held as an inflation hedge as the next long wave expansion begins.

Clearly we now find ourselves in the midst of another global long wave banking crisis that has brought the global economy to the edge of the abyss. However, the beauty of long wave theory is that this is where it turns optimistic about the future. We are now in the midst of the global crisis, what the future offers is for true leaders to take bold action to find our way out of the global crisis and into a new global economy.

The emergence of DGC makes me more optimistic than ever about the potential for positive change in the global banking system and international finance and the growth of the global economy in the next long wave advance. DGC will play a major role as the true market based international currency that provides daily feedback on the job of governments and central bankers in managing their national or regional currencies. This chapter reminds us that history has proven that gold has survived what nothing else will, and that only gold is as good as gold.

Chapter 21:

THE CRISIS OF CAPITALISM

"The modern world-system in which we are living, which is that of a capitalist world-economy, is currently in precisely such a crisis, and has been for a while now. This crisis may go on another twenty-five years to fifty years. … The period of transition from one system to another is a period of great struggle, of great uncertainty, and of great questioning about the structures of knowledge. We need first of all to try to understand clearly what is going on. We need then to make our choices about the direction in which we want the world to go. And we must finally figure out how we can act in the present so that it is likely to go in the direction we prefer."

Immanuel Wallerstein

"Marx's theory of the inevitable decline of capitalism isn't accepted by any of the influential economists... There is also a transition in the highest levels … toward accepting that the capitalist economies are self-regulating, not self-destructive."

Andrey Poletayev, Russian Economist

"What they have to discover, what all the efforts of capitalism's enemies are frantically aimed at hiding, is the fact that capitalism is not merely the 'practical,' but the only moral system in history."

Ayn Rand

Mainstream analysts–be they political scientist, economist, or sociologist–as well as financial analyst, have historically not accepted the evidence for long waves in the international political economy or global financial markets. They do not recognize the importance of its impact on global economic and financial market activity. Academic analysis of the long wave is limited.

It may be that academia has overspecialized and somehow missed the comprehensive theory of the long wave. Researchers and advocates of long wave theory are few and far between in academia, particularly in the business schools. However, the most current long wave winter season is providing substantial long wave hypothesis confirmation. The growing body of evidence for the existence of long waves, including the research by the System Dynamics Group at MIT and other approaches, may correct the shortfall of academic acceptance of long waves in the future.

The long wave is essential to understanding history, current developments and the future in economics, financial markets and international politics. However, for the present there is no meaningful body of time-honored research in the literature with accepted terms, theory and framework of thought for discussing, conducting research, or integrating the long wave in a comprehensive manner into established, economic, financial and political systems of thought in mainstream academia. The findings in the System Dynamics Group at MIT have not been accepted in other areas of academic research. However, there is one school of thought, known as World-Systems Analysis, which does grasp the importance of long waves. It is typically the domain of left-of-center thinkers; however, its framework is useful as a starting point for other areas of academia to explore long waves. World-Systems Analysis helps explain where we have come from and where we may be headed in terms of international political economy and other fields of inquiry.

World-Systems Analysis is an exception to the long wave void in modern academic political economy and social system literature. This relatively small group in academia does recognize the remarkable power the long wave brings to any relevant analysis of the international political economy. They even appreciate and have great insight into how the long wave drives profitability, manufacturing trends and the flow of trade. They recognize the powerful impact of the long wave on capital flows and even financial markets. Ironically, most adherents to the World-Systems Analysis are socialist and neo-Marxist. They tend to believe every long wave is bringing us closer to the end of international capitalism, the rise of global socialism.

World-systems analysts present thoughtful and detailed arguments that we have now entered the great crisis of capitalism. They believe that this global crisis marks the accelerating end of international free market capitalism. Such thinking argues that economic long waves are the birth pangs of global socialism and will ultimately produce crises so severe that a new global socialist, left-of-center, social-democratic, redistributive order will rise from the ashes of international capitalism, a capitalist system that is so badly damaged by the current crisis that it cannot recover. Unfortunately, such thinking cannot be dismissed and needs to be addressed, since socialist solutions look more attractive and are, in fact, being embraced and aggressively implemented during this long wave winter crisis.

Although the intent of this book is to present an objective analysis of the evidence for long waves, we all have our own unique perspectives. It should be clear at this point in this book that this author approaches long wave analysis from the perspective of and advocates what most would view as classical liberal or libertarian international free-market capitalism.

The approach this book takes to long wave analysis and its extended implications for the international political economy is a right-of-center or even a classical conservative approach to World-Systems Analysis. It is a lonely domain to date, but is an open field, and others are expected to join this approach to long wave analysis due to the clarity it brings to complex global system and international financial market analysis. What is enjoyable and helpful about reading world-system analysts is that, to be blunt, they understand capitalism far better than most capitalists. They were not surprised in the least by the financial and economic crisis that has hit international capitalism in recent years. Please note that this author believes that most world-systems analysts are wrong in their ultimate conclusions, but most capitalists could learn a great deal from the systematic world-systems approach to understanding where capitalism has come from, which dynamic forces drive its expansion and contraction phases, what the key threats to international capitalism are, and what our options are for the future.

The father of World-Systems Analysis is Immanuel Wallerstein (1984). Wallerstein is a Senior Research Scholar at Yale and received his Ph.D. from Columbia University and is the former President of the International Sociological Association. Wallerstein continues to write a column for *Agence Global.* Wallerstein is a very clear writer, effective communicator and insightful analyst. Anyone that desires an understanding of where we have come from as a civilization and where we are headed should read Wallerstein and become versed in the approach of World-Systems Analysis, in order to prevent most of its adherent's conclusions and predictions for our future.

One reason Wallerstein's approach to World-Systems Analysis is so clear is that it could be viewed as object oriented in its approach, with parallels to the object-oriented programming paradigm. He categorizes what could be viewed as the objects, classes, domains, attributes, fields, properties, roles, characteristics and functions of important world-system participants and subsystems. He understands their relationships with each other and has developed World-Systems Analysis to integrate the relationships. Object-oriented thinking is exceedingly helpful for any subject that requires theoretical thinking. The National Security Agency would be well advised to build object-oriented models for computer simulations that incorporate World-Systems Analysis structures for the purpose of running scenarios on the medium and long-term risks of systemic crisis and the inherent risks to national security.

While working on this new edition I came to realize that my own approach to long wave analysis regarding possible outcomes to the international political economy and markets is that of a world-systems analyst of sorts; however, the approach presented is from the fundamentally different perspective of advocating a libertarian approach to international free-market capitalism as the greatest system ever devised by man, one to which we may return during this global crisis.

Each long wave is driving capitalism toward a new era of prosperity, driven by increasing individual liberty, freedom and trade liberalization. It is technological innovation that drives freedom of access to information, market efficiency and increasingly economically relevant databases and stable information systems. These forces drive efficiencies in pricing and distribution systems.

World-Systems Analysis can be viewed as a framework for discussion and analysis of the options for capitalism moving forward. It provides a coherent framework for arriving at the outcome options of this long wave winter season and future ones. It is my recommendation that long wave analysis in the field of international political economy, sociology, economics and finance adopt the framework of World-Systems Analysis created by Wallerstein. The system of thought is highly adaptable. World-Systems Analysis can be used to effectively make the case that long waves are not the birth pangs of global socialism, but the birth pangs of a new era for international free market capitalism that will exceed all others in human liberty, freedom, economic opportunity, growth, financial stability and progress.

The speed with which the advocates of global socialism have reasserted their arguments during the current global financial and economic crisis of capitalism has stunned many free market advocates and observers. International free market capitalism was riding high only a few years ago, as more countries were incorporated into the fold. A stunning rebound of calls for global socialism during this long wave winter season was exactly what was predicted in prior editions of this book.

Socialist solutions have already been embraced by the United States and other historically capitalist countries. Relatively new capitalist countries on the periphery of the developed world may be tempted to turn away from market-based solutions and embrace solutions the socialists have to offer. These various left-of-center, socialist and neo-Marxist arguments must be countered and free market advocates need to explain why socialist interpretation of the ultimate outcome of this and future economic long wave crises are flawed and wide of the mark.

Mainstream rejection of the long wave's existence does nothing to advance the cause for free market-based solutions during a global long wave winter crisis; it has in fact done a great deal of damage. World system theorists are remarkably insightful and articulate regarding the intricate details of capital flows and the spread of capitalism to new countries and regions. Where they go wrong is in their conclusions of the long wave producing the final crisis of capitalism. They fail to understand the full potential of international free market capitalism to rejuvenate and emerge into a new and more powerful advance. However, they do realize that capitalism is weakened temporarily in crisis and that is the time to advocate and push for greater socialist agendas for governments and non-government organizations (NGOs). We cannot fault socialists for intelligently seeking to advance their cause, but we must counter their arguments and allow true international free market capitalism to prove them wrong.

It is important to briefly examine World-Systems Analysis thinking regarding long waves and rebut their conclusions. The current crisis of this long wave winter already has, and the next will certainly once again bring the belief in the crisis of capitalism and the rise of socialism to the forefront of popular discussion.

Left-of-center thinkers, be they social-democrats, socialist or neo-Marxist, are arguing that the Soviet Union was not true socialism or Marxism. There are now vicious attacks being made on free markets. Left-of-center thinking is once again asserting itself in a call for socialist world government. This was predicted in earlier editions and is now occurring in this long wave winter.

Wallerstein (1984) espouses that there have been three types of social systems throughout history and that a fourth is yet to develop as an "invention of the future." The first type of social system he discusses in his book, *The Politics of the World Economy*, is the reciprocal minisystem such as the Greek city state. The second type is the redistributive world empire, such as Rome. We will review the possibilities of a redistributive world empire in more detail later on.

The present international system is an example of the third type of social system Wallerstein (1984) defines and examines.

Most of Wallerstein's work examines what he calls the capitalist world economy, which he argues has been evolving since the 14th century. In his discussion of the capitalist world economy, he presents the typical and predictable two-class position that the surplus capital of the direct producers–the working proletariat–is extracted from the system in the form of profit and distributed via the market to the bourgeois capitalist class.

Wallerstein's (1984) basic thesis is that we are now in the midst of a transition from the capitalist world economy into the fourth type of social system, which he believes will be some form of left-of-center government-led redistribution-based system, but I do not claim to completely understand his thinking in this regard. As I understand it, this would be a system where profit and private property would be abolished and all ownership of production would be held by the public–in other words, the state. Wallerstein sees the capitalist world economy as being in a systemic crisis that began with the Russian Revolution in 1917, one that will give birth to a socialist government-led redistributive system at the end of a transition lasting 150 years; so we are now in the final decades of this transition.

Although Wallerstein fails when he attempts to show that the capitalist world economy will of necessity be replaced by a government-led redistribution system, he does a good job of outlining the long wave characteristics and development of the free market capitalist system. His analysis of the inner workings of capitalism is insightful.

The following excerpt comes from Wallerstein's *World-Systems Analysis: An Introduction* (2004). This short book is recommended to anyone that seeks to understand how the long waves fit into World-Systems Analysis and wants an introduction to Wallerstein's approach. This excerpt demonstrates Wallerstein's insight into some of the important mechanisms of international capitalism and how they fit into the ebb and flow of long wave dynamics:

> The normal evolution of the leading industries—the slow dissolution of the quasi-monopolies—is what accounts for the cyclical rhythms of the world-economy. A major leading industry will be a major stimulus to

the expansion of the world-economy and will result in considerable accumulation of capital. But it also normally leads to more extensive employment in the world-economy, higher wage-levels, and a general sense of relative prosperity. As more and more firms enter the market of the erstwhile quasi-monopoly, there will be "overproduction" (that is, too much production for the real effective demand at a given time) and consequently increased price competition (because of the demand squeeze), thus lowering the rates of profit. At some point, a buildup of unsold products results, and consequently a slowdown in further production.

When this happens, we tend to see a reversal of the cyclical curve of the world-economy. We talk of stagnation or recession in the world-economy. Rates of unemployment rise worldwide. Producers seek to reduce costs in order to maintain their share of the world market. One of the mechanisms is relocation of production processes to zones that have historically lower wages, that is, to semiperipheral countries. This shift puts pressure on the wage levels in the processes still remaining in core zones, and wages there tend to lower as well. Effective demand which was at first lacking because of overproduction now becomes lacking because of a reduction in earnings of the consumers. In such a situation, not all producers necessarily lose out. There is obviously acutely increased competition among the diluted oligopoly that is now engaged in these production processes. They fight each other furiously, usually with the aid of their state machineries. Some states and some producers succeed in "exporting unemployment" from one core state to others. Systemically, there is contraction, but certain core states and especially certain semiperipheral states may seem to be doing quite well.

The process we have been describing—expansion of the world-economy when there are quasi-monopolistic leading industries and contraction in the world-economy when there is a lowering of the intensity of quasi-monopoly—can be drawn as an up-and-down curve of so-called A-(expansion) and B-(stagnation) phases. A cycle consisting of an A-phase followed by a B-phase is sometimes referred to as a Kondratieff cycle, after the economist who described this phenomenon with clarity in the beginning of the twentieth century. Kondratieff cycles have up to now been more or less fifty to sixty years in length. Their exact length depends on the political measures taken by the states to avert a B-phase, and especially the measures to achieve recuperation from a B-phase on the basis of new leading industries that can stimulate a new A-phase.

A Kondratieff cycle, when it ends, never returns the situation to where it was at the beginning of the cycle. That is because what is done in the B-phase in order to get out of it and return to an A-phase changes in some important way the parameters of the world-system. The changes that solve the immediate (or short-run) problem of inadequate expansion of the world-economy (an essential element in maintaining the possibility of the endless accumulation of capital) restore a middle-run equilibrium but begin to create problems for the structure in the long run.

Consider Wallerstein's insight above in light of the current state of the global auto industry, global banking services or housing. We are presently in a classic B-phase or Kondratieff contraction winter phase. The G-20 and governments around the world are implementing all out policies and programs to try and get out of the current B-phase. As pointed out by Wallerstein, the solutions foisted upon the global economy by government can create problems for the structure of global capitalism in the long run. It is possible that governments implement solutions that jeopardize the future of international capitalism. However, if they do not realize that long wave exists, they risk overcompensating for the natural rhythms of capitalism, and thus producing a true crisis of capitalism in the future.

Most of us would agree that capitalism is going through a period of violent adjustment. I would argue that this is due to the long wave decline, not a greater systemic crisis. It is far from clear, as Wallerstein argues, that the adjustments we are experiencing are terminal and will create an entirely new social system.

In light of the collapse of the Soviet Union, the replacement of socialist governments in Eastern Europe with regimes friendly to the capitalist world economy, reunification of Germany, and the many losses of revolutionary (i.e., antisystemic) movements internationally in recent decades, e.g. China embracing capitalism, there could be a temptation to write off the work of Wallerstein and his general thesis altogether. The current crisis of capitalism in this long wave winter season now clearly puts such a write off on hold.

Until a few years ago, it appeared that the capitalist world economy had turned the tide on the socialist challenge. However, Wallerstein (1984) himself predicted some of the shifts and changes in the 1980s and 1990s, especially the opening of Eastern Europe to Western market influences. His work provides a great deal of reactionary fodder for those with socialist revolutionary tendencies, as well as food for thought for those of us who would like to preserve a free market, capitalist, international economy, and, therefore, need to be aware of prominent socialist and neo-Marxist thinking.

Critical to Wallerstein's explanation of how the capitalist world system functions and how it will meet its fate is the notion of patterns in the system. Wallerstein's work is most creative and insightful when he looks at long waves. I should note that long waves are only one of the patterns he considers. Wallerstein (1984) believes that long waves have been present in the capitalist world economy since its emergence in the 14th century. Wallerstein clearly sees the capitalist system as having a natural tendency to overshoot necessary supply and overproduce as the "anarchy of production" seeks to maximize profits. We have reviewed this long wave principal and tendency of overproduction in detail in this book, although have not cast it in such a negative light. The notion that all trends go too far and evoke their own reversal would be clear to Wallerstein.

Like most socialists, Wallerstein (1984) sees economic demand as strictly a "function of the sum of political arrangements." He believes that when these political arrangements supporting demand are stable for a period of time, production overshoots demand and major bottlenecks are created in cycles lasting 45 to 55 years-the Kondratieff wave. We agree with this interpretation, although government intervention has clearly extended the range of long wave bottlenecks.

Wallerstein argues that over the centuries, each long wave decline and advance has deepened the capitalist system. He believes they forced the capitalist system to further penetrate the entire globe in order for the system to pull out of the long wave contraction phase and into the next long wave expansion. He believes that to ensure the capitalist system's survival, capital must always seek greater returns both in peripheral and in entirely new regions and countries. This is the reason most socialists believe the developed world exploits developing countries, to ensure the profitability of capital and, therefore, the future of the system.

Wallerstein (1984) basically argues that now, after many long waves that have driven capitalism into previously remote regions, the entire globe has basically been penetrated by the capitalist world economy. He argues that the capitalist world economy has reached or will soon reach the end of the line, a point where there are no more undeveloped and untapped regions and peoples to bring into the periphery of the capitalist system. In a sense, he is arguing that capitalism is reaching the point where it has run out of victims. The rapid rise of the BRIC countries of Brazil, Russia, India and China are an example of this long wave phenomenon, but this is a process that is closer to its beginning than its ending. International capitalism is in many respects only now hitting its stride, and the forces of socialism at work during this particular long wave winter crisis must be held in check and turned back.

The periphery countries that are being integrated into capitalism were never victims, but are being offered the opportunity to participate in the greatest economic system ever devised, and consequently a better way of life. Sure, some victimization has occurred, but it paled in comparison to the good produced by improved living standards. It could also certainly be argued that, although most of the globe has been touched by capitalism, the development of the global economy has only just begun. It will take many more long waves to get anywhere close to full development of the global economy, and even then, the system would not need new territory and people to pull out of a long wave decline. But Wallerstein (1984) believes the engines of capitalism have no more long-term fuel and that a systemic crisis greater than that triggered by a severe long wave decline will produce a socialist world government. He believes we have already entered this systemic crisis and are close to the point of capitulation to a new system of global socialism.

There are clear problems with Wallerstein's arguments. Even he (Wallerstein, 1984) argues there are other ways for capitalism to pull out of a long wave decline and stimulate a new long wave era of growth. Further expansion into new regions to create a new periphery for exploitation isn't critical for free market capitalism to pull out of a long wave decline. During much of the cold war, the capitalist system was losing territory on its borders and was still expanding nicely in a long wave advance. There are numerous issues with Wallerstein's argument in this regard.

One reason I wanted to review Wallerstein and expose some of the general flaws in his thinking is that I believe he has something significant to contribute on long wave analysis and a very useful framework for discussion and analysis of international political economy. He has a few insights into how the free market system pulls out of long wave declines, although many of his ideas borrow heavily from Kondratieff's original work. Wallerstein's (1984) observations, however, undermine his own argument of the ultimate systemic crisis of capitalism. He believes that, since its inception in Western Europe in the 13th and 14th centuries, the capitalist system has pulled out of a long wave stagnation phase in four basic ways.

The first way that capitalism can try to pull out of a long wave decline is by further mechanizing to save labor costs or by simply shifting production to the low labor costs of the periphery. This basically means that industry buys more machines to cut labor costs and increase productivity or moves production to a developing region or country with cheaper labor. This is to a great extent what the North American Free Trade Agreement (NAFTA) is all about: the United States wanted to shift some of its production to Mexico. This shift has been seen in other areas of the globe as well. Japan has shifted production to countries with lower labor costs in Southeast Asia. Western Europe is shifting production to the newly opened markets in Eastern Europe.

When production is shifted to countries with low labor costs, demand is stimulated in these areas. Products are produced more cheaply for the developed core countries, and demand is generated in the peripheral areas of new production due to the wages paid. What we are currently witnessing is precisely what Wallerstein (1984) expected to occur. The problem is that this process produces a drag in developed countries as good jobs in textiles, auto production, etc., emerge elsewhere. In the early going, this process creates more of a drag than a boost on wages because the new jobs in the periphery pay a lot less than the old job in the core country (i.e., deflation), but it creates better margins for capital investment in the periphery. The real boost to the system will come during the next advance and spring season of the long wave as the peripheral areas become even more developed. That new spring season is dead ahead.

Wallerstein's (1984) elaboration of some of Kondratieff's thinking is important in the present stage of this long wave because of the massive political restructuring that has taken place globally in recent years, particularly in former socialist nations. The new markets for shifting production into Eastern Europe, Russia, China, and Latin America, which includes the BRIC countries, surpass anything ever seen in a long wave decline. At no time in history, have so many markets been opening up with potential for stimulating demand and expanding the penetration of capitalism in general. These drastic differences with the 1930s are one reason it could be argued that we are in for a mild long wave winter season rather than a severe one.

The vast new markets for international capitalism are critically important for how bad things get in this long wave and how long we are in this long wave winter season, and how fast we will accelerate out and pull into the next advance. If trade wars and protectionism do not erupt during this long wave winter season and the domestic economies of the new markets of Brazil, Russia, China, India and many other countries begin to pull into the next advance, they could pull the core countries with them, in a powerful way. This is what the powers that be are attempting to engineer, but the timing is going to be critical as this long wave winter unfolds and the next spring season begins.

Never before in history have so many new markets with skilled workers opened up so close together during a long wave decline. The deflationary winter season of this long wave is and will remain obvious, but many negative effects of the long wave winter could be muted by the opening of these new markets and their economic growth. High costs and excess production can be exported to these new markets. They also provide new outlets for capital in search of higher returns. Losses in one region can be made up with gains in another.

The one big potential problem is if one of the major new markets, such as China or Eastern Europe, is taken out of the equation. A military coup, trade wars, shooting war, revolution, civil war, extreme nationalism, or any number of other events could threaten these markets during the present long wave winter season. If the trend toward opening these markets reverses, this long wave winter could easily be more severe than the 1930s, but I believe it will be sharper and recovery will come faster. If one or more of these markets are shut down in this long wave winter, the consequences will be disastrous for a global economy that is in crisis. Trade wars and protectionism are likely the single biggest threat to disrupting the spread of capitalism.

The second way Wallerstein (1984) sees capitalism pulling out of a long wave winter crisis he takes directly from Kondratieff: the innovation and new technology that invariably arises during a decline to set the stage for an advance. By creating new businesses and industries around new innovations, overall demand is stimulated in the economy. The new technology and new industries that come with it create the new jobs for the next long wave advance in the developed core countries. The new technology and industries have quasi-monopolies and sometimes monopolies based on patents and thus better margins than the old industries. New jobs replace the old jobs that were shifted to the periphery in the decline.

A third way Wallerstein (1984) sees the capitalist system pulling out of decline is with redistribution of world surplus in both core and periphery areas of the capitalist system. This is a unique contribution to long wave thought and is a late 20th-century phenomenon. This redistribution is an effort to increase demand and stimulate the system. Wallerstein sees this as the planned bourgeoisification of the proletariat. This could be seen as the central effort of the New Deal during the Great Depression and many of the policies during this decline. Redistribution of wealth is an attempt to stimulate the system by shifting wealth from the few to the many. Even though I argue that the attempt fails and actually hampers recovery, Wallerstein is correct in observing that it is one way governments of capitalist states have tried to stimulate the system to move out of a long wave decline. This is proving to be the case once again, only a Global New Deal is in the offing.

Finally, Wallerstein (1984) argues that demand was stimulated in past long wave declines by expanding the outer boundaries of the capitalist world economy. New periphery countries were created, areas previously untouched by Western capital. It should be noted that Wallerstein sees the globe as fully absorbed into the capitalist world system at the close of the 20th century. In his analysis this final option for pulling out of decline no longer exists. This is the primary reason he believes the capitalist system has entered its systemic crisis.

Only one of Wallerstein's (1984) four observations on how capitalism pulls out of crisis depends upon the borders of the capitalist system being expanded, at least on earth. The other three can come internally and dynamically and do not require exploitation or incorporation of new land or peoples.

The capitalist system is less dependent than ever upon the capital and labor relationship with which socialists are so obsessed. There is also the final frontier: space. Expansion into space doesn't take more room on earth. Elbow room in this regard is unlimited. New lands and peoples do not have to be exploited, as far as we know. Of course, it is not exploitation, but opportunity. Call it expansion. However, avenues for deployment of capital are limitless on earth, even in old markets that can be rejuvenated. Capitalism will not die because it runs out of room, even if the space industry doesn't pan out. However, we are clearly seeing space exploration beginning to pick up steam in this long wave decline and winter season. Space tourism is only beginning. Space exploration is expected to boom in the years ahead.

However, I will concede that Wallerstein's (1984) thinking is very important in terms of increased activity in peripheral markets in Russia, Eastern Europe, China, Mexico, South America, and Southeast Asia, i.e. the BRIC countries plus many others, in this long wave winter. Expansion of capitalism into these markets is laying the groundwork for the next long wave expansion and could dampen this winter season decline. Economic growth and development in these areas as a means to reduce production costs and to provide an outlet for capital as well as markets for surplus production are one reason we could manage a mild long wave winter this time around. Financial markets appear to be expecting the benefits of this dramatic turn of events. Once again, if something unforeseen closes these markets-such as an international crisis: civil war in Mexico, Russia, or China, or an upheaval such as a global trade war-then a mild long wave winter could turn nasty-and fast.

Wallerstein's (1984) strongest argument for his dream of the emergence of socialist world government was his observation of the increasing socialization of the means of production. This was taking place up until the late 1970s and early 1980s. Socialism, the public ownership of production, was expanding, and many believed it was working in some countries. However, this trend reversed when socialism appeared to have hit a wall. At least it did until the latest long wave winter season crisis in the last few years. We now see even the U.S. government rushing headlong into the ownership of production and services, even bank ownership. The speed with which we are seeing the reemergence of the global forces of socialization as this global crisis unfolds is remarkable.

At the time of the last edition of this book, privatization was the new trend globally. That has now reversed with the long wave winter crisis, with the U.S. government leading the way. In the last edition I noted that it was hard to conceive of a socialist world government coming about when the global system is rushing toward privatization. The world economy has scarcely entered this long wave winter season financial crisis when socialization has seen its fortunes soar. In the last edition, I stated, "A severe long wave winter crisis will renew the calls for socialist solutions and could potentially reverse the global trend toward privatization and market economies in the West."

In the 1995 edition, I wrote, "Clearly, many of Wallerstein's (1984) arguments concerning the capitalist system being in systemic crisis are having a hard time finding validity these days. Most observers are declaring that what Wallerstein calls the capitalist world economy is the victor over a socialist world government. However, dismissing Wallerstein would ignore the dangerous relevance of some of his observations and predictions." Wallerstein's writing's are now getting much more attention with the drastic shift to socialist oriented solutions during this global long wave crisis.

Many of his predictions are coming to fruition as a period of economic stagnation forces the capitalist world economy to retrench and seek to stimulate new demand and fight to keep open new markets. This is exactly what Wallerstein (1984) argued the capitalist system would do. The applicability and accuracy of some of Wallerstein's insights should make the reader cautious about ignoring his prognostication that proponents of a government-led socialist redistributive government will once again assert a claim for being the next logical world social system when hard times hit capitalism once again; indeed, this is happening now. Exact timing isn't crucial for Wallerstein since he allows for a transition process taking 150 years after the Russian revolution. With such a broad time parameter, Wallerstein would seem to argue that what appeared to be the receding tide of socialism was only a surface aberration in good times. Indeed, a renewed call for socialist world government has emerged as capitalism's chips are down in this long wave decline and the trend of the 1980s and 1990s toward privatization has suffered a major reversal of fortunes.

Wallerstein's arguments (1984) in favor of a socialist redistribution world government are certainly flawed. For many reasons, a socialist world government would prove to be a greater social disaster than the Soviet Union, but on a global scale. However, during a long wave winter crisis, people will be looking for answers and many will undoubtedly turn to socialist solutions. They won't buy the arguments for capitalism self-rejuvenating; not surprising, since, clearly, it does not appear to be rejuvenating very effectively during the final years of this long wave winter season.

It would therefore be wise to understand the socialist arguments and the flaws in those arguments. The long wave cleans out the capitalist system for a new beginning; it will never kill it, unless socialist theory espousing a new social system is once again taken seriously by government leaders as well as the more radical revolutionaries.

Once again, Wallerstein has a great deal of insight into the intricacies of capitalism. His more recent thinking was updated in an October 16, 2008 article entitled "The Depression: A Long-Term View", in *Monthly Review*, when he made the following observations on the global crisis of the current long wave decline and winter season:

The depression has started. Journalists are still coyly enquiring of economists whether or not we may be entering a mere recession. Don't believe it for a minute. We are already at the beginning of a full-blown worldwide depression with extensive unemployment almost everywhere. It may take the form of a classic nominal deflation, with all its negative consequences for ordinary people. Or it might take the form, a bit less likely, of a runaway inflation, which is simply another way in which values deflate, and which is even worse for ordinary people....

If one asks why this Kondratieff B-phase has lasted so long, it is because the powers that be–the U.S. Treasury and Federal Reserve Bank, the International Monetary Fund, and their collaborators in western Europe and Japan–have intervened in the market regularly and importantly–1987 (stock market plunge), 1989 (savings-and-loan collapse), 1997 (East Asian financial fall), 1998 (Long Term Capital Management mismanagement), 2001-2002 (Enron)–to shore up the world-economy. They learned the lessons of previous Kondratieff B-phases, and the powers that be thought they could beat the system. But there are intrinsic limits to doing this. And we have now reached them, as Henry Paulson and Ben Bernanke are learning to their chagrin and probably amazement. This time, it will not be so easy, probably impossible, to avert the worst....

As for our immediate short-run ad interim prospects, it is clear what is happening everywhere. We have been moving into a protectionist world (forget about so-called globalization). We have been moving into a much larger direct role of government in production. Even the United States and Great Britain are partially nationalizing the banks and the dying big industries. We are moving into populist government-led redistribution, which can take left-of-center social-democratic forms or far right authoritarian forms. And we are moving into acute social conflict within states, as everyone competes over the smaller pie. In the short run, it is not, by and large, a pretty picture.

What I find to be one of the more interesting aspects of Wallerstein's (1984) work is that he believes that in the ancient world, world economies gave way to redistributive world empires. This would be an empire like Rome or ancient China, where there was a single center of political power. Wallerstein never clearly explains why, this time around, the capitalist world economy will be transformed into a socialist system, instead of producing another redistributive world empire. I actually think Wallerstein is onto something here concerning the possibility of the rise of an authoritarian redistributive world empire, which would be a potential right-of-center authoritarian form of government-led-redistribution. The single political center for this redistributive world empire would be the United Nations combined with other supranational organizations such as the WTO and IMF as administrators of the globalization infrastructure of a loosely coupled international system of state capitalism and interventionism (i.e., a redistributive world empire). This appears to be what is now occurring, more so than global socialism.

A redistributive world empire is far more likely this time around than what he has termed left-of-center social-democratic or socialist government. There is a good chance that during this long wave winter season decline the global financial crisis is allowing at least some form of a modern redistributive world empire to emerge. A redistributive world empire would have a massive international, interventionist, bureaucratic-government structure, which appears to be the trend.

In the last edition I did not give the rise of left-of-center socialist world government a chance as a system to emerge out of the current long wave crisis. However, I've come to believe the risk of Wallerstein's arguments for socialist solutions being given more credit deserve greater consideration. This comes in light of the rush to public ownership and wealth redistribution solutions in this crisis around the world. The U.S. has led the way in this trend. Wallerstein's projection of the rise of socialist world government 150 years after the Russian revolution means that the final push for global socialism would be during the next long wave winter season. Presumably, this long wave winter season would be a major step in that direction.

This new edition proposes that there are three options vying to become the dominant global system that takes us out of this global long wave decline and winter season crisis, and into the next spring season of the global long wave. Rest assured, we will take clear steps on one of these three paths out of this latest long wave decline and winter season of global financial and economic crisis. One of the following three scenarios is coming sooner rather than later:

1) The least likely scenario for the future is in my view the case made by Wallerstein and presented in this chapter. This scenario suggests we are in the long awaited crisis of capitalism that will force us to take steps toward global socialism and a left-of-center government-led redistribution system. This now has to be considered a possibility based on U.S. and other government's aggressive state ownership based response to the global crisis. Wallerstein sees the full transition to a new future of global socialism coming by 2067, which will be close to the end of the next long wave winter season. It remains my conviction that Wallerstein's (1984) prediction of a socialist world government does not have a significant chance during this long wave winter season crisis or the next. The socialists will once again be disappointed and not see their dreams fulfilled.

2) The next chapter considers the second scenario and what Wallerstein termed a redistributive world empire. It could also be viewed as a right-of-center government-led redistribution system, where the world will end up looking more like the Roman Empire, with managers of global institutions being the modern day Roman senators and major world leaders being the modern Caesars. These would invariably lead the world into new Dark Ages a few centuries hence. This is a far more likely outcome than left-of-center democratic-socialism.

3)   The third and final option considers a return to true
     international free market capitalism in the form of
     what we term in this book as The Great Republic, a new
     era of high-technology-driven limited government
     and private-property market based international free
     market capitalism. The Great Republic becomes the
     more likely option if U.S. fiscal and monetary policy
     efforts to boost the global economy fail. When this
     happens the debt deflation will accelerate, and the
     necessity of radically reducing the size of government,
     reducing the tax burden on citizens and international
     capitalism and more intelligent market based
     resource management and allocation become the
     clear alternatives. Individual liberty-based political
     movements will take the world in the direction of The
     Great Republic.

We are indeed in the long wave winter season and a limited
crisis of capitalism. However, it would be more accurate to
explain the global crisis as a crisis of "state" capitalism not true
capitalism. The extent of the mess we are in was not caused by
international free market capitalism, but by a mixed system of
limited free markets, government intervention and trillions of
dollars in state capitalism sponsorship and implicit mortgage
guarantees that were leveraged beyond all reasonable levels. In
state capitalism the losses are increasingly being socialized and
the gains are privatized, such a model has little in common with
true capitalism.

The most attractive alternative to address the crisis for the
future of the global economy is a return to true international
free market capitalism, with less government and more individual
responsibility and liberty, in other words, The Great Republic.
This option may actually get a fair hearing in the years ahead.
Whether it will emerge victorious is an entirely different matter,
as there is a risk of the forces of state capitalism and intervention
aligning globally in supranational organizations that create a
modern redistributive world empire.

Chapter 22:

A REDISTRIBUTIVE WORLD EMPIRE

"Great occasions do not make heroes or cowards; they simply unveil them to the eyes of men. Silently and imperceptibly, as we wake or sleep, we grow strong or we grow weak, and at last some crisis shows us what we have become."

Bishop Wescott

"Civilization is the progress toward a society of privacy. The savage's whole existence is public, ruled by the laws of his tribe. Civilization is the process of setting man free from men."

Ayn Rand

We should begin our discussion of the potential rise of a redistributive world empire with the position that, no matter what happens during this long wave winter season, we will emerge into another long wave advance. No matter how mild or severe this winter season and the low economic tides it brings, there is always the rising tide on the other side that creates a new more advanced global economy. Therefore, the long wave is really an optimistic theory of economic progress. My hope is that this book is clearly communicating the positive aspects of long wave theory. There are great and rewarding days ahead; don't let the gloom and doom that is dominating the media or the risk of a world system you would rather not see emerge during this long wave crisis get you down.

Prognostication regarding the details of the technology, currency, and nation that will lead the next long wave advance can be a complicated and difficult exercise. However, there is a question more important than those concerning the technology or currency that will lead the global economy into the next long wave spring season, or the particular nation or region that will lead the global economic charge. A more fundamental question must be asked concerning the overall political, economic, and financial international system that will emerge in this age of a global economy. What world system will rise to the occasion?

We have already discussed in this book the creeping state capitalism and interventionism of the 20th century, which is the natural progression of the New Deal that was launched in the 1930s long wave winter season. The New Deal was not limited to the United States. It was a global phenomenon that has seen government bureaucracy expand its tentacles into every aspect of the lives of citizens and economic activity around the world.

The forces opposing and undermining free markets and capitalism appear to arise from within the capitalist system itself. These include well-meaning lifelong politicians and their constituents and supporters in business that are or become government contractors. An elite class of such state capitalist operators and interventionists have emerged and grown in number over the decades; a libertarian may categorize them as looters. They simply don't understand the damage they are doing to a market economy by constantly expanding the role of government. The government fills roles the market should be filling.

Adam Smith's principle of the "invisible hand" is not a force state capitalists and interventionists appreciate, but a force they mistrust. They are insulated from the life they create for the middle and hourly working classes, who pay the bills of state capitalism. Elites, through their access to government leaders or their roles as government leaders, have accelerated the rise of state capitalism, a mixed system of capitalism and government funded programs and projects. The international free market system has been slowly but surely compromised. By lobbying for government contracts with the rising number of government agencies and programs, elites have played an important role in the rise of state capitalism and interventionism that has grown to include or directly impact a large portion of GDP in most countries.

Creeping state capitalism and interventionism in mortgage and financial markets, combined with purer forms of capitalism in financial markets, producing a toxic mixed system without requisite regulation. The trillions of dollars in debt this system created, some with explicit and some with implicit guarantees by taxpayers, began to implode. The crisis brought us to the very edge of the global financial and economic abyss.

The crisis of this long wave winter season, magnified by the rise of state capitalism, created a situation where government had to step in with increased intervention. If government had not stepped in, the entire global financial system could have melted down and international chaos would have ensued. There would have been blood in the streets. If this had occurred, we would likely now be on the door step of Wallerstein's vision of the true crisis of capitalism and the birth of global socialism—or worse, in a backlash to the social chaos that would have engulfed the world. There would have been shuttered financial markets and a collapse in economic activity, far worse than has already occurred.

Wallerstein is correct in observing that governments implement changes in long wave B-phase declines that create problems in the long run for global capitalism. However, these will not likely lead to the ultimate crisis of capitalism that many anticipate and the birth of a new world system of socialism. The United States and the rest of the developed world are caught in a vicious cycle that is now rapidly moving the world system of creeping state capitalism toward a redistributive world empire.

The emerging redistributive world empire began as a loosely coupled world economy of nation states that have increasingly embraced state capitalism. The interventionism and bureaucratic growth of state capitalism, since the New Deal of the 1930s, now threaten to give birth to a Global New Deal. Nation states are increasingly relinquishing their national sovereignty to supranational organizations and raising taxes on their citizens to pay for growing government expenses.

Wallerstein has observed that world economies have transitioned into redistributive world empires in the past. A redistributive world empire needs unified political power. The forces at work during this long wave winter, such as calls for a

Global New Deal, risk the emergence of a redistributive world empire. This will occur if sovereign nations turn too much power over to supranational organizations such as the United Nations, IMF and WTO. National governments, even the United States, are increasingly bureaucratic national models of emerging state capitalism and interventionism that is turning its sovereignty over to supranational organizations and global treaties. A new redistributive world empire is rising and clearly appears to be the route we are taking during this long wave winter season.

The New Deal was the attempt by government to regulate and tax and spend away the inevitable pain of a natural long wave winter season that was worse than it had to be because of government intervention. Clearly government has stepped up in an even bigger way this time around. Government is still trying to cure all the ills of the system, while in reality government intervention and meddling for the past five decades have made things worse and will make things worse in the long run. Interventionism is an attempt to fix perceived failures that the market could address on its own, and it feeds the growth of state capitalism. Clearly, Wallerstein's assertion that government attempts to end B-phases is a fact, and is creating problems for the capitalist world system.

The New Deal rejected self-regulating free markets, and we haven't looked back since. From the 1930s to the present, state capitalism and interventionism has been on the rise, with only a few brief respites. A Global New Deal during this long wave winter season threatens to accelerate state capitalism and interventionism on a global scale and take the world a few steps closer to a redistributive world empire, where state capitalism and interventionism are expanded and usurped by supranational organizations, be they regional or global.

The emergence of a more closely-linked global economy in the latest advance has brought world society to a great fork in the road. The new paths diverge ahead of us. We have to choose which of them we will pursue out of the latest long wave decline.

It is only during major financial, economic, and political upheavals that major structural changes in political and economic direction can take place. The population is too content during a comfortable long wave advance. It is only in a long wave decline that the international system is thrown into crisis and turmoil and that anything can happen. New roads are cut in crisis and the destiny of billions of people will follow in the ruts.

The New Deal and big government would have never flown 20 years earlier; it took the Great Depression to take us down that road. It is a road that has brought us to the present era, where out-of-control government growth consumes an ever-growing amount of the productivity of the citizens of the globe.

A chief characteristic and mark of a redistributive world empire is the socialization of risk and the privatization of profits. This has been the hallmark of government action in this long wave winter crisis thus far. We all know that a system that pays million dollar bonuses to people who fail miserably, inevitably paid for by taxes and higher costs of goods and services on the hourly working class and middle class, is not a system we want to see advanced. Nevertheless, it is the system in effect today. The problem with such a system of elite globalization is that it makes socialism look like an attractive option to the masses, which have an increased tendency to riots and to respond favorably to overt populism and nationalism. These are growing forces in a long wave winter season. This creates ongoing instability for such a system.

If we continue along the redistributive world empire path out of this long wave winter crisis, the rising empire will be required to vastly expand its power. A redistributive world empire will become dependent upon excessive taxation of property and income to supply its spending requirements. Redistribution of wealth to the protected elite class and the non-working class, to maintain power and control over its subjects, becomes an expensive proposition. Inefficiencies increase and resources become scarcer. An armed bureaucracy will ultimately be charged with keeping order, as the Roman legions did 2,000 years ago.

Such a redistributive world empire would have many characteristics of socialism, but would look far more like a global police state. Individual freedom would likely be significantly restricted. Such a system would not be socialist because it would not be based on public ownership of all property and public ownership of production. Private property would exist but would primarily be controlled by a wealthy elite class that controlled the system. This was the case with the last redistributive world empire, the Roman Empire.

A new redistributive world empire would very likely be built on three foundations: North America controlled by the United States, Europe controlled by Germany, and Asia controlled by China. This trilateral approach to the world's political and economic institutions can already be seen in much of the government policy and planning in all three blocks.

A redistributive world empire would basically be an all-powerful government run in the interest of the rising elite class that controls government and multinational corporations directly and through quasi-governmental organizations. Through excessive taxation of the middle-class and redistribution of wealth, the redistributive world empire is held together and maintains power. Taxation of both the working and middle class funds the redistributive world empire.

Those who run the system own and control both property and production; they are not taxed. Through foundations and creative accounting, they keep their wealth intact, away from the reaches of the government minions. It is the middle class who, through taxation, pays the interest on the debt that is income to the elite class.

In a redistributive world empire, we will witness the emergence of a growing layer of interventionism and bureaucracy at the global level. Much of this system is already in place, but it lusts for more power and legitimacy. The current global financial and economic crisis could be the excuse for plunging the capitalist world system beyond the point of no return.

Many would argue that there is no turning back from this path; I beg to differ. The Great Republic is a much more attractive option and, for a number of reasons, it may have higher odds of emerging from this long wave winter season and global crisis than presently realized.

Chapter 23:

THE GREAT REPUBLIC

"Destiny is real"

PQ Wall

"The progress of the human race is marked by periods of economic distress when want, poverty, and unemployment set the minds of men to thinking. These were periods when convictions were sharply and vigorously stated and men, by force of extremity, took their complaint to the fountain head. Great changes in government, leading to the emancipation of mankind and to the democracy which exists today were the result of movements that grew out of economic adversity."

Otto C. Lightner

"...there is in all great commercial countries a good deal of bullion alternately imported and exported for the purposes of foreign trade. This bullion, as it circulates among different commercial countries in the same manner as the national coin circulates in every particular country, may be considered as the money of the great mercantile republic. The national coin receives its movement and direction from the commodities circulated within the precincts of each particular country: the money of the mercantile republic, from those circulated between different countries. Both are employed in facilitating exchanges, the one between different individuals of the same, the other between those of different nations."

Adam Smith

"Ask yourself whether the dream of heaven and greatness should be waiting for us in our graves —or whether it should be ours here and now and on this earth."

Ayn Rand

Most advocates of World-Systems Analysis and other left-of-center socialist leaning thinkers and actors in the global system believe that the capitalist world economy is even now meeting its slow and irreparable demise. They believe capitalism is in its death throes; that the current long wave winter crisis is doing irreversible structural damage. The next long wave winter crisis is expected to deliver the final *coup de grace* for international capitalism. However, it is my contention that the framework of World-Systems Analysis can be utilized to make the case for a capitalist world economy and the regenerative forces of long waves, and demonstrate that we can stop the slide of capitalism into a government-led redistributive world empire, if we take another path: The Great Republic.

World-Systems Analysis clearly articulates that the increasing costs in the capitalist system of (1) taxes, (2) material and other non-labor production costs, and (3) labor costs are leading to the demise of capitalism. This is, in fact, true. It is time to recognize this and actively pursue policies to reverse, mitigate and better manage these forces to ensure a new golden age of capitalism. The Great Republic represents the active pursuit through human action of an aggressive return to an individual liberty and freedom based free market capitalist world economy. It is the only way to stop the rise of the redistributive world empire or global socialism and ensure the long-term survival of America and international capitalism.

The Great Republic is the best and most viable option for the global economy to extricate itself from the current long wave decline and enter the next long wave advance, preventing capitalism's slide toward a redistributive world empire. The Great Republic is a real and emerging option for the world system that is in competition with the forces that are aggressively driving for establishment of a redistributive world empire. The Great Republic is taken from Adam Smith's notion of an international system of unrestrained free trade based on the available option of a stable international currency in the form of digital gold currency.

What we term the Great Republic is being advanced by rapid technological innovation in communications, with the next wave of the Internet and the object-oriented programming (OOP) paradigm coded systems running under the hood. The OOP paradigm allows the global network of computer systems to more effectively represent the real world digitally, accelerating discovery, progress and efficiency, with astounding stability and speed on a global basis.

The Great Republic, in object-oriented programmer's parlance, is a loosely coupled distributed object model of sovereign nations serving its free and independent citizens, driving liberty, fraternity and economic opportunity. The Great Republic is creating and will accelerate a new global marketplace by capturing and magnifying the power of individual liberty and free international association for ideas, trade, travel and commerce. Economic and financial decision making will increasingly be removed from the politicians and their elite class of managers, which are increasingly a pariah to true international free market capitalism. Power and process will return to the free marketplace and be subject to survival against the best and brightest of ideas.

The dawning redistributive world empire will be snuffed out, rejected by the rising hourly working and white-collar middle class of citizens of The Great Republic around the world. Out of the ashes of the latest long wave winter decline will emerge a powerful new global economy based on limited government, free markets, national sovereignty, and individual liberty. It will be a global economy that thrives on global competition born of free markets. The unfit pet projects of politicians will not survive the competition.

Granted, the response to the current long wave winter season of global financial and economic crisis has thus far been a major expansion of federal government powers and intrusion into business, financial markets, and the global economy. What is disturbing is how fast the center of the financial and business world shifted from New York to Washington. This same paradigm shift occurred in most developed countries. The trend is troubling for anyone who believes in free markets, the power of human action and individual responsibility.

I believe The Great Republic offers another way out of this global crisis and long wave winter season. The Great Republic is emerging now and will continue to emerge, increasingly shining through in the midst of the chaos of global crisis. There is a backlash growing in the hearts and minds of Americans and those around the world who recognize the power of free markets and the forces of international free market capitalism. If it was only a matter of hope, the future would be dim, but facts are a far more powerful thing. Only a free market system can solve our problems. It is the only system that places the future where it should be, in the hands of those who will create it.

If the power of the free market and potential of The Great Republic was just another idea in a smooth political speech, we would be in trouble, but the free market is far more than an idea or an ideology. The free market is the real deal. The free market naturally produces long waves, but it did not produce the magnitude of the long wave crisis we currently face. Why has the natural long wave become a tidal wave of financial disaster around the globe? Government intervention and state capitalism prevented the market from weeding out the buffoonery, before it got to big too fail. Government intervention and its side kick of state capitalism is what turned this long wave into a government sponsored tidal wave of economic and financial disaster and its ensuing human misery.

If there is one core message to the basic concept of *Jubilee on Wall Street*, it is take heart; the invisible hand of the free market is already at work, creating solutions to our problems. Hundreds of millions of hard working individuals, in virtually every industry and marketplace around the globe, are hard at work, stepping up to solve the problems. I remain confident that in due time it will be clear that the government needs to step aside and let powerful free market forces address the problems. Whole new industries and entirely new ways of doing things are being created that will carry the day as we emerge from this long wave winter and into the next long wave advance.

The end of big government is a real option. It is increasingly evident that a majority of the citizens and taxpayers, not only in America, but around the world, are fed up with the hollow promises of government at every level. They have been promised education, prosperity, healthcare, increasing living standards, happiness, financial security, banking insurance, and a lot of other pie-in-the-sky utopian nonsense. The results of government interventionist attempts to create a government run perfect world are examples of good intentions gone bad. Government has increased its appetite for the hard-earned productive resources of the people of the globe, always needing just a little bit more of the total pie to solve our problems. Government has failed miserably at every turn in the road.

The government cut of GGP (Gross Global Product) has constantly increased in recent decades, while the standard of living of the majority of hard-working people has continued to decline; decade-after-decade, in country-after-country, government has made promises and failed to deliver the goods. Not because government hasn't tried; it has tried. Government is also full of good hardworking people. There are important roles that government must play. But government simply cannot achieve what only a true free market system motivated by free, self-preserving individuals who enjoy liberty and the fruits of their labor are capable of achieving. This fact is becoming obvious to a growing number of citizens in a growing number of nations in the global economy that is staggering under the load and burden of too much government.

Individuals must be accountable for their actions for better or worse. Government can't level the playing field, holding up the losers and holding back the overachievers. Worse yet, reward bad behavior and punish good behavior and expect the global system to produce its best or even second best results. It is a laughable and preposterous proposition. Such a system will in time only produce failure and misery across the board. This long wave winter season crisis has produced prime examples of government rewarding bad behavior and punishing good behavior. Such moral hazard is an evil that is self evident. It cannot and will not last. The people will not allow it.

Roosevelt was a consummate politician and was able to rally the people into believing that government could lead the way. Government intervention has been a yoke around the neck of not just the economy, but individuals ever since. Government has consistently expanded its influence. From those with the greatest ability to those with the least ability, we have all been held back by the noble intentions of misguided politicians who have tried a grand experiment. It has failed. Now we are facing the next horrifying specter in the experiment of big government: The Global New Deal in the form of a redistributive world empire.

There are those of us who still hold the old-fashioned view that America is the leader and last hope of real freedom from government tyranny in the world. Americans must demand a return to freedom and the road of the private sector and free markets to solve the problems faced by the accelerating global long wave crisis. I have my doubts that any other nation or nations can or will carry the torch for human liberty and freedom at this important juncture in human history if America does not lead. If not, the outcome will be a redistributive world empire from which we will not escape.

It must be noted that there are nations and regions that are definitely moving away from government and toward free markets and private solutions to society's problems. Southeast Asia is an excellent example of this trend. The trend away from government intervention and toward private solutions is one of the primary reasons I believe Southeast Asia will lead the world into the next long wave advance. They appear to already realize that government does not have the power to solve problems or improve living standards. China, along with the little tigers of Southeast Asia, is trending toward what could be the foundations of the private rather than public path for the new global economy, but they still need American leadership.

The real question is whether these new market economies can survive the onslaught of the redistributive world empire if the

United States doesn't change its ways and join in the trend away from government solutions. Maybe these nations can prosper without the moral support of the United States. They may surpass the United States in economic growth for the simple reason that they embrace the principles that made America great.

The backlash against global New Deal interventionism is spreading. A tiring of government intrusion and a weariness of the self-interest-motivated folly of politicians is a global phenomenon. The tide is turning. We may be just seeing the tip of an iceberg of popular revolt against government intervention in society that will rise to the surface as this long wave winter progresses.

Hope takes many forms. Many of my readers will undoubtedly question my judgment on this, but I believe that President Obama and his administration will come to realize that government does not have all the answers. They will realize that markets must be given the freedom to work it out and emerge into the next long wave advance. We are now clearly in the most critical years for political decision making during this long wave winter season. The United States and the world are depending on President Obama to make the right decision and lead us from the brink of a redistributive world empire; it is now or never. My expectation is that advocates of free markets will be pleasantly surprised at the decisions the Obama administration will make before the long wave winter comes to its close.

This long wave represents a unique confluence of global financial and political forces. The U.S. dollar as the world's reserve currency, in combination with dollar dominated individual, business and government debt, are a powerful force at work in this long wave winter. Before this long wave winter season is over the market forces they are unleashing are going to make our major trading partners view our fiscal and monetary re-inflation policies as a form of subsidies to U.S. business and protectionism. This will in fact be an accurate assessment on their part. Every action produces a reaction. The U.S. will be forced to end our aggressive fiscal and monetary policy to avert the disaster of the onslaught of a major global trade war. This will trigger continued debt deflation. This will require cutting government spending as a matter of necessity.

The long wave forces at work must be considered along with the fact that a revolt of the middle class is a real possibility in a number of countries, especially the U.S. The political situation will be exciting in coming years as the long wave unleashes major new forces in the political debate and process. The grass roots revolt that is now waiting in the wings is not a typical political revolt for some new grand political scheme, schism, or "-ism."

We are seeing the beginning of what appears to be a revolt against political interference across the board and at all levels. Ross Perot in the 1990s and recent tax tea parties only scratched the surface. These are macro trends that continue to build under the surface. What we are seeing is not a revolution for a cause, but a revolution against government, an anti-cause.

As already discussed in the chapter on politics, government has set itself up to take the blame for this long wave decline by claiming to have the solutions. The backlash against government failure this time around could be revolutionary. A global political climate change not seen since the American Revolution may be in the wings as we approach the end of this long wave winter season, and enter the next long wave spring season and advance.

The lines are clearly beginning to be defined for the choice of paths to be taken out of this long wave decline. The proponents of a return to genuine international free market capitalism are the underdogs at this point. As the next few years unfold and the failure of government intervention becomes more obvious to the masses, look for acceleration in the desire and call for free market capitalism and the end of big government.

A popular revolt may call for an end to the trend toward a U.N.-dominated redistributive world empire and global welfare state. The curtain is being jerked back, concealing the true nature of the Land of Oz in Washington, D.C., Tokyo, London, Peking, Moscow, Paris, Bonn, Brussels, other capitals around the globe, and the United Nations. The political wizards will be seen for the fakes they are and the revolt will swell.

The new economy created by the next long wave advance may well blow right past government interventionists and world empire builders, leaving them wondering what happened to their control of the world system. The new long wave economy will create information and communication systems, along with prosperity, that governments will not be able to control.

We are likely to see a rekindling of the vision of America's founding fathers–this time, internationally. It was a simple vision. The early American government was for defense and to maintain the domestic peace. It was understood and accepted that a free people, free to work hard and succeed, could handle the rest. Freedom from the tyranny of government was the vision that inspired people to come from every nation on earth to the new world.

You may doubt the feasibility of this potential path toward The Great Republic developing out of the latest long wave decline. You might be right. Such doubts have a basis. Maybe society has gone too far in the wrong direction to turn back. Maybe a new redistributive world empire is inevitable. A little doubt is certainly warranted, but the potential return to America's political roots and freedom from excessive government intervention is a far greater possibility than most realize at this point. All trends go too far, and politicians taking millions in campaign contributions from Fannie Mae and Freddie Mac as they inflated the housing mortgage bubble is too much for most Americans to stomach. They were quite literally taking money from your home in broad daylight. And that crime is just for starters. The American people are far smarter than that, and the pendulum of political will is invariably beginning its swing back.

The pendulum has only recently swung far enough in the direction of government intervention and control and the potential tyranny of a redistributive world empire to begin its swing back to liberty and individual accountability, driven by market forces that cannot be put back in the bottle. The voters may well demand that government get out of education, child care, art, lending, bank insurance, etc. and turn these roles over to the private sector. In certain instances, these things will be managed by the private sector for government and in others jettisoned from government involvement completely.

We can't really talk about the options out of this long wave crisis without at least briefly discussing the international monetary and financial outcome of each path. Obviously, each path will produce a major difference in the money system.

The monetary system advocated by the path of the redistributive world empire will most likely be run by the IMF as a subsidiary to a more globally powerful United Nations. Central banks of the globe would work closely in concert with the IMF and World Bank under new international laws and potentially a U.N. resolution. A U.N. resolution would force the new money system on the nations of the world without choice.

In the worst years of the long wave decline, in the next several years, potentially during a new banking crisis, the world builders who advocate the redistributive world empire may take bold steps. World leaders, probably the G-20, could get together and offer a new global money system as a solution. The trilateral currency blocks of the U.S. dollar, the Chinese yuan, and the euro would be the foundation of the system. The goal would be to merge these three currency blocks in time–potentially immediately, but certainly within a decade–into a single international currency unit. The first steps in such a money and banking system would be created in the midst of a global banking crisis.

The only way the people of the world would accept such a system in a crisis would be if it were tied somehow to the perceived stability of gold–even if it was not a true gold system. Keep in mind that during long wave declines, nationalism is a powerful force. Rising nationalistic movements would likely have to be crushed to see a Global New Deal type of money system implemented. This system would have a model in the present euro. The likelihood of a partial gold basis to such a system makes owning some gold a wise move. However, eventually gold could be dropped from this system, and we would have a single international fiat currency backed in nothing but faith in the world-empire builders and politicians. If we take this path, the economy would still enter the next long wave advance, but under such a new monetary system there would be much slower growth than without it. Controlled by the all-powerful redistributive world empire, human potential would be restrained. There is a much better way. Please note that most of this was written in the 1995 edition of this book, 15 years before China and Russia stepped forward during the global financial crisis of this long wave winter in early 2009 and offered exactly such an IMF-managed system.

However, in the worst years of this decline, we may well see the forces in favor of a redistributive world empire become disarrayed. The European Union is showing signs of strain already. We may see the nations of the globe recoil from recent trends toward the redistributive world empire. We will likely see a new wave of nationalism, even micro-nationalism and isolationism not seen since the 1930s. Micro-nationalism, nationalism, and the many movements that seek smaller circles of political sovereignty and autonomy are taking the world in one direction and the forces of the emerging world empire are trying to take the world in another. Eastern Europe, Africa, Northern Ireland, Quebec, China, Southeast Asia, and India all contain examples of the trend toward smaller rather than larger circles of government power.

One of the reasons I am growing more optimistic and believe The Great Republic will become a reality, is that it now appears that the most likely currency system to emerge during this crisis is the hybrid system of regional fiat money and digital gold currency (DGC). DGC represents the free market's response to a massive market need during the decline of an economic long wave. Advances in technology have made DGC possible. DGC is a game changer.

DGC as the optional currency of The Great Republic provides a standard for all participants to readily ascertain and measure the value of their work and unique contribution to the global economy. The Great Republic represents a return to genuine, robust and sustainable technology-driven modern international free market capitalism as the world system. The Great Republic will preempt the rise of a redistributive world empire and prevent the ultimate crisis of capitalism anticipated by many.

DGC represents a form of pure gold deposit accounts that can be utilized with ease for local, national and international transactions and settlements. DGC will increase in use and will provide the ability to move into and out of various fiat currencies with growing ease and sophistication. It may be difficult to imagine at this point, but in the future DGC has the potential to ride herd over major and minor fiat currencies. It is already happening to some extent for those who use it as a means to avoid the danger of irresponsible and inflationary fiscal and monetary policies.

DGC is digital gold representing a fixed amount of real gold in secure insured vaults, in many cases in Switzerland, but vaults in New York, London and Fort Knox will also suffice. Sovereign states and their governments may choose to administer and offer a DGC to their citizens to encourage economic growth and financial stability. DGC will serve to keep a check on national fiscal and monetary policy as their impact will be felt in real time on fiat currencies through their conversion rates to DGC. It will force fiat currencies to be managed effectively by more prudent central bank monetary and national government fiscal policy, or risk being crushed by the powerful global forces at work and the free flow of information in The Great Republic.

In conjunction with the growth of the use of DGC and inevitable increases in its use and sophistication, the world appears to be headed toward three dominant regional fiat currencies, the dollar, euro, and Chinese yuan. The dollar will remain the dominant one of these three for some time, and it is in the interest of the U.S. to maintain this dominance. Sound government fiscal policy and sound central bank monetary policy will be cheered by users of DGC, which will switch back into fiat currencies and, therefore, buoy their exchange prices relative to DGC.

Smaller government, radically reduced taxes, and the widespread use of a high-technology-driven loosely coupled DGC system, would position the world for explosive growth during the next advance of the long wave. The global economy could see rising prosperity and economic growth levels not seen since the 19th century. This is particularly interesting because many of the nations of Southeast Asia that are poised to lead the next advance have enough gold reserves to issue their own DGC.

Advances in communications, namely the Internet and object-oriented programming, that have already occurred during this long wave winter, and their deployment is accelerating. They will organize and disseminate new ideas that determine the allocation of capital resources for consumption, production and investment during the next long wave advance. The backbone of The Great Republic would be the availability and widespread use of DGC. Fiat currencies may even gain in value against DGC, because they are kept in check by the watchful eye of the market.

In the years to come, peaceful political revolt against the status quo and bigger government could become popular movements, which might even seize political power through the ballot box. Political, market and long wave forces are still beyond the control of the architects of the redistributive world empire. It is not too late. Those involved in peaceful political revolts around the globe against larger government would totally distrust financial and economic solutions managed by the empire builders. In short, we could see a wholesale rejection of the trend toward government solutions on a local, state, national, and global scale.

Just as communism was rejected, the citizens across The Great Republic, and citizens of their respective countries, will reject the creeping redistributive world empire. We may well witness wholesale rejection of what big government offers. This growing force would likely reject most government solutions for a return to a modern technology-driven international free market capitalism. Government and its role would be cut drastically in The Great Republic.

There is good reason for my optimism. The following may sound like a bit of a reach in light of where we find ourselves today, but radical measures are needed and major political change is in the air and coming fast. The following are my proposed twelve foundations for U.S. policy to position the U.S. to lead the rise and show the way toward The Great Republic as a new model of international political economy. The coming long wave advance is the optimal time to maximize our potential. This list is not intended to be exhaustive, but as a start, to set a new tone for the discussion of our true potential and the necessary steps to get there. The greatest generation is not in our past, it is in our future. The Great Republic has the potential to deliver the greatest era in the history of humankind:

1. Tax reform: Individual and corporate income tax, as well as all social security taxes, should be scrapped for a simple national sales tax system. The basic approach of FairTax.org is solid; however, the national sales tax they propose is too high. The sales tax rate needs to be capped by a constitutional amendment and, once implemented, the sales tax rate needs to be systematically reduced over time, in conjunction with a measured reduction in the size of federal and state government as a percent of GDP. This can only be done if the 16th amendment is repealed. Both a national sales tax or value added tax (VAT) and an income tax would be an unmitigated disaster for the U.S.; if this occurs, the dawning of The Great Republic will be jeopardized.

2. Limited Government: Government spending needs to be cut aggressively. A cut in federal government spending equal to 1% of GDP per year should be implemented until total government spending, including Social Security, represents only 15% of GDP. GDP will be growing sharply under the tax reform above, so the reductions in the percentage of GDP are expected to actually be an increasing government budget in actual dollar amounts. Any government activity that can be privatized should be. A vast number of government agencies can be privatized, including government operations that are large and extensive.

3. Balanced budget amendment: Pass a constitutional amendment to balance the budget, which only allows deficit spending when GDP is negative, and in times

of war, with any such deficits required to be repaid by spending cuts over 3.5 years (the regular business cycle) after GDP returns to positive, or the war has ended in victory. The initial pursuit of a balanced budget, due to the current deficit, will need to be phased in over 7 years, with a required percentage reduction of the current deficit of ~15% per year.

4. U.S. Patent and Copyright Laws: Intellectual Property laws in the United States need to provide the greatest protection anywhere in the world for any and all intellectual property, making the U.S. the world's number one market for research, development and commercialization of new products and services. Such policies will go a long way to ensure a great global economic boom with the U.S. leading the way, as other nations will follow our lead.

5. Social Security: Unfortunately, there is no other option to save the country from the social security disaster and bankruptcy that is barreling down on us. The math just doesn't work; we must means test Social Security. A means test for Social Security is more than fair because the reduced taxes in No. 1 above will more than cover the loss of social security benefits to those with means. If you have income over a certain multiple to the poverty level, your Social Security payments need to be reduced.

6. Healthcare: The healthcare system needs to be built on private, high-deductible health plans that financially penalize poor health decisions and financially incentivizes individual responsibility and healthy behavior. Catastrophic unpreventable health events could be generously covered in a system that reaps the savings from effectively incentivizing good health behavior. Medicare must also be partially means tested, which increases the deductible amount for those that can afford it. Medicaid benefits need to be cut back across the board and only be available

for the truly indigent. We must design health care
insurance and delivery systems to incentivize good
health behavior.

7. Digital Gold Currency (DGC): A constitutional
amendment establishing the right of U.S. citizens to
own DGC accounts in U.S. private and public DGC
banks and international DGC banks is required. The
amendment should also grant foreign citizens the
right to hold public and private DGC accounts in the
United States. The U.S. Treasury should be required to
convert Fort Knox into the most advanced and secure
DGC bank vault in the world, as it will be a boon to
the U.S. economy and the government will earn fees
in gold. A Fort Knox DGC will have to compete with
private U.S. and foreign DGC banks, so it will have
to be competitively run. DGC and fiat money systems
must be kept separated. If they are combined it will
only lead to the corruption of the gold basis to the
system. Technology now allows for totally separate
systems and a firewall should remain between them
forever. A key role of DGC is to constantly monitor
and price in the marketplace in real-time the job
government and central banks are doing in managing
their fiat monetary systems.

8. Federal Reserve Board: A significant increase
in commercial bank reserve requirements and
corresponding decreased use of debt leverage is
required. Without a Year of Jubilee, international free
market capitalism needs the government to regulate
the use of debt leverage in commercial banking. With
responsible government fiscal policy the Federal
Reserve System will be able to more effectively manage
stable fiat monetary policy. Economic growth will take
care of itself if the above policies are implemented.
The Federal Reserve will not be required to juice the
economy with easy monetary policy to compensate
for reckless government fiscal policy that saps the

vitality out of the U.S. economy. DGC will provide a market alternative to fiat money at all times. DGC will likely find more widespread use when the Federal Reserve cannot manage monetary policy effectively due to bad government fiscal policy, but will decrease in use when government maintains fiscal discipline and the Federal Reserve can more effectively manage monetary policy.

9. Free Trade: The U.S. must be the world's leading defender of free trade, by reducing tariffs and subsidies and all other forms of government assistance to all industries and businesses. We must get government out of business and end the failed experiment of U.S. "state" capitalism that risks the U.S. being the primary accomplice in its own destruction and the corresponding rise of a redistributive world empire, or even worse, global socialism.

10. Drug Policy: Most terrorism and major crime, including the Taliban, is funded by the international drug trade. Illegal drugs should be legalized to defund international terrorism and crime. This creates regulatory issues, so a new class of drugs needs to be created that has the regulatory status of non-approved. Such substances would be taxed at a higher rate than the regular national sales tax rate. Such drugs could be taxed at a high rate to fund public and private drug prevention and rehabilitation programs at the local level, but not so high as to incentivize illegal activity. Employers would have the right to terminate employees for use of non-approved drugs. Such a policy will go a long way to stabilize the border with Mexico and defund the Taliban, allowing the U.S. to win the war in Afghanistan, which is critical to national and international security.

11. Federal budget surpluses: If the proposed actions above are implemented and government spending is reduced to 15% of GDP, the U.S. government

will begin to run budget surpluses during the next advance of the long wave cycle. These surpluses will be managed by the U.S. Treasury, partially invested in U.S. DGC in the Fort Knox DGC Bank, and various other investments, including foreign treasury debt investments to complement U.S. foreign policy goals; however, the buildup of government surpluses needs to be limited. If surpluses exceed 10% of GDP in any quarter, any such government surpluses should be paid out equally to U.S. families using the prebate system proposed by FairTax.org, and managed by the Social Security Administration. Federal budget surplus bonus payment distribution to all American families could be made in U.S. dollars or DGC, at the discretion of the U.S. Treasury. This is the only bonus program in which the U.S. Government should be involved, paying all American's for jobs well done that have produced federal budget surpluses.

12. Election Reform: The use of election law to prevent third-party competition needs to end. The two party oligarchy and their lobbyists are reducing U.S. political freedom and threatening individual liberty. The populism that is building in America is an unstoppable force; it must be channeled into the power and reward of international free market competition, and not the dead end road of isolationism and protectionism. Election reform must allow for fair ballot access for new third-party participation that seeks to reform Washington for more effective government, and unleash the potential force for good in the rise of The Great Republic.

Don't confuse these proposed policies as opposition to strong and effective U.S. government. The U.S. Federal government must maintain the greatest military and defense capabilities in the world. If we implement these policies, consistent with the principles of The Great Republic, the U.S. economy will boom to a $50 trillion and growing economy within a decade and the federal government will have a $7.5 trillion dollar budget in a low or no inflation global economy. If we implement these polices the U.S. will lead the next advance of the global long wave and take the world along with it on a global boom that will give new meaning to U.S. shock and awe policy. If the existing two party oligarchy in Washington can make it happen then fine, but it may take a third-party to force real change. The American people are clearly ready for such a major change in U.S. politics.

Taking either the path of a redistributive world empire, or The Great Republic, the global economy will emerge from its long wave decline and enter another long wave advance in the coming years. The political, economic, and financial systems that emerge, depending on which path is chosen, will be very different. Before the current long wave global economic crisis is over, we will know what we have become politically, economically, and financially. We will either be citizens of an all-powerful redistributive world empire that rivals the power of Rome at its apex, or we will be citizens of free nations, in a new age of technology-driven, international free market capitalism, known as The Great Republic.

The redistributive world empire would likely be a highly regulated system that would have less personal freedom and liberty and would never see very high growth rates. Individual financial and economic opportunity would exist but would be limited. The standard of living would rise slowly. Large multinational corporations would dominate the economy and national policy. National governments, agents of state capitalism, would surrender power, authority, and sovereignty to the United Nations and other supranational organizations. Such a system would see new government-regulated and subsidized technologies and industries lead the next long wave advance. However, in time, the redistributive world empire would choke the system and create a major breakdown of currently unimaginable proportions, very likely in the next long wave decline. It is at that point that Wallerstein's vision of a new future of global socialism could in fact be in the cards.

Ian Bremmer (2009) noted the critical role the U.S. must play to survive the global pressures that are mounting in an age of state capitalism when he wrote in *Foreign Affairs* in 2009:

> U.S. policymakers must try and sell the value of free markets, even though this is a difficult moment to do so. If Washington turns protectionist and keeps a heavy hand on economic activity for too long, governments and citizens around the world will respond in kind. The stakes are high, because the large-scale injection of populist politics into international commerce and investment will obstruct efforts to revitalize global commerce and reduce future growth.

The Great Republic, a reinvigorated system of international free market capitalism, would see explosive growth and prosperity in the coming long wave spring season and advance. Its dominant feature would be the shrinking size of government as a percentage of GDP. The system would see global competitiveness push national economies to great new heights of achievement. National sovereignty would be insured. New industries and technology would come to the market with phenomenal speed and effect. Small businesses and corporations led by visionary entrepreneurs would produce the greatest economic force on the planet. The standard of living of the hourly working and middle class would see drastic gains. In The Great Republic, human dignity, liberty and freedom, and the economic opportunity they will bring would create the greatest international political economy ever known to humanity.

Chapter 24:

A NEW BEGINNING

"An honest man is one who knows that he can't consume more than he has produced."

Ayn Rand

"The only real solution to the problem of over indebtedness is to reduce the value of the outstanding debt."

Nouriel Roubini

"Times of general calamity and confusion have ever been productive of the greatest minds. The purest ore is produced from the hottest furnace, and the brightest thunderbolt is elicited from the darkest storm."

Colton

"I like the dreams of the future better than the history of the past."

Thomas Jefferson

The basic theme of this book is that the long wave cycle is international free market capitalism's manifestation of the Jubilee, creating a new beginning for the global economy. Although a long wave, particularly the winter season, isn't much of a celebration, it has an impact on the global economy similar to the Jubilee. It cleans the slate and gives the economy a new beginning.

The Jubilee laws would have countered the primary forces that produce a regular long wave, a natural phenomenon only discovered by Kondratieff thousands of years later. It could be argued that the Jubilee laws were a form of government regulation.

A closer look reveals that the Jubilee reflected something far deeper than regulation or structured rules of commerce. The laws seem to have anticipated, even predicted, the natural long wave seasons that would inevitably be played out in the global economy.

The Jubilee was clearly an effort to control three areas of the economy: debt, prices and production, the three areas that tend to get out of control in a free market economy. There is no evidence that the Jubilee laws were ever implemented, so we have no evidence of how they would have worked to control the long wave. However, the objectives of the laws are clear.

The unique laws would have had the effect of discounting prices against year 50, the Year of Jubilee. The value of land was to be figured by how many years it could be used until Jubilee. The further away you were from Jubilee, the more expensive the land; the closer you were to Jubilee, the cheaper the land, which was the chief means of production in those days. It should be noted that the Jubilee laws were written for an agricultural economy. These laws would have the effect of giving us the exact opposite of what we have been reviewing in the long wave. In the long wave, we have prices beginning low in the spring season and moving constantly higher until reaching a peak. Prices collapse late in the long wave decline and winter season.

A system that incorporated the Jubilee laws would have the highest prices in the first year following the Year of Jubilee. Prices would constantly fall until year 50, the next Year of Jubilee. This would bring falling prices rather than inflation to the entire economic system. The Jubilee rules appear to be followed involuntarily in a long wave decline in a very imperfect manner.

The Jubilee laws would have a major impact on total economic production. Production and expansion would be based on predictable falling price patterns and not misguided anticipation of inflation, as is the case in our global system today. The flow of capital into the forces of production in a Jubilee system would be smoother, based on predictable price movements. You wouldn't have the buildup of excess capacity in the economy.

In our system, you have virtually every industry overproducing in winter. Global capacity utilization is presently collapsing. This leads to trade wars, bankruptcy, and unemployment. The buildup of excess production is what eventually brings the deflation that bursts the speculative debt bubbles in the long wave. The Jubilee control of production occurs naturally in the long wave, albeit painfully. That is if government doesn't step in and prop up companies that are overproducing. We have clear overproduction in autos and banking services today that needs to be removed from the system.

The third force tackled by the laws for the Year of Jubilee was something we hear a lot about these days because we have a lot of it in the global economy: debt. All debts were to be eliminated in the 50th Year of Jubilee. This prevented a buildup of inefficient and dangerous debt levels in the economy. In such a system, you wouldn't actually have excessive debt cancellation. No bankers in their right minds would lend money beyond the Jubilee–since they knew the loan would legally be forgiven. Loans would not be made with maturities beyond the Year of Jubilee, because they would not be repaid. Debt could not be refinanced and snowball into a massive debt berg that sinks the global economy.

There would be a tendency for the most debt early in the cycle in a Jubilee system and total debt in the system would constantly decrease until the next Jubilee. In our economy, as evidenced by long wave history, we have low debts early in the cycle and more debt late in the cycle. In fact, debt levels explode in the last years before the long wave bust.

Outstanding debt would constantly decrease in a Jubilee system as prices decreased. Debt can be a very useful tool in our economy, but it is clear that too much of a good thing can be disastrous. Debt reached unprecedented levels in every sector of the economy in recent years. At the same point in a Jubilee system, debt would be virtually nonexistent. Debt is not inherently evil in and of itself, but when used as indiscriminately as it is in our system, it is bound to eventually create severe problems. The defaults and failures of a long wave winter achieve the same thing as the Jubilee cancellation, with a great deal more human pain and tragedy.

The long wave winter, as with all long wave seasons, lasts "ideally" 14 years, but can range from 10 to 16 years and consists of four Kitchin cycles. The last one or two Kitchin cycles of a long wave winter may be very mild and have many characteristics of spring. In the current long wave it looks like we postponed the worst of winter until the final Kitchin cycle. Jubilee was a one-year transition, while our system takes years to get out of its winter season of debt collapse and deflation.

The principles of the Jubilee are timeless. The Year of Jubilee acknowledged and constrained the end results of human nature that would cause the system to get out of control. Jubilee was to act like a safety valve. The author of the laws for the Jubilee appears to have understood the generational forces and tendencies within a society.

Recognition of the economic forces evident in the Year of Jubilee can also be considered in a more socially responsible and spiritually relevant context. This has not been the focus of this book, but it is important to note in our attempt to present the full picture of the long wave. The Year of Jubilee was addressing prices, production and debt in order to address potential economic imbalances in society. These economic imbalances will ultimately have social and spiritual implications and consequences, which are evident today. The consequences can be severe and do great social and spiritual damage.

In a message delivered by Dr. John Akers (2009) to the L. Nelson Bell class in Gaither Chapel in Montreat, North Carolina, he did an excellent job of reducing the economic forces addressed by the Year of Jubilee to their socially and spiritually relevant dangers; 1) the dangers of greed that always seeks to gain more at the cost of others, 2) the oppression of debtors, often the poor, and 3) the destruction of natural resources. These would all have been held in check in the Year of Jubilee. A high standard for principles of stewardship and compassion in social behavior was required by the ancient Jubilee laws.

Dr. Akers pointed out that these standards were not ends in themselves. The purpose behind the Year of Jubilee was to produce socially and spiritually important results. By upholding these principles the people would be reminded of God's goodness and compassion. The end results would be spiritual renewal, social harmony and long term stability. The selfish tendencies of the human heart would be held in check. Although the Year of Jubilee is not practical today, the principles are more important than ever. Such principles are not effectively administered by law; they need to be written on our hearts. This author's belief is that a global long wave crisis has a way of adjusting our perspective on these matters, giving us a chance to reconsider our priorities.

The unique and clear perspective on the long wave given by the Jubilee is clear, not in the economic laws it outlines, but in acknowledgement of the flaws in human nature itself. Humans run the system, so it is human relationships and human action in the field of the long wave that create forces that determine the economy's direction. The Year of Jubilee appears to have been designed as much for the governance of our human relationships as for economic regulation.

Clearly, the Year of Jubilee wasn't just another set of regulations or rules for intervention in the economy when things go wrong. They were integral laws that prevented the excesses from ever occurring in the first place. In retrospect, the Jubilee law appears to have acknowledged the natural long wave trends and the likely lengths of those trends in the economy and checked them in advance.

By looking at the Year of Jubilee, we more clearly understand and appreciate why the global economy overexpands and overproduces, has inflation and deflation, and builds up debt bubbles that must burst. By controlling prices and thus excess production and by forcing the elimination of debt, the Jubilee system would be stabilized, rather than forced to decline every half century as the free market system does. Unlike Jubilee, which was to create a new beginning immediately, the long wave winter season is a far more painful and lengthy process that cleans the slate, forces drastic change and, out of necessity, ultimately creates a new era of growth and prosperity for the system.

Government regulations that try to stop the natural long wave forces once they have gotten out of control only do more damage. This was the case in the 1930s and may be the case this time around. Once a decline is underway, regulation is futile. Jubilee wasn't a law that would bailout banks, farmers, and industry; it would have kept them from taking a good thing too far and getting in trouble in the first place.

Don't get me wrong, over the past 200 years the capitalist system has proven to be the most productive and effective form of economy. I'm not advocating new Jubilee-style regulations. The economic system of today has seen great advancements in wages and overall prosperity. Our system allows for anyone to work his or her way up in the system, if he or she is only willing to put forth the effort and the energy necessary.

The fact that the long wave decline is truly a Jubilee and a new beginning in our modern system can be difficult to accept, especially during the pain of a long wave winter. The swing from prosperity to depression tills the economic soil for spring planting. A new work ethic wrought from tragedy and experience is also imparted to the average individual during a long wave winter, so the necessary work will be sure to get done during the next advance.

A new beginning comes as the long wave purges inefficiency and recklessness out of the economic and social system. Inefficient and excessive debts are purged from the global system due to corporate failures of those who used too much debt to finance operations and are contributing to overproduction. The long wave decline produces a new beginning by forcing the implementation of new technology. It promotes more efficient corporate and manufacturing processes as companies look for new ways to ensure their survival, giving the global system new life.

There are those who believe global capitalism will one day no longer have a cycle, short or long, but will be in a perpetual state of stable growth. Those who believe this have the notion of perfectibility for the economy, which appears to stem from belief in the perfectibility of human nature.

Here is where their ideas are flawed. Human nature is full of extreme tendencies, including greed and arrogance. The forces that drive the system will always be present in humanity and show a tendency to rise and fall in long waves. The system that gains its vitality and strength from this competitive nature, as does capitalism, will never reach a state of perfection or equilibrium without flaws or cycles. A system that tried to produce perfect and stable growth through government interventionism in a mixed economy of state capitalism and free markets would eventually be caught in the same trap that sunk Communism. It would need so many controls to maintain stability, it would produce only stagnation. Such an experiment would ultimately fail, although we have already tried it to various degrees, and here we are in another long wave winter debt bust.

The business ventures of humanity must be free to fail as well as to succeed in order to produce the growth and success we require from international free market capitalism. As we are free to move from a state of risk-aversion to a state of risk-proclivity, we create the business cycle. If the system ever reached a state of growth equilibrium, we would most likely find ourselves bored.

A controlled society that sought to eliminate the long wave cycle would have to suppress the desire to assume risk, the desire to achieve or invent something new. It would, therefore, stifle productivity and progress. Yes, the business cycle could be eliminated with many restrictions and regulations, but this would not be the sort of economic and political system you would enjoy and appreciate–just ask the hundreds of millions of former Communists in Russia, Eastern Europe, and China.

The concept of equilibrium is actually an illusion; disequilibrium is the true reality. The theory of efficient markets is dead. We must be free to move too far in one direction as well as too far in the other. We pursue the center for our own safety over time, but we always overshoot. Jubilee law simply acknowledged these tendencies and was an effort to make the results of such swings less severe. Jubilee wasn't an attempt to regulate the system, as we think of regulation today, but an effort to give the market freedom within boundaries that would keep the system from driving itself over the edge.

Only by allowing freedom of movement from one extreme to the other can participants in the system have a shot at finding economic success and happiness. The market system must be allowed to take its course, unconstrained and unregulated, if it is to be productive and competitive and provide the highest possible standard of living for all citizens of the world. However, the risk and losses must not be socialized and born by taxpayers. They must be paid by those who take the risks.

Free market capitalism isn't perfect–but then neither are humans–which is why the system works for us. A modern-day Jubilee in the form of a long wave winter season, which produces a new beginning for a global system that has pushed prices, production, and debt too far, is just what the global economy needs to insure its longer-term survival.

This book was an effort to establish that long wave theory has merit and warrants serious consideration and analysis. If my interpretations of the theory that were presented in this book are somewhere in the ballpark of accuracy–and evidence would suggest that they are–then we have now sailed into the critical long wave winter season and a global debt bust.

Very few heeded the warnings in the earlier editions of this book. It is now time to proclaim the good news. This edition suggests that an explosive new economy will emerge in the years just ahead and will offer incredible opportunity.

Just as in all long wave advances, as Nikolai Kondratieff (1951) observed, the new economy that will emerge will be driven by advances in communications and transportation. A great number of technological advances are already under development. Many of the new ideas are still forming in the minds of their inventors scattered in all the nations of the global economy.

The deflation of computer prices as we have entered this decline will likely have a major impact on the next advance. Powerful desktop systems capable of tasks limited to mainframes a few years ago are getting into the hands of virtually all mechanical engineers, physicists, electrical engineers, biologists, and product designers, as well as workers in a vast number of other fields, and weekend inventors. New technology alone isn't a cure for an economy in decline, but it will be part of the fuel mixture for the propulsion of the next long wave advance.

The Internet now provides access to vast databases of scientific data and new generations of search engines and interfaces are providing immediate access to that information that is triggering an acceleration of discovery and invention. My own company, ALP Life Sciences, LLC, is a great example of these forces at work with the basic application of nanobiotechnology that we are pursuing. The prior company I founded used object-oriented programming to build powerful online research tools that accelerated research times and greatly reduced research cost structures for many Fortune 500 life science companies.

Lower computer prices simultaneous with a drastic increase in their power and their connection to the Internet are changing our society and economy in remarkable ways. One big change that is well underway is that our education system is being drastically altered by low-priced computers linked with digital video transmissions, new software, massive data banks, and new technologies that cater to education.

The educational system is riddled with problems and is growing less responsive to the needs of the competitive global economic system. We will likely see a marriage between recent and future advances in low-priced computing and telecommunications with entirely new approaches to Internet based education. The costs and failure of the existing educational system will of necessity demand such change. Internet based home schooling is booming and will likely be used to drastically cut education expensive and inefficient federal, state and local education budgets.

Out of necessity, Internet-based home schooling is a wave of the future. Students are able to log onto the latest computer system and connect to lectures, lessons, and question-and-answer sessions with the best teachers and minds in the world. Vast libraries, data banks and other sources of information are available on-line. The best available lessons on every subject are increasingly available online and can be downloaded or streamed.

With less time wasted on an inefficient educational system, students will be able to spend more time in positive social settings with family and friends in their communities, developing solid interpersonal skills. This is already happening. Internet home schooling doesn't mean the children of the next long wave advance will be anti-social. A sense of smaller local community will likely be a strong force in the next long wave advance, which we are only now seeing in its early stages.

Many new or reorganized schools will be sponsored and supported by the free-enterprise system. Individual companies and industries desperately need skilled and well trained workers. The private sector will get involved in education by necessity. There will be plenty of brick-and-mortar schools for students to attend, but they will be drastically different from today's. They will no longer be controlled by a central bureaucracy. We have seen this trend accelerating. Don't get me wrong, brick-and-mortar schools are not going anywhere, but they will increasingly be driven by new technology and the trend toward privatization will accelerate. You may be one of the millions who are called to this field and are making it happen, or you may have kids that are already participating.

In short, our education system has, in many ways, become obsolete. The market is responding with new solutions during this decline and will continue to do so in even bigger ways during the next long wave advance. Ten or twenty years into the future, education will look nothing like it does today. Children will receive better educations at only a fraction of today's cost. The influence this will have on the future will be astounding. But education is only one area that will see change. New forms of better education will help create the talent to drive the new engines of the new economy.

The same advances that alter education will alter virtually all aspects of our working and recreational lives. Very few white-collar workers will go to work at the office when they can work from home more efficiently and effectively over the Internet. This will likely alter the demographics of our cities and the development of real estate. If I don't have to go to the office, why do I have to live within an hour of the city? When I do have to go to the office, I will be able to take a super-efficient, magnetically levitated train.

These trains will travel up to 300 mph on a magnetic cushion–so why not live a few hundred miles from the office? A quick trip to the local terminal and you're in the city in no time at all for your weekly or monthly meetings. These forces may cause our big cities to deteriorate even further in the years ahead as technology allows workers to flee the crime and decay of the megalopolis. There is likely to be a great shift from the hassle of the cities to the security and comfort of small town life. This trend is now booming.

Other major changes to transportation will come from space research programs. A space plane will likely be a reality by early in the next long wave advance. Fleets of these planes will follow. Manufacturing and development in space will be a primary engine of the next long wave advance. Manufacturing facilities on the moon and Mars will likely be a reality midway into the next advance. Developments that come in the exploration of space will be applied to many aspects of life on earth. The next price peak in real estate may well see inflation on crater-front condos on the moon. Electric and other alternative energy cars will likely outnumber gasoline-powered cars by the end of the next long wave advance with breakthroughs in new batteries and manufacturing materials.

Whole new technologies and industries are being developed during this decline and will be expanded and/or implemented in the coming long wave advance. Job opportunities will come from sources never dreamed possible after unemployment reaches its highs in this long wave winter. Unemployment will fall as the new economy gains momentum. People will adjust to the changes. Humans are far more resourceful than politicians give them credit for being. Take them off the free lunch line and they learn quickly.

If needs arise and there is not sufficient talent to fill them, the market will respond and educate the needed employees who will have a powerful new work ethic after a long wave winter.

They will be ready and willing to do what it takes to succeed in the new economy of the next advance. It will be the late 1950s work ethic and desire to achieve all over again, with tomorrow's technological advances in the areas of transportation and communication as the catalysts.

The rapidly approaching spring season of the long wave will be an exciting, fulfilling time. Since the United States was the leader of the long wave advance and speculative fall season that ended in the depression of the 1930s and Japan was the leader of the advance and fall season that ended most recently, a legitimate question is what nation will emerge as the next leader? Looking at history, we see that the leader of the long wave tends to move west.

China will clearly be the leader of the next long wave advance and will carry along its neighbors, Malaysia, Indonesia, Thailand, and Singapore. I don't believe China will become a hegemonic power in the 21st century as great as the United States was in the 20th century, but it may well come close.

The true leader of the long wave doesn't usually emerge until well into the advance of the cycle in terms of standard of living, national wealth, and so on. Certainly China has many changes to go through before it becomes a leader in the free market, capitalist system. The Chinese government is allowing significant free market growth and activity at the local level. Larger scale operations are still run by the state, but there are signs this is changing. It appears as though the people will create a bottom-up free market revolution in China that will peacefully overturn the communist government by the sheer forces unleashed by the marketplace.

In the Southeast Asian countries, we are actually seeing a trend toward free markets, more established property rights, and less government regulation and intervention, while the United States and Europe are going in the opposite direction.

China and Southeast Asia will suffer crisis and setbacks as the global economy moves deeper into the latest long wave decline—along with all other nations. However, when you're close to the bottom, you don't have far to fall. You can't really talk about depression in the Western sense when a nation is only beginning to develop and build its infrastructure.

If the Chinese government hinders the free market revolution taking place in that country and takes a nasty turn for the worse politically, obviously China will not end up as the next long wave leader. However, I believe that it will be the next leader and that some of the greatest investments of the next advance will be in China-along with its Southeast Asian neighbors. Timing investments in this region will be critical.

The runner-up to China and Southeast Asia for the next long wave leader may well be Russia and the Commonwealth of Independent States. If movement toward free markets continues in Russia, this will be a real possibility. But Russia is likely to suffer more significant setbacks than China on the way to a booming economy. Russia is blessed with natural resources exceeded only by those of the United States. Will we see speculation in high-priced dachas on the Black Sea before a bust at the peak of the next long wave advance?

The name Kondratieff will surely be kicked around by a few market contrarians, if the Moscow stock exchange, along with the Beijing stock exchange and other Asian exchanges, is leading the globe in speculative excesses with a classic long wave fall-season and speculative blow off during the next peak of the long wave. Russia may suffer its own setbacks on the way toward free markets, but I believe it will succeed in the long run and participate in the next long wave advance–even if it doesn't lead it.

Don't misunderstand me. The United States will remain a major world power. It could easily remain the major world military power for a few hundred years. However, the United States will only remain the political and economic leader, or close to the top, if the right decisions are made in the years ahead. Regardless of the important decisions to be made and actions to be taken by the United States, the competition will continue to get tougher. The United States could even trump China and lead the next advance if we pursue and lead the world on The Great Republic pathway out of this global crisis.

It may be wise to at least consider whether something could be done to prevent the extremes of the long wave; it is only natural to try. The question must be asked as to whether we should just accept its inevitable effects on the economy and financial markets. I don't think we should give up on finding ways to prevent the extreme pain of the decline of the cycle. In so doing, we must acknowledge that the extremes of the speculative upswing would likely have to go as well. This might not be so bad. Still, even if we find a way to smooth the roughest edges, the long wave itself will always exist.

I'm convinced that controlling or stunting the extremes of the cycle, if it is to come at all, must come internally within the free market system, with economic and financial decisions based on knowledge of the cycle in the private sector. It is my contention that a true free market economy would make the cycle less severe anyway. The Great Republic will have long waves, but the crisis they produce will be over faster and they will produce less damage than a system juiced by loose monetary and fiscal policy and government intervention and guarantees.

The work on the System Dynamics Model at MIT will help in the decision-making process for industry. The individual participants, corporations and industry groups, and financial leaders within the economic system must make the decision to pull back from over expansion. With more research, the System Dynamics Model may prove to be a very helpful tool. Even then, the long wave and smaller cycles will not be eliminated, but the extremes could be avoided.

It is questionable whether such advanced thinking on long waves will ever happen. The next generation always forgets. It is certainly too late to avoid extremes in the latest decline of the long wave as we have sailed right into a global debt bust. There could be real dangers in trying too hard to control the long wave. By avoiding the pain of the long wave decline, the growth and prosperity of the advance would most likely be stunted. It should be remembered that if you believe in free markets the long wave is natural and healthy. You would not end the natural winter season if you could. The earth would burn up.

This book has illustrated that a new generation always drives the next cycle to its extremes. Because they didn't learn the lessons of pushing the system too far, they don't see the danger at the top and they push the system over the edge once again. At the peak of the next long wave, it is highly unlikely that long wave theory will be any more accepted than it is today.

As we conclude our study of long waves, it would be helpful to review the extensive terrain covered. We have examined past civilizations and looked at the factors that led to their demise. The history of the free market system we have today, its qualities and drawbacks, have been reviewed. The work of the Russian economist Nikolai D. Kondratieff (1951) and what he saw in the data he gathered on the long wave in free market economies since 1789, has been examined.

The work in the System Dynamics Group with the System Dynamics Model at MIT gives us a different perspective on the long wave. We learned that the long wave is generated internally within a market system by decision makers in the public and private sector. We learned that the System Dynamics Model is one of the few tools available for industry to look inward and make the decisions that could help to avoid the extremes of the cycle.

Field theory has had a dramatic impact on the hard sciences and on how interconnected, naturally occurring phenomena in space and time are understood. The idea of interconnected fields was examined as a possible clue to the social system activity occurring in space and time that appears to produce the long wave phenomenon. We concluded that long waves and smaller cycles are fields of human action in space and time.

We have come to realize that Kondratieff could not as fully appreciate the long wave as we are able to do as a result of our experiences of the last century, and now the first decade of the new millennium has provided extensive additional information that has confirmed the long wave perspective. The emergence of an increasingly interdependent global economy in recent decades has given us a unique look into the long wave and its character, and is playing a major role in the current global long wave winter and will undoubtedly drive the next long wave advance.

Psychology has shown a powerful relationship between the long waves and how society relates to the economic world and what people expect and anticipate from the system. Now we will be better equipped to observe our own reaction to the different phases of the cycle.

Human conflict has been found to be directly related to economic circumstances and surroundings. War was discovered to be far more likely during a time of expanding economies than contracting ones. In hard times nations look inward; in good times, they observe their neighbors raw materials and covet them with their growing industrial power and ability to wage war.

The banking system and the condition the financial system was in during past peaks and declines of the long wave, and how similar those conditions are compared to the international banking system today, has been reviewed. It is clear that during this long wave winter season major change and a restructuring of the international banking system and global currencies will occur.

We have looked closely at the forces at work in the long wave and their enormous impact on global trade. One can't help but look forward to truly free trade in an open global economy where the consumer has unlimited access to the global economy during the next advance.

Technology and invention have been seen as important elements to both long wave expansion and long wave contraction as humans seek solutions to their stagnating economic condition. We are now beginning to experience and we look forward to even greater advances in technology, new inventions and ideas that will propel us into the next expansion phase of the long wave.

The political atmosphere of the day has been seen to have a direct relationship and to be enormously influenced by the location in which we find ourselves in the long wave. We can only hope the right political decisions are made in this winter season crisis. The Great Republic may come to fruition this time around, and genuine free markets may have a chance, although a redistributive world empire ruled by a new type of Caesar is certainly a possibility. Major political upheaval on the part of the middle and hourly working classes are a distinct possibility.

Our study of the long wave has brought us to the investor's dilemma in facing the cycle. Both inflationary and deflationary scenarios have been examined. We reviewed the basic investment instruments of stocks, bonds, real estate, commodities and how they typically perform in different phases of the cycle. We have recognized that gold will once again play a monetary role as digital gold currency gains in use and functionality.

We have speculated on how we could best profit from the long wave and its effect on financial markets and the economy. We hope to emerge in the next advance ready to profitably ride the next upswing in the global economy.

The misconceptions of socialist and neo-Marxist long wave analysis have been evaluated. We have concluded that we are not experiencing the crisis of capitalism, but the crisis of "state" capitalism. It was determined that socialist world government is not a likely outcome of this decline, but it cannot be ruled out due to the aggressive role governments have chosen to play in this long wave winter crisis. Finally we have considered the paths to be chosen in the midst of the decline in the global economy. We have come to realize that we will soon learn what political and economic system will dominate the next spring season and advance of the Kondratieff long wave. It is yet to be determined whether a new golden age of decentralized free markets of The Great Republic are in store, or a disturbing, all-powerful redistributive world empire.

Taking a look at the nature of the free market system and its relation to human nature and the Year of Jubilee gave us clues as to the real nature of the long wave that passes through the global economy on a regular basis. In the process of our review, we have considered the tendencies of human nature that lead our system through periods of prosperity and depression.

We have taken a look at the three foundations of evidence available on the long wave, including Kondratieff's research, the System Dynamics Model at MIT, and the Year of Jubilee. We are now brought to a point of decision as to our acceptance or rejection of the long wave hypothesis. It is clear to any observer that looks at the evidence that we are now in the midst of the global financial and economic crisis of a long wave winter season. What remains to be seen is whether the worst of the long wave damage has been contained with government intervention. It is still possible that poor political and monetary decisions will allow this crisis to reach critical mass during this long wave winter season and throw international capitalism into a systemic crisis.

My own view is that this long wave season will be milder than the last one and a new long wave spring season and advance will begin around 2012. However, the remainder of this winter season is fraught with danger, and major mistakes can be made as we seek a new global economy and long wave spring season. Powerful forces are at work.

The right decisions must be made in the years ahead. Reason must win out. The forces unleashed during this long wave winter season are forcing the inevitable and unstoppable rise of The Great Republic, a new age for international free market capitalism.

EPILOGUE

"Tetelestai" Jesus of Nazareth

The most debt-ridden global economy in human history is in crisis and has experienced a gut-wrenching financial crash. For billions of people around the world, in the words of Charles Dickens, "It is the worst of times," unless of course you are on the receiving end of a taxpayer funded million dollar bonus.

Fear and anxiety over actual and impending job loss, investment losses, retirement fund losses and even basic survival for many families and individuals are hitting hard. Most are shell shocked by world financial and economic events. There are growing numbers of unemployed hungry living in tent cities and on the streets of virtually every city of every country on every continent.

The scale of the unfolding global crisis means it likely already has, or will have, a major impact on your life. Regardless of who you are, where you live, or what your profession may be, this crisis will touch your life and your relationships in many ways, both negatively and positively. It will create remarkable opportunities, as well as obstacles. The breadth of this global crisis we are now in the midst of is almost unimaginable in its far reaching impact. The many aspects of your life that could be affected include your job, your home, your retirement plans, your children's future, your friendships and your spiritual life. These areas of your life will be–or may have already been–impacted in minor and major ways.

The unfolding global long wave economic and financial crisis will likely be the defining historical event for a generation or more, as the Great Depression was for previous generations. However, my belief, and possibly your own, is that there is always a spiritual dimension at work in the events of our lives, the small events and the big ones. The global crisis we are now experiencing is no exception. In the major crisis events of our lives, we become more predisposed to recognizing that there are forces at work in our lives that are bigger than our ability to control them, no matter how hard we try. My sincere hope is that this book has challenged you to look for the purpose and potentially positive forces at work in this global crisis, in both the major and the seemingly insignificant ways it is affecting you.

Adam Smith, author of *Wealth of Nations*–still the most relevant work on international political economy, though it was published in 1776–called the force that is always present and at work in our lives the "invisible hand." My own view is that it is the intersection of our free will with the invisible hand that guides our decision making, impacts the outcomes of our lives and has a relevant impact on those we interact with: our family, friends and those we encounter in all aspects of our life and work. It is interesting that almost any modern reference to the work of Adam Smith mentions his notion of the invisible hand.

Many are not aware of the fact that Smith was likely referring to the providence of God in our lives and our world in his reference to the invisible hand. Some seek to refute this, but many analysts conclude the invisible hand Smith referred to was attached to the long arm of a sovereign, active and omniscient God. You may find this notion encouraging, or then again, you may find it disturbing, even terrifying. What this suggests is that the ever-so-slight nudge you often sense directing you to take action or exercise caution in your work and personal or family life, is in fact the hand of God that works His purposes through your own actions and participation in His ongoing work.

There are obviously those who will disagree with this interpretation of the invisible hand and the role it plays in our lives. Of course, you have a free will to take or leave my view on this matter. You may view such invisible forces at work, if at all, as a destiny that is determined by your actions alone. You may believe that, indeed, you are the captain of your soul and divine providence plays no role in such matters. Granted, this view does have its appeal and we all find ourselves operating under this *modus operandi* on occasion. You may view this global crisis as just another force coming at you that you will manage to work your way through. Either way, my hope is that this book provides relevant input to your thinking on these matters.

My take is that the invisible hand is always at work, even in this global crisis, and specifically in your uniquely valuable and important life and situation. The invisible hand has worked, and will work, through your life and actions in powerful ways that you may not even imagine. One purpose of this book is to try and help you see past how this crisis is affecting you negatively and discover the purpose and potential in this crisis to change your life—as well as the lives of your peers, those under your authority and those over you in authority, and those you love—for the better.

Like most, you have likely pursued riches in one form or another. This crisis may encourage the pursuit of real wealth in your life, wealth that will last far beyond the impact of mere riches and be passed down for generations. The plans that the invisible hand has for you are good. My hope is that this global crisis and this book will play a small role in pointing you to a higher power that has a vested interest in your life and in you fulfilling your greater purposes than just accumulating riches. The accumulation of riches may come, but your success and happiness has much more important things at stake than mere monetary gain or the passing material things of this life.

Our attempt to fill the spiritual void in the human heart with material things invariably plays a role in the swing of the economic long wave. We put too much emphasis on acquiring things we don't need with debt that we cannot afford. Collectively our appreciation for the real value of things becomes distorted in the later years of a long wave and we lose proper perspective. The price we are willing to pay in debt, dollars, our time and the sacrifice of relationships for what we think will bring us happiness is too high. We confuse a debt-financed lifestyle of passing riches with true and lasting wealth created by the day-in-and-day-out application of our individual talents and calling to the work we were created to do here on earth. A personal Jubilee and the adjustment it brings to our priorities and way of thinking is required. It is my contention that the collective sum of these individual Jubilees drives the ebb and flow of the economic long wave.

History has shown that it is often only in times of difficulty that we are forced to return to basics and consider what it is we were put on this planet to accomplish. Crisis in our lives helps us find our purpose, true talent and calling, which we may never discover without it. This is why a long wave decline and winter season is filled with innovation, new ideas and inventions that drive the next advance of the long wave. People are rediscovering the work for which they are most suited and were created to accomplish. It is possible that you were created to achieve things that you would never have considered without the global crisis that is now taking you back to the drawing board. This long wave decline may well be a new beginning for you in the same way that the Jubilee was to provide new beginnings to all debtors. The long wave decline is a wake-up call. During a long wave decline our priorities change, family and spiritual values take precedence over acquiring more things with debt we have no hope of repaying.

The author of Leviticus understood the tendencies and machinations of the human heart, and suggested the Jubilee as a safety valve. It reflected a desire to prevent people from being overly burdened by debt, freedom from all forms of slavery. The global economy does not have the Jubilee safety valve. It has the boom-and-bust of the economic long wave that wipes away excessive debts with the defaults and bankruptcies of the winter season.

The size and scope of the global crisis reveals that it goes beyond finance, politics and economic theory to the heart and soul of mankind, with all its need for fulfillment, ambition, pride, fears, and even some greed. Economics is not merely driven by greed, but other good and far more powerful forces at work in the human heart. I encourage you to seriously consider how the invisible hand is at work in your life in this global crisis and how you need to respond to its direction. Decisions made at important intersections guide your future and the futures of all those impacted by your decisions.

My genuine hope is that this book will provide you with a new perspective and realistic hope in these difficult times. It is my conviction that the greatest years for the United States and the world lie directly ahead as the current long wave ends and a new long wave begins. The years directly ahead are fraught with risk, as well as full of remarkable opportunity. Your greatest years of contribution and participation in the global economy can be ahead of you. Find what you were created to do and put your hand to the plow.

However, before we end our journey seeking an understanding of the long wave and the forces that drive it, there is just one more relevant historical note required regarding the long wave. I would prove negligent in my duty of relaying the story of the long wave, as it relates to the Jubilee, if this final information were not passed on to you. Only the mystery of the spirit behind the deeper principles of the Jubilee can fully convey its meaning; the power of the written word will surely fall short.

My hope is to bring clarity of heart and mind to readers during the current global financial and economic crisis, which I recognize is the sum of untold millions of personal stories of crisis and unfinished endings. You need to be aware that the Year of Jubilee, first and foremost, reflected the heart of a compassionate and loving God for his people. He yearned to set them free from their debts, so that they could enjoy an unencumbered life of freedom and lasting fulfillment in a relationship with Him. He wanted to provide a legal way out for his people to escape a life under the burden of unworkable debt loads. His heart's desire was to provide a way to free His people from the crushing bondage of debt that brings trouble to the heart, and weariness to the bones.

Theologians have long recognized that many passages, stories and events in the old covenant serve as a portent of what was to come under the new covenant. The Year of Jubilee was no exception. To this end the final word Jesus cried out before his death on the cross was *tetelestai*. At the time of His death, during the height of the Roman Empire's power, in Greece and the region of Palestine, the word *tetelestai* was used to stamp a debt as "paid in full."

When debt exists between debtor and creditor, it creates a strained relationship. This is especially true when the debtor has no possible way to secure the resources required to pay the debt that is owed. This fact is evident throughout the global economy today, as debtors with no ability to pay their debts are facing the wrath of their creditors, who themselves are often debtors to even larger creditors. With one word *tetelestai*, the greatest and most important debt cancellation in human history was transacted. The terms were established under which you can be restored to a right relationship with the creator of the universe who wants to free you from your debts and enter into a meaningful relationship with you for eternity. No government, business, credit card, or loan shark can change, renegotiate, or roll your debt over.

This debt cancelling transaction was the fulfillment of the heart of God for his people, first reflected in the proposed laws for the Year of Jubilee, and His recognition of our natural tendency as humans to go into debt. A debt cancelling has been transacted on your behalf. The debt owed has been paid in full, no matter what the balance. There is no other name, means or terms, by which this debt cancellation can be secured. You could not pay it if you had all the gold in The Great Republic, but all your debts, denominated in the currency of sin, have been paid in full once and for all. However, you must personally accept the terms of this debt deal, without caveats, call provisions, debt swaps, or confusing derivative instruments attached by you.

In conclusion, the restlessness of the human heart in search of fulfillment is a driving force in the long wave. The evidence for the long wave makes us personally accountable to our need of a personal Jubilee, a new spiritual beginning. Freedom from the burden of debt in the spiritual realm could be the greatest force to carry you into the future and the spring season of the coming long wave advance. A new life of purpose and peace with God beckons. If the notion of a personal Jubilee of debt cancellation resonates with you on a level deeper than mere market cycles, further pursuit of the subject is highly encouraged. The invisible hand may be nudging you even now to explore your personal Jubilee. Please visit the link "Your Personal Jubilee" at LongWaveDynamics.com for more information.

BIBLIOGRAPHY

Aharonov, Yakir and Aage Petersen. 1971. "Definability and Measurability in Quantum Theory." *Quantum Theory and Beyond.* Ted Bastin, ed. Cambridge: Cambridge University Press.

Akers, John. 2009. "God Calls His People to Compassion." L Nelson Bell Class Message, Gaither Chapel, Montreat North Carolina. July 12, 2009

Andres, William A. 1985. "The Case for Open Trade" *Vital Speeches,* August.

Bernstein, Jake. 1991. *The Handbook of Economic Cycles.* Homewood, IL: Business One Irwin.

Berman, Jeff. 2009. "BDP Survey: Protectionism Will Worsen Recession." *Supply Chain Management Review,* April.

Bremmer, Ian. 2009. "State Capitalism Comes of Age." *Foreign Affairs,* May/June.

Carey, Nick; Grenon, Andre. 2008. "Foreign ownership of U.S. companies jumps." Thomson Reuters, August.

Chen, Shiyin; Lin, Liza. 2009. "Global Crisis 'Vastly Worse' Than 1930s, Taleb Says." Bloomberg.com, May.

Clausen, A.W. 1983. "Third World Debt and Global Recovery." *Vital Speeches,* April.

Dewey, Edward R. and Edwin F. Dakin. 1947. *Cycles; The Science of Prediction.* New York: Henry Holt and Company.

Dula, Arthur M. 1985. "American Business: Heading into Orbit." *Saturday Evening Post,* March.

Eckes, Alfred E. 1985. "International Trade in Turbulent Times" *Vital Speeches,* July.

Evans-Pritchard, Ambrose. 2009. "Biblical debt jubilee may be the only answer." UK *Telegraph,* 19 January.

Feinberg, Andrew. 1987. "The Crash of 1989." *Gentlemens Quarterly,* February.

Forrester, Jay W. 1984. "Managing the Next Decade in the Economy." Address to the Joint Economic Committee of Congress in Washington, D.C. Germeshausen Professor of Management, Sloan School of Management, M.IT.

Forrester, Jay W. 2003. "Economic Theory for the New Millennium." Plenary Address at the International System Dynamics Conference, New York, July 21, 2003.

Fuhrman, Peter. 1988. "Another Stake Through Stalin's Heart." *Forbes,* December 26.

Graham, Benjamin. 1949. *The Intelligent Investor.* New York: HarperCollins Publishers.

Green, Timothy. 1981. *The New World of Gold.* New York: Walker and Company.

Hendrick, Bill. 1992. "MIT Scholar Sees Historical Pattern in Downturns." *The Atlanta Journal and Constitution,* February.

Herrick, Tracy. 1993. *The Money Analyst.* Los Angeles: Jeffries and Company.

Henske, John M. 1982. "The Changing World Environment for International Trade." *Vital Speeches,* October.

Hindle, Tim. 1982. "Banking's House of Cards." *World Press Review,* May.

Hochgraf, N. 1983. "The Future Technological Environment." *11th World Petroleum Congress,* London: John Wiley and Sons.

Homer, Sidney. 1963. *A History of Interest Rates.* New Brunswick: Rutgers University Press.

Johnson, Paul. 1991. *Modern Times.* New York: Harper Collins.

Kondratieff, Nikolai D. 1951. "The Long Waves in Economic Life." *Readings in Business Cycle Theory.* Translated by W. F. Stolper. Homewood: Richard D. Irwin.

Kennedy, Susan Estabrook. 1973. *The Banking Crisis of 1933.* Lexington: University Press of Kentucky.

Kondratieff, Nikolai D. 1988. "Purged Economist Kondratyev Market Ideas Hailed." *National Affairs.* Reprinted from Sotsialisticheskaya Industriya (in Russian), Moscow.

Krugman, Paul. 1999. "Can Deflation be Prevented?" web.mit. edu/krugman/www/deflator.html.

Krugman, Paul. 1999. "Deflationary Spirals" web.mit.edu/ krugman/www/spiral.html.

Krugman, Paul. 2003. "Fear of a Quagmire?" *The New York Times,* May 24.

Lightner, Otto C. 1991. The History of Business Depressions. New York: Burt Franklin.

Leffler, George L. 1957. *The Stock Market.* New York: Ronald Press.

Levy, Jack S. 1983. *War in the Modern Great Power System, 1495-1975.*Lexington: University Press of Kentucky.

Lightner, Otto C. 1922. *The History of Business Depressions.* New York: Burt Franklin.

Lodwick, Seeley G. 1983. "Are Farmers on the Way Out?" *Vital Speeches,* June.

Malabre, Allred L. 1987. "Debt Keeps Growing, With Major Risk in the Private Sector." The Wall Street Journal, February 2.

Malabre, Alfred L. 1986. "Kondratieff Rolls on, As Does the Economy." *The Wall Street Journal,* January 20.

Mandel, Ernest. 1980. *Long Waves of Capitalist Development.* Cambridge: Cambridge University Press, 41.

McCormick, John. 1984. "A Riches-to-Rags Story" *Newsweek,* April 2.

Maxwell, James Clerk. 1982. *A Dynamical Theory of The Electromagnetic Field.* T. F. Torrance, ed. Edinburgh: Scottish Academic Press.

Meier, Paul. 1993. *The Third Millennium,* Nashville: Thomas Nelson Publishers.

Murtino, Joseph P. 1985. "Does the Kondratieff Wave Really Exist?" *The Futurist,* February.

Opinion Asia. 2009. "Protectionist Rubber Meets the Road." *The Wall Street Journal,* April.

Paul, Ron. 1982. *Case for Gold.* Washington: Cato Institute.

Peterson, David. 1987. "Neo-Conservatism." *Vital Speeches,* February.

Porter, Roger B. 1983. "International Economic Challenges of the 1980s" *Vital Speeches,* January.

Prechter, Robert. 1989. *A Turn in the Tidal Wave.* Gainesville: Elliott Wave International.

Prechter, Robert. 2002. *Conquer the Crash; You Can Survive and Prosper in a Deflationary Depression*. Gainesville: New Classics Library.

Prechter, Robert. 1993. *The Elliott Wave Theorist*. Gainesville: Elliott Wave International.

Quinn, James. 2009. "Shock Warning on U.S. Municipal Bonds." *Telegraph*. April.

Roubini, Nouriel. 2008. "The Beginning of the End of the Crisis? Reactions to Authorities' 'Bad Bank' Solution" *RGE Monitor*, September 19.

Samuelson, Paul. 1947. *Foundations of Economic Analysis*. Cambridge: Harvard University Press.

Schmookler, Jacob. 1966. *Invention and Economic Growth*. Cambridge: Harvard University Press.

Schumpeter, Joseph A. 1939. *Business Cycles*. New York: McGraw-Hill.

Schumpeter, Joseph A. 1954. *Business Cycles*. New York: Oxford University Press.

Selfridge, Gordon. 1943. *The Romance of Commerce*. John Lane Company.

Sheets, Kenneth R. 1985. "Farmers up in Arms" *U.S. News and World Report*, March 11.

Sheets, Kenneth and Collins, John. 1985. "Ailing Farm Economy-Damage Spreads Wide" *U.S. News and World Report*, July 29.

Sherrid, Pamela. 1985. "The Great Bull Market of 1985." *U.S. News and World Report*, December 16.

Simmons. 1983. "Washington Memo: Worst-Case Scenario." *Financial World*, October 15.

Snyder, Julian M. 1983. "An Economic Theory for the Real World." *Vital Speeches*, August.

Spengler, Oswald, 1928. *The Decline of the West*. New York: Knopf.

Steil, Benn. 2007. "The End of National Currency." *Foreign Affairs*, May/June.

Sterman, John D. 1985. "The Economic Long Wave: Theory and Evidence." Working Paper 1656-85. Cambridge: MIT Press.

Stoken, Dick. 1980. "The Kondratieff Cycle and its Effects on Social Psychology." *The Futurist,* February.

Terrones, Marco E.; Scott, Alasdair; and Kannan, Prakash. 2009. "From Recession to Recovery: How Soon and How Strong?" *International Monetary Fund,* April.

U.S. Treasury Department. 2009. "Major Foreign Holders of Treasury Securities." February.

Waldman, Peter. 1986. "Severe Deflation Hits Commercial Properties in Many Areas of U.S." *The Wall Street Journal,* September 4.

Wall, PQ 1993. *PQ Wall Forecasts.* New Orleans: PQ. Wall Forecasts, Inc. 5:2., February.

Wall, PQ 1998. *Destiny is Real.* New Orleans: PQ Wall.

Wall, Wendy L. 1986. "U.S. Agriculture Faces Still More Shrinkage, Many Economists Say." *The Wall Street Journal,* December 24.

Wallerstein, Immanuel. 1984. *The Politics of the World-Economy.* Cambridge: Cambridge University Press.

Wallerstein, Immanuel. 2004. World-Systems Analysis. Durham and London: Duke University Press.

Wallerstein, Immanuel. 2008. "The Depression: A Long-Term View." *Monthly Review,* October.

Whalley, John. 1985. *Trade Liberalization among Major World Trading Areas.* Cambridge: MIT Press.

Wilson, John Oliver. 1985. "Trade Wars." *Vital Speeches,* June.

Woche, Wutschafts, 1982. "Banking Crisis Ahead?" The Stanley Foundation. *World Press Review,* November.

Yamani, Ahmed Zaki. 1983. "Control and Decontrol in the Oil Market." *Vital Speeches,* June.

Zahorchak, Michael, Raymond A. Wheeler, 1983. *Climate: The Key to Understanding Business Cycles.* Linden, New Jersey: Tide Press.

INDEX

APPENDIX

Stay current with the impact of the powerful forces of long wave dynamics on financial markets and your investments by visiting LongWaveDynamics.com and subscribing to *The Long Wave Dynamics Letter,* edited by David Knox Barker. Every monthly issue provides an update on the long wave family of cycles for investors and traders. Tracking the trends of the long wave family of cycles is essential for the success of both investors and traders. Subscribers also receive access to exclusive cycle tools and resources, and access to current market analysis in the Weekly Update blog.

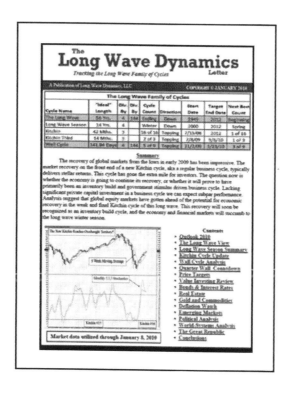

Learn more at: LongWaveDynamics.com

Made in the USA
Lexington, KY
02 November 2011